BUG OUT
VEHICLES AND
SHELTERS

BUG OUT
VEHICLES AND
SHELTERS

Build and Outfit Your Life-Saving Escape

SCOTT B. WILLIAMS

Ulysses Press

Published in the United States by
ULYSSES PRESS
P.O. Box 3440
Berkeley, CA 94703
www.ulyssespress.com

ISBN 978-1-56975-979-0
Library of Congress Control Number 2011926016

Acquisitions Editor: Keith Riegert
Managing Editor: Claire Chun
Editor: Bill Cassel
Proofreader: Jessica Benner
Production: Abigail Reser, Judith Metzener
Index: Sayre Van Young
Cover design: what!design @ whatweb.com
Cover images: shack © PiLensPhoto/fotolia.com; sky lightning © Paul Lampard/
    fotolia.com; truck © Oksana Perkins/fotolia.com
Interior photos: See page 254

Printed in the United States by Bang Printing

10 9 8 7 6 5 4 3 2 1

Distributed by Publishers Group West

For my brother Frank,
a true vehicle enthusiast who has owned and tested just about
every kind of automobile, motorcycle, boat, RV, ATV, and bicycle
known to man.

TABLE OF CONTENTS

ACKNOWLEDGMENTS

As always, I am grateful for the love and support of my dear fiancée, Michelle, for her help and encouragement in putting all this together and keeping me motivated through another big project.

Keith Riegert and the rest of the staff at Ulysses Press have once again steered me in the right direction to distill this information into a better book than I envisioned, and I am grateful for their continued faith in my work that has led to this series of survival titles.

Most of what I know today about motor vehicles began with what I was taught by my father, who insisted from the time I learned to drive that I know how to maintain and repair my own vehicles, and from my two older brothers, Frank and Jeff, from whom I've learned how to choose and repair a variety of cars, trucks, and motorcycles. I also want to thank a longtime reader of my *Bug Out Survival* blog and previous books, Dustin Tarditi, for his advice regarding off-road driving and off-road vehicles.

My experience with boating goes back to childhood youth group trips led by Dr. F. W. Tripp of my hometown. That experience was later enhanced by thousands of miles of canoe trips with my longtime paddling partner, Ernest Herndon. I'm indebted to sea kayaking legend John Dowd for tips and pointers that probably saved my life on my first solo kayaking voyage to the Caribbean, and I'm grateful to Ben and Sylvia Olsen of Whisper, Lawrence Pitcairn of Heron I, and Josephine Adams of Celebration for teaching me how to sail cruising boats on that same trip. From my good friend and master boatbuilder David Halladay of Boatsmith, Inc., I have learned skills that have taken my understanding of yacht carpentry and boatbuilding to a whole new level and allowed me to write about the subject of DIY boats from extensive personal experience. I am also indebted to another friend, yacht designer Reuel Parker, for his insights in boat design and the practical aspects of living aboard and bugging out on a variety of unique, shallow-draft craft.

Finally, over the years I gained an entirely different perspective on long-distance bicycling and proper pedaling and training techniques from my cousin Rick Venturini, a lifelong cycling and road racing enthusiast who was occasionally willing to ride with a novice like me.

INTRODUCTION

Mobility can be the key to survival. You only have to watch the current news to see how natural disasters, outbreaks of disease, acts of random violence, and terrorism and larger-scale conflicts overtake those who are unable to get out of the path of danger. Certainly there are times when staying in place and seeking shelter is appropriate; but there are also situations where your current location quickly becomes untenable and if you wish to survive, along with your family and other loved ones, you had better be prepared to leave—or *bug out*. At the most basic level, this will entail walking or running on foot. But with the huge array of machinery available today to move us from place to place, we have more and better transportation options than any of our predecessors in human history. This book looks at how you can use those options to survive in an emergency, as well as how some of the means of travel that we take for granted in everyday life may quickly cease to be viable. This information will enable you to consider the options and make the best choices to enable you and your family to be self-sufficient when it comes to mobility. Forget about any form of public transportation, as such systems will likely be inoperable or crowded beyond capacity. One only has to look at the lessons from a natural disaster like Hurricane Katrina to realize that those without their own means of evacuation can easily become helplessly trapped and at the mercy of whatever events unfold next.

People have always desired to move about on land and water, whether out of necessity or simply to satisfy their curiosity about other places, and have long endeavored to develop new and more efficient ways of doing so. With our ability to travel at high speeds, long distances mean little today, and for many the simple act of being in motion is such an enjoyable experience that for them the use of vehicles is more recreational in nature than essential. Regardless of whether you drive a car, ride a motorcycle, pedal a bicycle, or operate a boat for pleasure or because you have to get somewhere, in the event of a major disaster or a change in conditions caused by a larger breakdown of society, the ability to get around that we all take for granted could suddenly become much more challenging. But unless you are reduced to the last resort of walking, chances are any planned or unplanned evacuation you might find yourself forced to undertake will involve some sort of vehicle. Choosing the one that is right for you is the main subject of this book, which is a logical expansion of one of the key elements of bug-out planning that I presented in *Bug Out: The Complete Plan for Escaping a Catastrophic Disaster Before It's Too Late.*

The heart of that book focused on the "where-to" aspect of bugging out, and I wrote it because I perceived a huge gap in that part of the equation among all the excellent "how-to" survival books available at the time. Most discussions of the specifics of where to go if you have to bug out were vague at best, and I wanted to offer my ideas on the kinds of places I would choose in different regions if I lived there and had to find a safe refuge in a hurry. Realizing I had spent a large part of my life seeking out and spending time exploring remote places and wildlands throughout the Lower 48 states, I wanted to share my experiences with readers who may not have had time to do the same. Breaking the country down into eight distinct regions, I discussed the available resources, potential hazards, probable weather conditions, and other advantages and disadvantages of each, then pointed out some specific locations that were representative of each region. I also covered the basics of how to find your own bug-out locations by using tools such as topographical maps, Google Earth, and, of course, your own preliminary scouting trips. Then there was a chapter that presented an overview of transportation options, covering such bug-out vehicles as trucks and SUVs, motorcycles and ATVs, bicycles, a variety of boats from canoes to large cruisers, and even pack animals.

Because I had a lot of ground to cover on the main subject of that book—the bug-out locations—the material on preliminary preparations such as the bug-out bag and bug-out vehicles had to be limited. Because there is so much more detailed information on the subject of bug-out vehicles that I wanted to share then but could not, I have now put together this guide to the vehicles, boats, and additional equipment needed to help you effect a timely escape in the event of a catastrophic disaster or major Shit-Hitting-the-Fan (SHTF) event. My intention is to cover not only the usual options people consider in their preparations, but also some alternative ideas you may not have considered or may be less familiar with. Being well prepared to bug out doesn't necessarily mean you must have the latest and greatest high-tech SUV, boat, RV, motorcycle, or bicycle. In this book, I will present lower-cost options such as fixer-uppers, do-it-yourself projects, or even build-it-yourself alternatives, wherever practical.

In addition, as the title suggests, part of this book also deals with bug-out shelters: some that are mobile, allowing your bug-out vehicle and shelter to be one and the same, and others that are prepared in advance in a fixed location that you will use one of these vehicles to reach. Many survivalists and prepping experts criticize anything that has to do with bugging out, saying that leaving your home is almost always a bad idea and that any kind of traveling after a SHTF scenario will make you a refugee, wandering aimlessly at the mercy of those who would do you harm. But in both this book and the original *Bug Out* I am trying to emphasize the concept of flexibility and leaving your options open. No one can predict when and where such an event will occur next. If you can stay in your home or expensive retreat in the country, that's all well and good. But if you've put all your preparation time and money into one fixed location, then all your eggs are in one basket, so to speak, and if that place happens to be ground zero of the event, you're out of luck. The fixed retreats described here are low-cost and simple enough that you could have more than one in different locations if you are concerned enough to make that much effort. If your bug-out plan is solid to begin with, you will have what you need to survive whether or not you can reach your retreat. Having the retreat is just icing on the cake that will make survival easier and more comfortable.

When considering bug-out vehicles and shelters, an important factor will be your starting location, which will dictate how far you may have to travel to find a safe refuge and whether or not your options are limited to overland travel or also include water travel. Another major consideration in your bug-out preparations is whether you have only yourself to be concerned about or if you will be traveling with others. A young and fit individual unburdened with weaker companions can of course, choose among more travel options and endure more hardships than a family with small children or elderly parents or grandparents to take care of.

Because bug-out vehicles and shelters can be broken down into various categories, I have organized this book into four distinct parts for your easy reference. These categories are Escape Vehicles, Mobile Retreats, Alternative and Back-Up Vehicles, and Fixed Retreats. The following sections give a brief overview of each category and look at what is covered in that part of the book.

Part One: Escape Vehicles

In this first part of *Bug Out Vehicles and Shelters,* I'll discuss the transportation options that could be classified as "escape" vehicles. Certainly any vehicle or boat described in this book could be used to make your escape in a bug-out situation, and if you choose an RV, cruising boat, bicycle, or ATV as your primary means of travel, then it *will* be your escape vehicle. But for the purposes of this section, I'm defining escape vehicles as those vehicles that are suited for making a quick exit from a danger zone to your bug-out location while having the capacity to carry your bug-out bag and anything else you need to survive while you're traveling and after you get there. This means you won't be living in the vehicle, but rather using it as transportation, and if overnight stays are necessary along the way, you will be camping beside the vehicle rather than in it.

Chapter One looks at "Bug-Out Motor Vehicles: Cars, Pickups, SUVs, and Crossovers," as these are commonly used for everyday transportation and are the vehicles you are most likely to own already. Any automobile can work as a bug-out vehicle in a pinch, though obviously some are better than others, and I will discuss ways to optimize them for this purpose. Most of these vehicles will work as transportation for individuals, couples, or small families and can carry the basic gear and supplies needed to make your bug-out plan work.

Larger, highway-capable motorcycles also fit in the escape vehicle category; they can be used in much the same way as four-wheeled vehicles and even offer some advantages that cars and trucks don't. Motorcycles aren't suitable for everyone, but in Chapter Two, "Bug-Out Motorcycles," there is information on options in the two-wheeled category and how they can also be optimized for bugging out with your basic gear if you prefer them over automobiles. This chapter does not cover smaller off-road motorcycles that are not suited for high-speed, sustained travel on the road, as those are discussed in Part Three, which deals with backup and alternative vehicles.

Also in the escape vehicle category are options for making a quick getaway on the water. Escape boats are an excellent transportation option to consider if your everyday living or working location is near a navigable river, large lake, or seashore, and/or your bug-out location is reachable by water. As I pointed out numerous times in the original *Bug Out,* in many parts of the U.S., especially in the more populated eastern half of the country, sometimes the best nearby bug-out locations can only be reached by a boat of some sort. Chapter Three, "Bug-Out Boats: Escape Watercraft—Power and Sail," looks at smaller powerboats and sailboats of the type many people already own and use for recreation. Boats in this class can carry sufficient gear for bugging out in the same way that an automobile or motorcycle can, but are not big enough to have sleeping accommodations like the self-sufficient cruising vessels that will be discussed in Chapter Six.

Part Two: Mobile Retreats

This second part of *Bug-Out Vehicles and Shelters* covers vehicles that merge transportation out of a danger zone with a shelter or retreat that can provide long-term support for you and your family while you're on the move or after you get to a safer location. One key difference between mobile retreats and escape vehicles is that you can live or camp *in* them, rather than relying on a tent or other extra shelter. The ability to sleep inside the vehicle means that it can be set up for more comfort as well as more security, and you don't have to stop and un-pack everything to set up camp or repack it to get back on the move again. The smallest mobile retreats have at least as much storage space as the largest escape vehicles, and the larger ones have many times more. Some can carry everything you need for months of self-sufficient travel or living.

I have further broken mobile retreats down into three distinct types. In Chapter Four, "Recreational Vehicles and Other Manufactured Mobile Retreats," I'll look at the suitability of various recreational vehicles (RVs) of the type that many people use for weekend or vacation travel and camping. These prefab mobile retreats are common and easily obtain-able in a variety of configurations, sizes, and price ranges, both new and used. They include pop-up campers that can be towed behind most any vehicle, larger camper trailers that are always ready to use but require bigger tow vehicles, and motor homes that travel under their own power and can in turn tow many types of escape vehicles, including automobiles and boats.

Chapter Five looks at the "DIY (Do-It-Yourself) Mobile Retreats" op-tion. This includes converting a vehicle such as a work van or old bus into a customized survival platform. The DIY option is usually cheaper than a prefab retreat and can be uniquely your own, set up to meet your specific requirements. This category also includes structures you can build from scratch, starting with a flat-bed truck or pickup and convert-ing it to a "house truck," or starting with a basic utility trailer and build-ing your own camper or cabin onto it.

The final type of mobile retreat is the "Liveaboard Boat," the subject of Chapter Six. Many people have the misconception that all larger boats are luxury yachts obtainable only by the privileged few, but this is not the case; this chapter looks at a variety of vessels that you can buy cheap and fix up, or build from scratch in your backyard using basic tools for less than the cost of a new car or truck. Boats in this category include houseboats and shanty boats, motorcruisers, and ocean-capable sailboats. Depending on the design you choose, such boats can allow you to bug out on rivers, marshes, or swamps, along coastlines or bays, or even across oceans to safety beyond the horizon.

Part Three: Alternative and Backup Vehicles

This section is devoted to the discussion of alternative and backup vehicles that do not fit in the other categories. Most of the smaller vehicles in this category can be carried with you on a larger escape vehicle or mobile retreat, making them useful as a backup in the event that the main vehicle fails or can't be used because of traffic jams, lack of fuel, or other problems. Other vehicles in this category are more specialized than motor vehicles and require a higher level of physical fitness to use, making them less useful to families with children or disabled or elderly adults.

Chapter Seven, "Off-Road Motorcycles, ATVs, and Snowmobiles," covers small motorcycles that do not fit in the escape vehicle category of Part One because of their size or unsuitability for long-distance travel on roadways. Four-wheel ATVs are also discussed, as many of these vehicles can traverse much rougher terrain than any other motor vehicle and all are small and lightweight enough to be carried in the back of pickup trucks or on small trailers pulled behind other vehicles. Snowmobiles are included here as well for those living in areas where they are useful in the winter months.

Chapter Eight, "Bicycles as Bug-Out Vehicles," takes a thorough look at pedal-powered machines as bug-out vehicles. I pointed out the suitability of bicycles for this purpose in the original *Bug Out,* but this chapter goes into more detail about choosing and outfitting various types of bikes for carrying your bug-out gear. There is also information on the tools and maintenance needed to keep them going, as well as the riding techniques and fitness preparations necessary if you intend to cover long distances on a loaded bicycle.

The final category of alternative vehicles is "Human-Powered Watercraft," which are covered in Chapter Nine. These vessels include canoes, sea kayaks, and various small rowing vessels and they can be a vital part of your bug-out plan or even your main bug-out vehicle, depending on your particular situation. In this chapter you will learn what you need to know to choose among many options in this class of boats. I'll also cover operating and outfitting such a boat for this purpose and the skills needed to use it efficiently, so that like a bicycle, it can carry you long distances under your own power.

Part Four: Fixed Retreats

The last section of this book is not about vehicles at all, but covers the "shelters" mentioned in the title, dealing entirely with temporary and semi-permanent shelters that you either build or move in advance to your pre-planned bug-out location of choice. In the original *Bug Out,* I focused primarily on the type of evacuation people think of when they prepare a bug-out bag to keep at home or in their vehicle: an emergency that requires leaving in a hurry with just what you can carry on your back. This is an important part of bug-out planning, and the basic bug-out bag and its equipment should always be ready for you to fall back on in case all your more elaborate plans fail. But because bug-out planning should take place well in advance of when it might be needed, it doesn't have to mean a last-minute dash for the hills with nothing but a backpack except in the worst-case scenario. That is where Part Four of this book comes in: fixed retreat shelters prepared beforehand at your bug-out location can be stocked with extra gear and supplies in advance, giving you much more security and comfort than most people could find living out of a backpack.

Chapter Ten, "Site-Built Natural Shelters and Longer-Term Portable Shelters," discusses the simplest forms of fixed retreats—those that are found naturally, such as caves and rock overhangs, and those that can be built on-site from natural materials. Such shelters can serve as excellent hideouts in a remote bug-out location, because they don't require you bring in outside materials, cost little or nothing, and can be made to blend nearly invisibly into their surrounding environment. Also included in this chapter are prefab primitive shelters such as tee-pees and old-school wall tents that you *do* have to carry in but are still portable enough to be moved into the most rugged terrain if you do the work in advance. They offer better long-term accommodations than ultralight backpacking tents, particularly in cold climates or in winter in the mountains, as they can be heated from inside with an open fire or wood stove.

Chapter Eleven, "Secure Bug-Out Shelters," covers the next level up in fixed retreats. This kind of retreat requires more pre-planning and more work to build or set up, but can offer even better living accommodations and security if you know for sure where you will be bugging out and feel confident that you can get there when you have to. Retreats in this category include prefab sheds and other small buildings; converted shipping containers; small, simple-to-build cabins and micro-cabins; and underground structures and tree houses. In most cases, secure shelters of this category will have to be built on land that you own or have permission to use for this purpose.

Finally, Bug-Out Vehicles Are Fun

One thing to keep in mind as you read through this book is that bug-out preparations don't have to be all about impending doom and constant fear of catastrophe or even TEOTWAWKI (The End of the World As We Know It). Although other aspects of survival preparation can be enjoyable, to most people researching, acquiring, and setting up various bug-out vehicles is nothing less than fun; this is one reason survival forums, blogs, and related websites spend so much time discussing the subject. There's nothing wrong with having fun with these vehicles.

Get the vehicle you fantasize about if you can afford it and it is practical for the purpose, and customize it to your heart's content. If a camouflaged Jeep makes you feel more prepared, then get out the spray paint. If you prefer a customized KLR or old Harley chopper that looks like it belongs on the set of *The Road Warrior,* then build it to your taste. Maybe a big battleship-gray sailing trimaran right out of *Waterworld* is more to your liking. Just because the S has not yet HTF does not mean you can't get a lot of enjoyment and experience out of getting outdoors with that four-wheel-drive jeep, dual sport motorcycle, sailboat, bicycle, or canoe. If you are using it this way for weekend fun, you will be more familiar with it when and if the time comes that you really need it, and the use you get out of it now will justify the time and money invested even if that time never comes.

Important Note/Disclaimer

I would like the reader to keep in mind that this book covers a vast range of vehicles, boats, alternate transportation, and retreat shelter types. It would be impossible in a single volume to go into great detail about specific models, so I have chosen to focus instead on the key considerations for each type of vehicle or shelter, including the advantages and disadvantages and how you can incorporate them into your bug-out plan. While I do give a few examples at the end of each section, it's certain that I've omitted a lot of favorites, so I want to make it clear that this was not deliberate, lest some readers say I overlooked the best choice or their particular favorite. Please use this book as a set of guidelines and basic principles to make your own choices that fit your specific needs and environment.

My hope is that the real value of this book will be to make the reader aware of the key advantages and disadvantages of each type of bug-out vehicle and how important it is to perform the necessary maintenance and/or modifications to make sure it will get you to safety. Having your vehicle fail along the way could put you and your family in even more danger than you would be in if you had stayed at home.

Part I

Escape Vehicles

1

BUG-OUT MOTOR VEHICLES
Cars, Pickups, SUVs, & Crossovers

In this chapter I'll discuss the class of vehicles that is in everyday use by the largest number of people and will likely be the first option the average person will consider if they have to get out of Dodge in a hurry alone or with the family. For the purpose of separating the different types of motor vehicles available for consideration, this chapter covers passenger vehicles with four wheels (although some of the larger pickups in this class have dual rear wheels). Vehicles that meet this definition include cars, pickup trucks, SUVs, and the newer class of "crossover" vehicles that blur the line between cars, SUVs, and pickups.

More automobile options are available today than ever before, and anyone shopping for a new or used vehicle will be faced with a mind-boggling array of choices to consider. If, like many people, you're not in a position to purchase another vehicle to set up as your bug-out vehicle, you won't have to worry about all these choices and can focus on optimizing what you're driving now. Depending on your particular situation and your personal bug-out plan, you may not need a specialized vehicle at all. In many cases just about anything will do, as long as it's well maintained and will be reliable when you need it.

How Does Your Bug-Out Vehicle Fit into Your Overall Plan?

To determine what you need in a bug-out motor vehicle, first you have to assess your particular situation in terms of where you live or work every day and how far those locations are from safe bug-out locations that you consider viable in the event that you can't stay where you are. Will you be starting from within a large city, among the sprawling subdivisions of suburbia, or from a smaller city or town? Have you assessed a variety of potential evacuation routes to determine if your everyday car or other vehicle can negotiate them in any weather or traffic conditions? Will reaching your chosen bug-out location require driving on unpaved surfaces or in other difficult conditions, or do you plan to switch to alternate or backup transportation once you get to the end of the pavement? Will the backup transportation be hoofing it with your bug-out bag, or will you need racks to carry a bicycle, canoe, or kayak, or perhaps a trailer hitch and the capacity to tow a boat, ATV, or motorcycle trailer? Will you be traveling alone, as a couple, or as a family? How much luggage space will you need for everyone's gear, considering that the minimum will be a well-packed bug-out bag for each person, plus additional food, water, and other equipment if possible? When asking yourself such questions, it doesn't take long to figure out whether you can make do in your convertible sports car or if something like a four-wheel-drive, full-sized SUV is in order.

Disadvantages to Traveling by Road

Before you begin thinking about buying or customizing that perfect bug-out motor vehicle, stop first and consider the reality that in a true SHTF scenario, particularly in a big urban area, there will be many real drawbacks to *any* kind of travel on public roads. The main such drawback, of course, is that practically everyone else will have the same idea of attempting to drive out because that's all they know to do. But all you have to do is watch the news reports of a major hurricane evacuation on the Gulf or East Coast to see the problems that ensue when a mass exodus from a big population center is attempted by road. There will inevitably be traffic jams slowing movement to a crawl or complete gridlock just from the sheer number of vehicles. On top of that will be more chaos caused by mechanical breakdowns, vehicles running out of fuel, carjackings, and possibly even road blocks set up by the authorities (or worse, those who would take advantage of the situation).

Travel by road of course limits you to known, defined routes where it could be hard to avoid those who would stop or ambush you along the way. This sort of concern would be more relevant in the later stages of the aftermath of a major SHTF event, but it's something to think about. If you are going to bug out by road, be prepared to make your escape early, before the potential for such trouble develops. Since escape vehicles are the focus of this chapter, I will address the kinds of issues you need to think about in choosing the vehicle and keeping it ready at all times to make such an escape. First, here are some key points to think about if, after considering the disadvantages of traveling by road, you still find a motor vehicle best for your particular needs.

Key Bug-Out Motor Vehicle Considerations

Gasoline vs. Diesel Gasoline is by far the most common fuel used by the motor vehicles of the class discussed in this chapter. Diesel is the only viable alternative, as electric motors and other experimental technologies are not sustainable options in a bug-out scenario, at least for the kind of full-sized vehicles discussed in this chapter.

One advantage of gasoline engines over diesel is that because they are so common, more people are familiar with them and they are easier to repair in the event of a breakdown. They are also cheaper to purchase initially, reducing the total cost of the vehicle as compared to the same model equipped with a diesel engine. Other advantages of gasoline engines include lighter weight for a given horsepower and more horsepower than a comparable-sized diesel. Gasoline engines also generally run more quietly than diesels.

A disadvantage of gasoline as a primary fuel, however, is that it is harder to store for long-term use, because it is more volatile and dangerous than diesel and must always be properly vented and kept in approved containers to reduce the risk of fire or an explosion. Gasoline also degrades over time unless it is treated with conditioning additives like STA-BIL to keep it fresh. And if your vehicle is powered by gasoline, once you exhaust your supply and it becomes unavailable in a post-SHTF scenario, it cannot be improvised at home, unlike diesel.

Diesel is most commonly used in work trucks, construction and farm machinery, and larger vehicles designed for a long, hard service life. Diesel engines are expensive and require more knowledge to maintain and repair, but tend to require less maintenance over a much longer lifespan than the typical gasoline engine. Diesel engines also get better fuel mileage. Perhaps the greatest advantage of diesel engines in the aftermath of a long-term grid-down scenario would be that biodiesel can be made from cooking oil and other organic byproducts, allowing you to keep using your vehicle even if gasoline isn't available.

Choosing between gasoline and diesel boils down to what kind of scenario you are preparing for—long vs. short term. For most people who already drive the vehicle they will likely use to bug out if needed, and for most bug-out situations that will probably be relatively short-term, a powerful and economical gasoline engine will work just fine for an escape vehicle.

Blending In There are many advantages to remaining inconspicuous and blending into your environment in your bug-out vehicle. In the urban environment and on the highway, a vehicle that obviously *looks* like a bug-out vehicle will attract a lot of unwanted attention. This is where an ordinary four-door sedan can be the best camouflage of all. It will be so plain and nondescript that it will be almost invisible among the traffic. This is especially true if you choose a model with no status-symbol branding and no especially attractive styling or color. A plain beige Toyota Camry or gray Ford Taurus comes to mind. There are so many such cars on the road that no one gives them a second glance.

On the other hand, if you are driving a massive four-wheel-drive SUV loaded down with backup vehicles like bicycles, canoes, ATVs, or boats, everyone who sees you will assume you are well equipped with supplies and gear. This can make you a target for those who are desperate. You should take every reasonable effort to cover or hide obvious supplies, especially those highly desirable jerry cans of extra fuel, until you get away from the city.

Once you get out of town, blending in is more about the ability to hide the entire vehicle. In the backcountry, earth-tone colors like green, brown, tan, or black are easier to hide. Flat paint is even better, and chrome and other shiny parts should be taped or painted over, or you should consider carrying camouflage netting of the type used by the military to drape over the vehicle once you have it parked. This can be supplemented with vegetation from the surrounding area.

One other point to consider is that if your plan involves traversing remote country or primitive roads at night, especially in the desert where lights can be seen at a great distance, you may want to wire in a manual interrupter switch so you can disable your brake lights in such situations. On many nights out in open country, you can see well enough to drive slowly without your headlights, but if your brake lights give you away, there's not much point. Some newer vehicles also have headlights that stay on all the time and this will have to be fixed as well. If your vehicle does not also have a switch to disable the interior cabin lights when the doors are open, you may want to wire one in or simply remove the bulbs of any lights that may come on at an inconvenient time and give away your position.

The EMP Threat Much has been written on the subject of the vulnerability of modern motor vehicles to a possible EMP (electromagnetic pulse) event. Whether caused by a deliberate attack involving a nuclear burst in the atmosphere or possibly extreme solar flare activity, a strong enough electromagnetic pulse is said to have the potential to render most modern motor vehicles totally inoperable. The reason is that such vehicles rely on complex electronic circuitry for their ignition and a variety of engine controls, and once this sensitive circuitry is destroyed it cannot be repaired short of complete replacement of the affected parts.

Survivalists concerned about the EMP threat advocate choosing an older model, usually pre-1980, because such vehicles do not have onboard computers to control ignition and other vital functions. Whether you base your bug-out vehicle choice on this advice depends on how real you consider the EMP threat. In the spectrum of all the possible SHTF scenarios that could cause you to need a bug-out vehicle, the likelihood of a man-made or natural electromagnetic pulse powerful enough to shut down modern vehicles is relatively slim. Still, if you are confident in your mechanical ability to maintain an older vehicle, it wouldn't hurt to have all your bases covered by taking the EMP threat into consideration in your choice.

Old vs. New and Proven Reliability Aside from the remote chance of an EMP attack as described above, better technology and fierce competition among auto manufacturers has resulted in vehicles that are much more reliable than those of 30 or more years ago. While some people may enjoy rebuilding an old American truck or utility vehicle from the 1970s or before, the fact is that such vehicles were forever breaking down even when they were in their prime and most had an average life expectancy of well under 100,000 miles, usually with many repairs required to get even that far. An influx of Japanese cars and pickups in the 1970s and 1980s that routinely ran 200,000–300,000 miles or even more changed the way all automakers built vehicles, and thanks to that change it's not unreasonable to expect that kind of mileage from most any modern vehicle, especially those built in 1990 and later.

With 20 years worth of such vehicles on the used market, you don't have to buy new to take advantage of this improved reliability, but it certainly pays to do your research because some models have a better track record than others. In the used market, popular and proven vehicles that have enjoyed a long production run are the most desirable, as any common issues with a particular model will be well-known, along with the fixes for it. Parts for such models will also be easy to come by, whether used, rebuilt or new. Today, it's easy to find reliable information about specific models on the Internet and read the owner reports and reviews to get a good idea of what you'll be getting into when you buy. The more popular models also will have online owners groups or forums where you can find solutions to any common problems or help with any modifications you may want to make.

Standard vs. Automatic Transmissions Though they have fallen out of favor with most of today's drivers, standard transmissions are simpler and less likely to fail than automatics, especially in older vehicles (today's automatic transmissions are much improved). Standard transmissions are easier to repair if they do fail, and cheaper and easier to replace if necessary. The typical vehicle equipped with a standard will also get better fuel economy compared to the same vehicle equipped with an automatic. Another important advantage is that vehicles with standard transmissions can be push-started in the event of a battery or starter failure.

A possible disadvantage of standard transmissions is that they require more coordination and both feet and both hands to operate, at least when you are starting off or shifting gears. This could become a problem if you are injured, or if you need to do other things while driving, such as the worst-case scenario of having to return fire to defend yourself from the occupants of other vehicles or would-be carjackers.

Four-Wheel-Drive (4WD) and All-Wheel-Drive (AWD) Four-wheel drive and high ground clearance are essential if you plan to drive to a remote bug-out location that requires traveling over rough terrain or long distances on unpaved, infrequently maintained roads. They may also be invaluable in an urban evacuation scenario where the roadway is blocked with various obstacles and you need to drive on the shoulders or across curbs, medians, or ditches. The disadvantages of four-wheel-drive vehicles are that they more expensive to purchase initially and will likely require more maintenance and repairs than simpler, two-wheel-drive vehicles.

Most four-wheel-drive vehicles allow the driver to switch from the four-wheel-drive mode to two-wheel-drive for traveling on the pavement. This is the arrangement used in most SUVs and in trucks designed for some off-road ability. But all-wheel-drive (AWD) systems are becoming increasingly common in passenger cars and car-based crossover SUVs. Whereas regular four-wheel drive can cause problems on dry pavement, all-wheel-drive vehicles use a center differential that allows the axles to turn at different speeds. All-wheel drive can make for improved handing on the road, particularly in adverse weather conditions.

Maintenance, Tools, and Spare Parts Any motor vehicle that is part of your bug-out plan should be mechanically sound to begin with and regularly maintained. All machinery is subject to breakdown at inopportune times and if your bug-out vehicle fails you when you need it, you could be in as much or more danger than if you had stayed put.

Long periods of slow driving in stop-and-go situations such as you might encounter even in the most orderly evacuations of a city are hard on engines and cooling systems. To prevent overheating, one of the most common causes of failure, make sure your radiator is topped off with fresh coolant and that all radiator hoses are in good shape. Drive belts should also be inspected and replaced when they show signs of age or damage. Many newer vehicles have a single belt that drives the alternator, air conditioning compressor, cooling fan, and water pump. Losing this belt will render your vehicle inoperable, so it's a good idea to carry a spare. (Recommended spare parts and the tools to change them are listed in the "Bug-Out Motor Vehicle Checklist" at the end of this chapter.)

Motor Vehicle Modifications and Optional Equipment

Towing Packages If you plan to pull any kind of trailer for carrying extra gear or large backup vehicles such as boats, motorcycles, or ATVs, you will need to make sure your vehicle has adequate towing capacity and is equipped with a trailer hitch that can handle the load. Even small cars can pull lightweight trailers, needing nothing more than a hitch and a signal light connection kit. Some hitches are a simple do-it-yourself bumper installation, or you can take the vehicle to a shop and have a frame-mounted receiver hitch installed. Large SUVs and pickup trucks are rated for much higher towing weights and often come standard with a heavy-duty tow package that includes a receiver hitch, surge brake connections, and a beefed-up cooling system for the engine.

Cargo and Utility Racks Even the smallest economy car can benefit from the addition of cargo or utility racks on the roof. The most versatile racks are the removable crossbar systems such as those sold to carry canoes, kayaks, skies, bicycles, and other sports equipment. Such a rack makes it easy to carry your backup bug-out vehicle as well as additional gear and supplies or other awkward loads that will not fit inside the cabin space. Racks like this are available for practically any style of car, SUV, or pickup truck. Make sure they are rated for the weight you intend to carry on them. Another option is to have a welder fabricate custom racks of the sort that construction contractors frequently install on their pickup trucks for carrying ladders and building materials. You can also build sturdy wooden racks for pickups or other vehicles. Needing canoe racks on a van I owned at one point, I built some sturdy mounting blocks and crossbars out of teak lumber and bolted them directly to the roof, using marine adhesive sealant to prevent any possible leaks.

Carrying and Storing Additional Fuel Other than mechanical breakdown, running out of fuel will be your biggest worry when bugging out by motor vehicle. You can't count on being able to obtain more fuel after the onset of a SHTF scenario, so you should make it a habit to always keep your tank topped off and to keep on hand enough jerry cans of fuel for a complete refill for when you burn through your first tank. This extra tank of fuel will give you quite a long range in most motor vehicles and allow the reserve you need for long delays in traffic jams and other unforeseen events.

Clearing Obstructions and Getting Unstuck In addition to spare parts for your vehicle that you need to carry to ensure that you can keep it running, there are few other items specific to bugging out by motor vehicle that you should carry to improve your chances of getting where you want to go. In the aftermath of a SHTF scenario, you may find that you need to get through a locked gate or a barbed-wire, chain-link, or other type of fence. Heavy-duty wire cutters will work on many types of fences and a pair of 36-inch or larger bolt cutters will defeat most padlocks and chains. You may also encounter a roadway blocked by fallen trees or other obstructions. These may be the result of hurricanes or other storms, or deliberate man-made attempts to close the road. A chainsaw in your vehicle will allow you to open up all but the worst of these, but if you choose not to carry one, at least take along a large handsaw or axe. Likewise, a powerful bumper-mounted winch or a handheld come-along can be used to clear broken-down vehicles and other obstructions out of the roadway. The winch or come-along will also be essential for pulling the vehicle out if you get stuck in mud or other soft conditions off-road. Don't forget to include a shovel as well; if you get stuck while traveling off-road or in snow, a good shovel can make all the difference.

Vehicle Armor   If you are willing to spend the money, there are companies today that can transform most types of ordinary cars, pick-ups and SUVs into bulletproof armored vehicles. This type of business has expanded exponentially in response to terrorist attacks, drug-related violence and kidnappings for ransom. Materials such as Kevlar, steel, and composites can provide varying levels of protection up to the ability to stop rifle rounds, and can be incorporated so that the vehicle appears ordinary. Although you may be able to fabricate some level of DIY armor protection for your vehicle, it won't likely be as effective as a professional job done by companies that specialize in building vehicles to protect heads of state, business executives, diplomats, celebrities, and other individuals at high risk of attack. One such company is Texas Armoring Corporation. Learn more about the possibilities at their website at www.texasarmoring.com.

Passenger Cars

While standard passenger cars do not usually fit most people's mental image of a bug-out vehicle, they should not be ruled out for this use, particularly if that is the kind of vehicle you have now and use every day. As already mentioned, one of the advantages of an ordinary sedan is that it does not look like a stereotypical bug-out vehicle. In such a car, particularly if it is a common one in an ordinary color manufactured in huge numbers, you can blend in and avoid drawing any undue attention to yourself, your family, and the survival gear and supplies you may be carrying. There's a lot to be said for not looking like a target for thieves or looters who may be less prepared and willing to take your gear or even your vehicle.

Other advantages that cars have over SUVs and pickup trucks include a lower initial purchase price and a large number of inexpensive choices in the second-hand market. Because of the popularity of luxury SUVs and huge, fully loaded pickup trucks, many plain, unpretentious cars are not as sought-after and can be had with a similar number of amenities for much less money. Most of them also get better gas mileage as well due to lighter weight and lower profiles that offer less wind resistance.

Consider also the on-the-road handling qualities of cars as compared to SUVs and pickups. Most police departments still use cars instead of other vehicles for their patrol cruisers, and the reasons include better handling, acceleration, and top-end speed. These characteristics are due to the lower center of gravity that allows aggressive driving with less risk of flipping over in high-speed maneuvers. A car could give you this same advantage if you find yourself in a situation where evasive driving tactics are required to escape pursuers. Even without the threat of other drivers, these same handling properties make cars safer in many situations on the road in bad weather.

Today there are numerous high-performance cars to choose from, many of which are wolves in sheep's clothing that do not project the image of muscle cars or sports cars, but look more like sedate family sedans. Some of these cars can match or nearly match many of the more exotic-looking sports cars that are marketed as performance vehicles.

Disadvantages of cars include the lack of four-wheel-drive in most of them and the lack of sufficient ground clearance or adequate suspension to negotiate rough terrain or other obstacles you may have to get around in a bug-out scenario. If you are planning on driving all or most of the way to a remote bug-out location, rather than switching to a backup vehicle or walking the rest of the way in, then a car will probably not be your best choice because of these limitations.

SOME PASSENGERS CAR EXAMPLES

Toyota Corolla This Japanese compact car has been in production since 1968 and is popular all over the world for its reliability and its excellent fuel economy. Current models begin at an MSRP of around $15,000 and the used market is full of good examples in price ranges from less than $2000 to more than $10,000, depending on age and condition. They can be had with either standard or automatic transmissions and in a variety of configurations from four-door sedans to three-door hatchbacks.

Ford Crown Victoria This American-made car is the classic full-sized, four-door sedan. It is the most popular police pursuit vehicle in the U.S. and is a popular taxicab and fleet vehicle because of its rugged construction, V8 engine, and rear-wheel-drive. Although 2007 was the last year a consumer version was available, excellent used examples are easy to find from a high of over $12,000 to less than $3,000 for an early '90s model.

Subaru Legacy Sedan All-wheel drive is standard on Subaru vehicles, and though many of the offerings from this manufacturer fit into the crossover or SUV category, the Legacy sedan is an AWD passenger car that has a great reputation for reliability and has long been popular in areas with tough winter driving conditions. For those who want better performance than the standard 2.5-liter engine, the Legacy is available in a turbocharged version with a five-speed manual transmission. The Legacy has been in production since 1990 and ranges in price from under $2,000 for the older models to about $20,000 for a new one.

Pickup Trucks

Pickup trucks are among the most versatile and useful of all motor vehicles, a fact that accounts for their current popularity across a wide spectrum of the population despite their origins as work vehicles. No other vehicle is better suited for carrying a variety of cargo or can be loaded and unloaded so quickly. This makes pickups ideal for those who want to carry backup vehicles such as small motorcycles, ATVs, bicycles, johnboats, canoes, or kayaks and other specialized gear as part of their bug-out plan.

Many modern pickup trucks are luxury vehicles with all the amenities of comparable cars and a correspondingly high price tag. But for bug-out vehicle purposes, if you can find a true work truck without all the bells and whistles, you'll have the advantage of simplicity and lower initial cost. Many of these are built for heavy loads and come with dual rear wheels. Base-model pickup trucks sold as work vehicles often come with standard transmissions and lack all the extra carpeting, fancy instrumentation, and in some cases even air conditioning and stereo systems.

SIZES AND CONFIGURATIONS OF PICKUP TRUCKS

Pickup trucks are essentially defined by that most useful of features, the bed behind the driver and passenger cabin that makes them so versatile. Some modern pickup trucks sacrifice much of this valuable bed space in favor of extra cabin space, especially the newer four-door sport utility models, in which the bed looks more like an afterthought than the primary design feature of the vehicle. Work trucks, on the other hand, often have a standard cabin with a single bench seat that can accommodate three people and a longer bed in the rear to serve the vehicle's primary purpose. If you need more room for additional equipment in the cabin, such trucks can be had in the extra or super cab versions with space behind the front seat or seats. Even larger cabins are available in the form of crew cab pickups that can carry six people inside. The various cab configurations found in work trucks can also be found in the more expensive, luxury versions of the same trucks that come with every amenity.

Choosing among all these different types of pickup trucks will require a hard look at what you need to carry in the back as well as the number of passengers, if any, that must fit in the forward cabin area. Like most vehicles, pickup trucks are a compromise, and here the choice is between enclosed, lockable, and climate-controlled passenger space and flexible, exposed cargo space in the rear. In addition to the passenger/cargo space layout considerations, pickup trucks come in a range of overall sizes from the compact mini-trucks that are the pickup equivalent of economy cars to behemoth, high-performance muscle trucks with huge, gas-sucking engines.

Compact pickups are simply smaller versions of the basic pickup design that first became popular in the United States when a flood of Japanese models entered the market under the Datsun, Toyota, and Isuzu names. These small trucks were popular for their fuel economy and later versions were sold under the Chevrolet, Ford, and Dodge names, as well as additional imported brands such as Mazda and Mitsubishi. Practically all the early versions of compact trucks came equipped with four-cylinder gasoline engines, and though smaller and less powerful than standard trucks, they were useful in many of the same ways as work and utility vehicles. Newer versions of compact trucks have crept up in size, weight, and engine power to the point where some of them offer few economy advantages in purchase price or fuel consumption over standard full-sized pickups.

Full-sized pickups are essentially the basic work vehicle from which all these other variations were derived. While they are rated for different load capacities, full-sized pickups generally have a bed designed to accommodate standard four-foot-wide construction materials such as plywood or drywall lying flat, unlike the compact pickups in which the rear wheel wells intrude into this four-foot space. Payload can range from 1,000 to 6,000 pounds, depending on the rating, which is one of the following: ½ ton, ¾ ton, 1 ton, or 1½ ton. These ratings do not indicate the true capacity, however, as the actual payload is much more. A ½ ton Ford F-150 can actually haul 1,400 to 3,000 lb., while a 1 ton Ford F-350 can carry as much as 4,000 to 5,800 lb. For most ordinary uses, a

standard ½ ton full-sized pickup is more than adequate, and this is the size that is most popular with pickup owners.

Crossover pickups are a new sort of hybrid vehicle that offer some of the features of a pickup with the comfort and interior space of an SUV. They resemble crew-cab pickups in that they have four doors, but the overall length is much shorter, so that the cargo bed in the rear appears to be more of an afterthought than a real feature. If you don't plan to carry a large backup vehicle like an ATV in the bed, a crossover pickup could be useful because the open cargo area is still more versatile than the trunk of a car or rear of an SUV for fitting a variety of loads. Examples of these crossover pickups include the popular Chevrolet Avalanche and the Honda Ridgeline.

Cargo space in all pickup trucks can, of course, be increased by towing a trailer, and for pulling really heavy loads such as large boats and RVs, full-sized four-wheel-drive pickup trucks with a heavy-duty tow package are the vehicle of choice. These trucks are designed to tow big loads on a regular basis, and can do so without damage to the engine or transmission. The biggest in the class will be fitted with dual rear wheels so that they can carry an increased tongue weight or much larger gooseneck trailers such as those used to haul cattle and horses.

In addition to differences in cab layout, size, and payload, most pickup trucks can be had in two-wheel-drive or four-wheel-drive versions, and many models are also available with either gasoline or diesel engines. The same general points already made about choosing among these options for other types of vehicles apply to pickup trucks as well, though if you've decided that a diesel vehicle will work best for your situation, you'll likely have more choices among pickup trucks (especially on the used market or at vehicle auctions, where you can find retired fleet vehicles).

Disadvantages of pickup trucks as compared to passenger cars and SUVs may include reduced interior cabin space, as discussed above, depending on the particular truck and its design configuration. Pickup trucks are generally more expensive, given the same age and condition as comparable passenger cars, because of their popularity and their usefulness as work vehicles, and in the used market you may find many worn-out and overworked trucks still commanding a surprisingly high price. Handling in wet conditions or at high speed is usually less than ideal in pickup trucks, mainly due to the light weight of the rear end when unloaded and the often higher center of gravity. While performance pickup trucks with hopped-up engines are popular as street cruisers, and many are as fast as or faster than the average car, they may not be as safe to push to the limits in evasive or other aggressive driving situations because of the increased risk of losing control.

SOME PICKUP EXAMPLES

Older Toyotas with 22-R Engine   If you can still find a clean example, the four-cylinder Toyota pickups with the 22-R engine are among the most reliable compact pickups ever built, with many exceeding 400,000 miles without an overhaul. I've owned three of these in the mid-'80s model years and put over 200,000 miles on them with few issues. They are economical to drive and can be found in the used market from under $1,500 for rough ones to well over $7,500 for later models with 4WD.

Ford Ranger/Mazda B-Series   The Ford and Mazda versions of this truck are essentially the same vehicle with the same engine and other components. Bigger and heavier than the true compacts like the older Toyotas and Nissans, they are still smaller than a full-sized truck and get decent fuel economy. They are available in a range of models from the basic four-cylinder with standard transmission to the 4.0-liter V6 versions with 4WD. I currently drive a 1997 Mazda B2300 with the standard transmission. It has 180,000 miles on it and has never been in the shop in the last 90,000.

Ford F-150   The Ford F-150 full-sized pickup is *the* most popular vehicle in America, and has been almost every year for the last 30 years, even including cars and SUVs. It has achieved this status thanks to its versatility in handling the needs of contractors as well as recreational users who need to haul cargo or tow boats and other trailers, as it is just the right size to get most jobs done without being overly heavy or fuel-hungry. The F-150 has been built in so many configurations that it would be impossible to begin to list them here, but you can buy any of them from the 1997–2003 generation up through the present models in production and be assured of getting a rugged pickup capable of extended service. New F-150s in the upper trim levels go for $40,000 or more, with the base model starting at about $23,000. You should be able to find a good older one starting at around $5000.

GMC Sierra 3500HD   The Sierra 3500HD is an example of a full-sized, heavy-duty truck available with a 6.0-liter V8 or 6.6-liter turbo-diesel V8 that puts out 365 hp. It's available with dual rear wheels and would be a good choice if you have to pull a heavy trailer such as one of the larger RVs, boats, or other mobile retreats discussed in the next section. Like other manufacturers' offerings, the Sierra 3500HD is available in several trim packages and configurations. The HD designation began with the model year 2007, but earlier variations of the Sierra 3500 have been around since 1990. Expect to pay over $30,000 for a new Sierra 3500HD, and at least $15,000 for a well-used 2007 model.

Sport Utility Vehicles (SUVs)

SUVs are probably the first vehicles that come to mind for most people when the term "bug-out vehicle" comes up. Most SUVs look the part because of their rugged, outdoorsy styling, which is usually enhanced by features like oversized tires and high ground clearance. Many come standard with four-wheel drive, towing packages, heavy-duty bumpers, and cargo racks. But vehicles that fall into the SUV category range over a broad spectrum and the term can include everything from rock-crawling custom Jeeps with roll cages to extravagant luxury vehicles bearing status-symbol names like Cadillac, BMW, Mercedes, or Porsche. They range in size from the tiny 2,000 lb. Suzuki Samurai to the over 7,000 lb. Hummer H1.

The typical SUV has the passenger-carrying space of a car but is built on a light truck chassis, with many manufacturers adapting the chassis from their popular lines of pickups in the same size class. The earliest SUVs of this type were designed for real work and were usually just as rugged as their pickup truck counterparts. Popular with survey crews and other workers needing more passenger space or interior storage space than a pickup could offer, the powerful four-wheel-drive vehicles of this type such as early Ford Broncos and Chevy Suburbans were often seen working far afield on poorly maintained roads. These vehicles later caught on with the general public as old-fashioned but practical station wagons were abandoned in favor of the SUV with its rugged "cool factor." During the 1990s, SUVs became so popular with

Four-wheel-drive Jeep SUV

those wanting to project an outdoorsy image that practically every automobile manufacturer began offering one or more models, whether they were in the business of building work trucks or not. Almost all of them had names with connotations of adventure: Explorer, Pathfinder, Discovery, Navigator, Yukon, Tahoe, Expedition, and on and on.

As a result of this fashion trend towards SUVs, not all of them are created equal, especially when it comes to off-road capability, where many of the luxury models are more show than go. Those models that do have serious capability are often selected by off-road vehicle enthusiasts for competitions and other events and are well supported with aftermarket accessories and add-ons for owner modifications. Examples include most Jeeps and many vehicles that are no longer in production, like the Suzuki Samurai. An example of a newer SUV that has found favor with enthusiasts is the four-wheel-drive version of the Nissan Xterra.

Disadvantages of SUVs include poor fuel economy in most models due to their heavy weight and excessive windage caused by their high-profile, boxy shape. Another weak point is the high center of gravity that results from the extra ground clearance built into most designs. SUVs have proven to be prone to rollovers because of this, particularly at high speeds on the road, where sudden evasive action can result in loss of control. Purchase price is another factor, with most new SUVs costing more than similarly equipped cars and used models often still holding a good resale value depending on the popularity of the model.

SOME SUV EXAMPLES

Nissan Xterra (4WD versions)   The Nissan Xterra is well regarded among off-road enthusiasts as a capable 4WD SUV. It gives up some of the better on-road handling of the smaller, car-based SUVs in favor of better performance when the going gets rough. When it was first introduced in 2000 it was intended to be a functional, compact SUV, but it was fairly underpowered until more recent years. The current model comes with a 4.0-liter V6 and can be had with either manual or automatic transmission. New prices begin at about $25,000, while the oldest examples can be found in decent condition for about $5,000.

GMC Yukon The GMC Yukon is one of the bigger full-sized SUVs, with seating for up to nine passengers in the newer models. Weighing 5,500 lb. and powered by a big 6.2-liter V8, its fuel economy is not great, but it is sturdy and rugged, with a heavy-duty towing capacity and lots of interior storage space. A new Yukon starts at about $39,000, and the current generation goes back to 2007. The model years from 2000 to 2006 are the best used examples and can range from around $6,000 to $15,000.

Jeep Wrangler The Jeep Wrangler and its predecessors have been around since long before the SUV craze of the 90s spawned the huge variety of vehicles with some pretense of off-road ability on the market today. Unlike most luxury SUVs, which are really best on the pavement, the Wrangler is not so great on the highway but can be quite capable in rough going due to its short wheelbase and good ground clearance. It's popular with off-road enthusiasts and with those who like the removable doors and fabric top. Today, the Wrangler comes in many levels of trim and different configurations and starts at around $22,000. Used models go back to the mid-'80s, when the Wrangler

Hummer H1 SUV

replaced the Jeep CJ series. You can find a decent 10- to 12-year-old specimen for around $5,000.

Hummer H1   Though today it has been replaced by less expensive and more road-friendly derivatives such as the H2 and H3, the original Hummer H1 was as close to the military Humvee as a civilian could get. At more than 7,000 pounds and just a tad under 8½ feet wide, the H1 is a burden in city traffic, but very capable off-road as long as you have fairly open terrain to maneuver in. Its main advantage over lesser vehicles is its 16-inch ground clearance, wheel placement that allows it to traverse 22-inch obstacles, and the ability to cross up to 30 inches of water. It certainly looks the part of a bug-out vehicle, but that may actually be a disadvantage, as mentioned previously. By its final year of production in 2005, the Hummer H1 cost more than $100,000. Today you can find a used one for under $50,000, in some cases as low as $30,000.

Crossover Vehicles

High fuel prices in recent years convinced a lot of the owners of big SUVs that perhaps they didn't need all that bulk, windage, and weight to haul their kids to the soccer game or the mall and that maybe the station wagon their parents had when they were kids was not so bad after all. Auto manufacturers offered a solution to this new need called the crossover. My first impression when I started seeing these vehicles was that they looked like updated station wagons on steroids, with their aggressive, raised stance on oversized wheels and wide tires. Many are available with all-wheel drive and they do offer some of the cargo capacity benefits of SUVs in a smaller, more manageable package. Although built on passenger car chassis, they feature SUV-like visibility all around with high seating that can, in some models, accommodate as many as eight people. Like SUVs, crossovers are designed to appeal to those who don't want to be perceived as boring, everyday family types. Crossovers do have potential as bug-out vehicles, especially when compared to other cars with low ground clearance. The combination of lots of lockable interior cargo space with good fuel economy and better handling than taller SUVs makes them something to consider.

SOME CROSSOVER EXAMPLES

Nissan Murano   The Nissan Murano is a classic example of a mid-sized crossover meant to serve as an alternative to the SUV. More car-like than some crossovers, it still offers a higher seating position like an SUV and plenty of cargo space. In production from 2003 until the present, the Murano can be had for around $10,000 for the oldest used models or just under $30,000 for a new one.

Honda Element   Unlike the sleeker Murano, the boxy Honda Element looks more like a mini-SUV than a car, but it is still a small vehicle, with the extra height giving it the illusion of being bigger. It offers large cargo space in a small package with unique clamshell rear doors and a lowering tailgate like a pickup, and is available in an AWD configuration. 2011 is the last model year to be produced, at an MSRP of just under $21,000. Used models go back to 2003 and can be found from about $7500.

Mazda CX-9   The Mazda CX-9 is one of the better-performing crossovers in its class and price range, with seating for seven passengers and plenty of cargo room. The current model features a 3.7-liter V6 with 273 hp and optional AWD. This vehicle was just introduced in 2007, so used examples still go for $18,000 or so, while a new one lists for a bit over $29,000.

Vans and Minivans

Many types of vehicles classified as vans, from minivans all the way up to the largest cargo work vans, could be used as escape vehicles in the same way as the cars, pickups, and SUVs already discussed in this chapter. The reason I'm not including them here is that because of their extra enclosed space (which often features removable passenger seats), most vans can be converted to mobile retreats, which are the subject of the next section of this book. Some thoughts on converting vans for that purpose are presented in Chapter Five. If you are interested in using a van or minivan solely as an escape vehicle, you can choose one based on your requirements using the guidelines already covered here for cars, pickups and SUVs. Some of these vans are well-suited to the purpose of escape vehicles due to their interior volume for carrying passengers and gear and available AWD option.

BUG-OUT MOTOR VEHICLE CHECKLIST

SPARE PARTS:
- [ ] Spark plugs
- [ ] Spark plug wires
- [ ] Alternator
- [ ] Drive belts
- [ ] Fully charged battery
- [ ] Thermostat
- [ ] Starter
- [ ] Fuel pump
- [ ] Fuel filter
- [ ] Headlamps
- [ ] Taillights and other bulbs
- [ ] Fuses
- [ ] Wiper blades
- [ ] Second spare wheel and tire (in addition to factory-supplied spare)
- [ ] Spare ignition key

OTHER SUPPLIES:
- [ ] Engine oil
- [ ] Transmission fluid
- [ ] Power steering fluid
- [ ] Brake fluid
- [ ] Coolant/antifreeze
- [ ] WD-40 lubricant spray
- [ ] Electrical tape
- [ ] Duct tape
- [ ] Nylon zip ties
- [ ] JB Weld metal glue
- [ ] Misc. fasteners (sheet-metal screws, nuts, bolts, etc.)
- [ ] Baling wire
- [ ] Can of tire repair/inflator (e.g. Slime or Fix-a-Flat)

TOOLS AND ADDITIONAL RECOVERY EQUIPMENT:
- [ ] Standard jack (usually supplied with vehicle)
- [ ] Hi-lift jack with long handle (can serve as winch)
- [ ] Tow strap (20', 20,000lb.-rated, looped ends)
- [ ] Come-along or bumper-mounted winch
- [ ] Lug wrench
- [ ] Tire plug kit
- [ ] 12-volt mini compressor or hand pump
- [ ] Air pressure gauge
- [ ] Socket set (standard or metric depending on vehicle)
- [ ] Open-end and adjustable wrenches
- [ ] Channel-lock pliers
- [ ] Vise-Grips
- [ ] Screwdrivers in several sizes (flathead and Phillips)
- [ ] Hammer
- [ ] Pry bar
- [ ] Spark plug wrench
- [ ] Allen wrench set
- [ ] Jumper cables
- [ ] Voltmeter or circuit tester
- [ ] Heavy-duty wire cutters/wire stripper
- [ ] 36-inch bolt cutters
- [ ] Chainsaw, large tree limb saw, or axe
- [ ] Shovel

2

BUG-OUT MOTORCYCLES

Many people formulating their bug-out plans overlook motorcycles as potential bug-out vehicles. This is probably because, in comparison to automobiles, motorcycles make up only a tiny percentage of the motor vehicles on the road, especially in the U.S. Motorcycles are not for everyone, for obvious reasons: compared to other vehicles they offer less protection from the elements, are limited in their ability to carry luggage or passengers, require more skill to operate in varying conditions, and expose the operator to more danger of serious injury or death when things go wrong. Among the non-riding general public there persists a negative perception of motorcyclists, much of it unfounded or illogical but fueled by the "outlaw biker" stereotype often portrayed in movies and by the anger motorists feel toward the small percentage of reckless riders on high-performance bikes who race through traffic pulling wheelies and splitting lanes like maniacs.

If you've never had a previous interest in riding motorcycles, then considering one as a bug-out vehicle may not be for you and it is not my intent in this chapter to convince you otherwise. If you are interested, though, it's never too late to learn. You can start by taking a motorcycle safety course and trying out a reasonably sized bike. I've been riding since my pre-teen years and have owned a variety of motorcycles throughout my life, but there have also been periods of several years when I didn't ride because I was exploring other pursuits. Like most people who ride, I keep coming back to it because the motorcycling experience offers a sense of freedom you can't get with any other land-based motor vehicle.

For many people who ride, motorcycles are only recreational vehicles to be used in sunny weather when the conditions are ideal for an open-air experience. Other recreational motorcyclists are much more serious about riding and use their machines for vacation touring or a variety of adventures like backcountry exploring on dual sport bikes. A smaller segment of the motorcycling community uses their two-wheeled transportation for economical daily commuting to work, as most motorcycles offer excellent fuel economy compared to automobiles. A smaller number still use motorcycles exclusively for all their transportation needs and do not even own "cages" (a derogatory term some riders use to refer to automobiles).

Better gear than ever before is available to make up for the shortcomings of motorcycles, and with the right combination of bike, equipment, and necessary skills, there is no reason why a motorcycle can't work as your bug-out vehicle. Since this chapter falls in the "Escape Vehicles" section of this book, the kinds of motorcycles discussed here have to be capable of sustained trips on the road at highway speeds. Smaller off-road-only motorcycles are discussed in the section "Alternative Equipment and Backup Vehicles." Still, like SUVs and four-wheel-drive trucks, many of the street-capable machines covered here also have remarkable abilities in the dirt and some can go places no full-sized four-wheeled vehicle could venture.

Disadvantages of Motorcycles as Bug-Out Vehicles

Since the motorcycles described in this chapter are primarily designed to travel on roads, whether paved or minimally maintained gravel, all the disadvantages that come with travel by road in general, as discussed in the previous chapter, apply to motorcycles as well. This includes the possibility of encountering man-made roadblocks, both the official kind set up by authorities who wish to limit or restrict movement and the criminal kind that may be set up by those who wish to

take advantage of the situation. While in some cases a motorcycle may allow you to go around obstacles that block larger vehicles, manned roadblocks will be more dicey, as you will be a wide-open target on a vehicle that offers no concealment, much less cover. This disadvantage can also manifest itself in any urban or traffic situation in a post-SHTF event, making you an easy target of opportunity to shoot at or hit with a larger vehicle.

You are exposed in other ways on a motorcycle too, to a greater risk of injury or death in a crash as well as to the elements. Although many riders survive high-speed crashes without injury thanks to a combination of the right protective gear and luck, if you hit a solid object (such as another vehicle, a guardrail, a tree, or a signpost) at high speed, no gear will save you. Exposure to the cold on a motorcycle is compounded by the wind chill of riding at speed, and when the temperature dips below freezing it can quickly lead to hypothermia unless you are wearing good cold-weather riding gear. Likewise, exposure to extreme heat or prolonged heavy rain can make your life difficult. In every way you are going to have to deal with the elements more on a motorcycle than in any automobile.

In addition to the increased risk of injury in a crash, there is also more potential for a crash to happen, since two-wheeled vehicles have a lot less rubber in contact with the road than automobiles. Loss of traction leading to a crash can happen fast and with little warning due to wet or icy roads, loose gravel, oil on the road, and other surface conditions that might not be a big deal in a car, truck or SUV.

Another potential disadvantage of the small size and lighter weight of motorcycles is that they are much easier to steal than automobiles. Two or three strong men can quickly hoist even a big bike into the back of a pickup and drive off with it, whether the fork is locked or not. In a post-SHTF scenario, all vehicles including motorcycles could be at a premium and a risk to leave anywhere for long, unless hidden completely out of sight. In an urban setting or anyplace else where you can't conceal it, you can use a heavy chain or cable to secure a motorcycle to a solid object like a tree or lamppost, but this will only deter those who are not equipped with bolt cutters. The best policy is to stay with the bike or keep it out of sight.

If this long list of disadvantages hasn't dissuaded you from thinking about a motorcycle as a bug-out vehicle, the rest of this chapter will help you choose and outfit the bike that's best for your needs.

Key Bug-Out Motorcycle Considerations

Ease of Concealment   This is a motorcycle advantage that many people overlook. As pointed out in the disadvantages above, motorcycles are easy to steal if left unattended, but because of their much smaller size and weight compared to automobiles, concealing one is relatively easy. If you need to leave it somewhere along your route or when you get to the farthest point you can ride to, a small camouflaged tarp or some natural vegetation from the surrounding area can make your motorcycle disappear. Often you can find a place to ride even a heavy street bike off the road and into the bushes or woods nearby, where you can camp unseen by others traveling by on the road. Even in normal times, this method of "stealth" camping is often used by adventurous motorcycle tourists who don't want to pay for a campground or other accommodations. In an urban setting, you can also hide and lock up your motorcycle inside your house, in a small storage shed, or inside a large van or box truck. Getting the biggest touring bikes through doorways might require removing the luggage systems, but the ability to move a motorcycle inside can be a big advantage in many situations.

Maintenance and Adjustments   Motorcycles generally require more frequent maintenance than automobiles. If you plan to use a motorcycle as an escape vehicle, you must know how to do the required routine maintenance and adjustments. You will greatly increase your self-sufficiency if you learn how to adjust cables, troubleshoot electrical problems, and replace your own tires (and drive chain or belt if your bike has one). Tires wear out much faster on a motorcycle than on a car or truck, and one big difference between automobiles and motorcycles is that you won't have the room to carry a complete spare wheel with a mounted tire—not to mention that the front and rear wheels are invariably different. You must have the tools and know-how to fix your own flat tires on the side of the road. Tubeless tires can often be plugged if the puncture is not too big. If you have inner tubes, you will need a patch kit and/or spare tubes, along with tire irons to remove the tube and a manual or 12-volt pump to refill it with air. You'll also need a means of lifting each wheel off the ground in order to remove it. Many motorcycles have center kickstands that make this easy; if yours doesn't, you can install one or carry one of the small jackstands made for the purpose. In a pinch, you can place a log or big rock under the frame to support it while you remove the wheel.

Motorcycles also generally require more frequent oil changes, and some engine designs require periodic valve adjustments, carburetor cleaning, and other maintenance chores that most automobile owners don't have to worry about. But despite the increased frequency of maintenance, most modern street or dual-sport motorcycles are as dependable as any other vehicle and can be expected to run 100,000 miles or more. A few of the important mechanical differences that you will encounter with a motorcycle are explained below, as well as how they might affect maintenance intervals and long-term durability.

Single-, Twin-, or Multi-Cylinder Engine?   Modern motorcycle engines come in a variety of cylinder configurations. Many of the dual-sport bikes discussed in this chapter use the simplest design of all: the single cylinder engine, often referred to as a "thumper." These bikes are designed to be lightweight and agile for their off-road function and give up some overall power and engine size to achieve this. Two-cylinder engines, such as the V-twins found on virtually all cruisers, allow for more displacement and power, especially low-end torque at lower rpm. Other two-cylinder configurations include parallel twins and opposed twins, such as the "boxer" engines BMW motorcycles are famous for. Multi-cylinder motorcycle engines include inline three- and four-cylinder variations and flat six-cylinder engines such as the 1832cc power plant found in the Honda Goldwing.

Your choice of engine type will depend a lot on the type of riding you want to do. A 650cc thumper is fine for an all-around, do-everything kind of bike, but if you plan on riding long hours on the highway, you will enjoy the extra power and torque of a rumbling V-twin or the smooth, high-revving top speeds of a multi-cylinder engine.

Final Drive Systems A motorcycle's engine power is transferred to the rear wheel by a chain, a flexible belt, or a drive shaft similar to those used in automobiles. Motorcycles designed for rugged off-road use are usually fitted with chain drives, which have a limited life before they need to be replaced along with the front and rear sprockets they run on. Of the three types of final drive, chains also require the most attention, such as adjustment and lubrication. But they work well on bikes with long-travel suspensions such as those typical on dual-sport motorcycles, and they hold up well to the abuse of grit, gravel, and water as long as they are cleaned and lubricated often. Chains can be replaced on the side of the road with a minimum of tools.

Flexible toothed belts, such as those used on almost all Harley Davidsons, typically last many times longer than chains, often up to 100,000 miles. They require practically no maintenance or adjustment, but could be replaced on the side of the road in the event of a failure. The only downside to modern belt drive systems is that if you plan to ride extensively off-road or on gravel roads, there is a chance that the belt could be damaged or broken by small rocks getting between the belt and the pulleys.

Some motorcycle manufacturers, such as BMW, have long used a shaft drive system like those on automobiles. These have the advantage of not requiring the maintenance or adjustment that chains do, but they are a lot heavier than either chains or belts, and when they fail they are much more difficult and expensive to repair. A shaft drive failure in a remote location will leave you stranded, but the modern shaft drive systems used on motorcycles today are quite reliable and many adventure bikes such as the BMW GS series use this system.

Liquid vs. Air-Cooled Engines The simplest motorcycles, such as older BMWs and all Harley Davidsons with the exception of the V-Rod, use the flow of air across their cylinders to keep the engine within operating temperature. Air-cooling eliminates the complexity and vulnerability to damage or failure of liquid-cooled engines, which have added components such as the radiator, hoses, and the water pump. A downside to air-cooling is that engine life can be shortened by the higher operating temperatures, especially if your riding involves a lot of slow going or stop-and-go situations where the air flow is reduced.

Liquid cooling is good for negotiating off-road conditions at slower speeds or dealing with long delays or gridlock in traffic. It also helps an engine endure for a long lifespan, which is why it is used exclusively in modern automobiles that are expected to run 200,000 miles or more. With motorcycle engines, the larger the displacement, the harder it is to cool with air flow alone. This is especially true on larger touring machines with fairings and side panels that block the air flow.

Equipment and Modifications

Riding Gear for Safety and Comfort Because you will be much more exposed to the elements and the danger of impact with the road, other vehicles, and flying objects, motorcycle riding requires special gear if you want to be reasonably comfortable and safe. Most states have laws requiring motorcycle riders to wear a helmet, at minimum. Full-face helmets are best in the event of a crash and also offer more comfort in cold or rain by keeping your entire head and face covered. Modern flip-up or modular full-faced helmets offer this comfort and protection with the option of raising the chin bar and shield if you need to talk to someone while stopped. If you wear an open helmet without a face shield, you should at least wear impact-resistance riding glasses or goggles, as your eyes will exposed to all sorts of dangers from flying insects to rocks and other road debris.

Safety gear shouldn't stop at the head, but should also include protective gloves, boots, pants, and a jacket. The best of these are reinforced with leather or Kevlar and not only protect you from abrasion if you go sliding down the road, but also incorporate armor in critical areas like the knees and elbows for impact resistance. In addition, most well designed riding gear will keep you warm in the cold and dry in the rain through a system of removable inner or outer layers. And with today's mesh gear designed for summer riding, you can ride in comfortable protective gear in the hottest weather without overheating.

For extreme cold-weather riding, there is also the option of electrically heated clothing such as vests that can be worn under your protective riding gear and are powered by being plugged into the bike's 12-volt electrical system. Some bikes are also equipped with heated handlebar grips and seats, or these can be added as an aftermarket accessory.

Luggage Systems: Carrying Your Bug-Out Gear on a Motorcycle To make a motorcycle work as a bug-out vehicle, you will need a way to securely carry your gear and supplies without compromising your safety while riding. This rules out wearing a backpack on your person, which raises your center of gravity and is tiring as well. Instead, the motorcycle should carry all the weight and bulk with a system of luggage racks and hard or soft panniers. Luggage systems vary widely, depending on the type of bike, but many sophisticated and reliable options are available due to the popularity of motorcycle touring. Adventure tourists on dual-sport motorcycles often carry everything they need for extended camping while traveling in remote terrain, enjoying a style of travel that comes close to simulating a bug-out scenario on two wheels.

Panniers or saddlebags that fit low over each side of the rear wheel are the best place to start loading up a motorcycle, because they keep the weight low and balanced. Your heaviest items can be carried in these, while bulkier but lightweight items like tarps, sleeping bags, and extra clothing can be packed in duffle bags or dry bags and strapped across the rear of the seat or on a luggage rack. Panniers can be of the rigid, hard-shell variety or made of fabric similar to backpacks and other soft luggage. (Color-matching hard panniers often come as standard equipment on dedicated touring bikes.) Adventure riders on dual sport machines tend to favor utilitarian aluminum hard cases or other waterproof lockable cases, such as Pelican cases or military surplus ammo cans bolted to racks on each side of the rear wheel. Those who ride in more extreme off-road conditions often prefer soft panniers, as the hard cases can break a leg or ankle in certain kinds of spills. Cruiser motorcycles usually look better with leather saddlebags that match the low-slung lines of the bike.

Cruiser-style motorcycles also frequently have an upright sissy bar/passenger backrest that can hold purpose-made T-bags or simply serve as a support to lash on a large duffle or backpack. An advantage of the tall sissy bar is that you could simply lash on your standard bug-out backpack and quickly remove it for hiking when you reach the end of the road. But any of the motorcycles discussed in this chapter can carry more than you would be able to carry in a simple bug-out backpack if you were traveling on foot. How much more depends on the particular bike and your own creativity when loading it.

Motorcycle Trailers and Sidecars Another way to increase the load-carrying ability and general utility of a motorcycle is to pull a trailer behind the bike or attach a sidecar to it. Originally meant to carry a passenger but also useful for stowing gear, sidecars are mostly a novelty item these days, but you can still buy them for many types of motorcycles or build your own. A sidecar will transform your bike into a three-wheeler, and handling will be different than a conventional motorcycle.

Some motorcycle tourists, especially couples who ride two-up for extended trips, like to pull their gear behind them in trailers. This could be an option worth considering if you are bugging out with your partner on a single motorcycle, as the passenger will take up much of the space that would normally be available for tying down extra gear. Some motorcycle trailers are strictly cargo carriers, but there are also pop-up camper trailers available that would cross over into the mobile retreat category discussed in the next section.

Solo or Two-Up Unless you are planning to use a trailer or side-car as discussed above, you will probably want to have two motor-cycles if you are bugging out as a couple. This will allow you to carry much more gear without being crowded or overloaded. If you were inclined to bug out on motorcycles as a family, two adults on separate bikes could also carry a child each, though this is not an ideal setup. But realistically, most people considering bugging out by motorcycle will probably be single individuals who will be riding solo and travel-ing light. It is in this application that motorcycles really come into their own as bug-out vehicles.

Dual Sport Motorcycles

When I was growing up in a small town in Mississippi in the '70s, prac-tically every boy in my neighborhood had a small motorcycle in the 75 to 250cc range. These motorcycles were invariably what we called "on-road/off-road" motorcycles at the time, and were usually Hondas, Suzukis, Kawasakis, or Yamahas. The "on-road" aspect meant that they were street legal, complete with turn signals, lights, brakes, and mir-rors, so we could ride them to school or zip up and down neighbor-hood streets. The "off-road" aspect meant that they came equipped with knobby tires and tall, long-travel suspension, and were lightweight enough that we could ride them on trails and logging roads in the woods and climb hills and jump homemade ramps in our attempts to imitate our motorcycle hero of the time, Evel Knievel.

Back then, most adults rode big street bikes such as Harleys and Goldwings, and I wouldn't have predicted that the on-road/off-road concept would continue to grow and develop into a category of motor-cycles known as "dual sport" bikes. But today such machines are avail-able in a range of sizes from a wide variety of manufacturers. Dual sport motorcycles can offer the best of both worlds, bridging the gap between long-distance highway touring machines and rugged off-road "enduros" that can eat up rough terrain. A dual sport motorcycle is the Jeep of the two-wheeled world and the popularity of this type of motorcycle continues to grow as more and more serious adventurers go out and show the rest of us what is possible with this type of bike. Dual sport adventure riders favor long-distance journeys in some of the least developed parts of the planet, and many ride north through Alaska to the Arctic Ocean, south through the most rugged parts of the Andes Mountains, through the heart of Africa, across Siberia, into the Australian Outback, and on and on. Because they are used in such remote areas, dual-sport bikes come equipped with larger fuel tanks than most motorcycles their size, and this makes them well-suited to being used as bug-out vehicles.

However, dual sport motorcycles also have some disadvantages compared to the other types discussed in this chapter. Like any other piece of gear with the "dual-purpose" or "multipurpose" label, dual-sport motorcycles are all about compromise. These motorcycles have the capability for both highway riding and off-road riding, but because they must be able to do both adequately, they do not excel at either. All but the smallest dual-sport bikes are much heavier than real dirt bikes (which are covered in Chapter Seven in the "Additional Equipment" part of this book), so they are limited when it comes to negotiating truly rough terrain or single-track trails. The heavier weight means that you have to be more careful climbing steep slopes or getting into situations where you might have to manhandle the bike or pick it up after a fall. Because they are also designed for the road, dual-sport bikes tend to have more breakable parts than true dirt bikes, including fairings and other plastic body parts, windshields, mirrors, turn signals, and headlights. Most serious dual-sport riders install various crash bars and other guards to protect these vulnerable parts so they can survive most of the minor falls and crashes that are inevitable in off-road riding.

Looking at dual-sport bikes in comparison to motorcycles built strictly for the road, we can see the other side of the compromise that is necessary in designing these machines. Because of the need for more ground clearance for negotiating off-road obstacles and the longer-travel suspension setup that is typical on these bikes to enable travel on rough terrain at speed, dual-sport motorcycles sit much higher and have a higher center of gravity than street bikes. Because they are taller they also present much more surface area to the wind, and some can be particularly treacherous in strong crosswinds with all of that surface area acting like a sail. Because of this height and windage, some dual-sport bikes produce a lot of buffeting to the rider at high speeds, particularly when traveling among big semi rigs that create turbulent air. This effect is more noticeable on the bikes of this type that are on the lighter end of the weight spectrum.

As long as you keep these compromises in mind, you can probably choose a dual sport motorcycle that will do the job for your particular purpose and location. If most of your expected route involves travel on good surfaces, such as pavement or well-maintained gravel, the bigger, heavier dual-sport bikes in the 800 to 1200cc range like the BMW or KTM twins will probably serve you just fine. However, if your bug-out location is closer to home, and reaching it necessitates traveling rough dirt roads, trails, or even going cross-country, a smaller, lighter dual sport bike with a 650cc or smaller engine like the Suzuki DR 650 will probably work best.

BMW R100 GS dual-sport motorcycle

The inexpensive Kawasaki KLR 650 is perhaps the quintessential dual-sport motorcycle, in production since 1989 and performance-tested by adventurous journeys all over the world. I currently own one of the second-generation (2008 to present) models of this bike and find it to be a great fit for most of the riding I do, which involves highway riding to get to remote national forest lands where I use it to explore logging and fire roads off the beaten path. It does all this while easily carrying everything I need to camp for several days or longer. With a six-gallon fuel tank and a fuel economy of around 50 mpg in most riding conditions, it has up to a 300-mile range. The KLR 650 is widely available in the used motorcycle market, often equipped with after-market add-ons that make it even more suitable as a bug-out vehicle.

Some Dual-Sport Motorcycles Examples

Kawasaki KLR 650   For the reasons mentioned above, the Kawasaki KLR 650 is one of the best all-around dual sport motorcycles out there. It is simple to work on and has great aftermarket support, as well as active enthusiast groups and online forums to answer any questions you may have. KLRs are reliable and people tend to ride them to the ends of the Earth, usually with few problems. One reason the KLR is so popular is that it's cheap. Although a current model may have an MSRP of around $6,000, dealers often sell them at considerable dis-counts—sometimes under $5,000 with a full warranty. Used examples of the first-generation models can be found for well under $2,000 for rough ones and around $3500 for a bike fully equipped for adventure. The second-generation model can be found used for as little as $3,000, though well outfitted ones generally go for more than $4,000. Information on the new model is available at www.kawasaki.com.

BMW 1150GS   BMW has long been a leader in the dual sport/adventure bike market, and their GS line includes bikes with engine

First generation (left) and second generation Kawasaki KLR 650 motorcycles loaded for touring

sizes from 650 to 1200cc. The bigger BMWs like the 1150 GS are particularly good at doing high-mileage days at high speeds with a heavy load. And in addition to this highway capability, they are quite able off-road, as long as you take the extra weight into consideration and don't get into situations you can't get out of. This bike has been made popular by the publicity it has received from many long trips, including around-the-world adventures, and has a good reputation for reliability. The 1150 GS is widely available on the used market since it was in production from 1999 to 2005 (it has since been replaced by the 1200 GS). You can find a good example of the 1150 GS for anywhere between about $6,500 and $11,000, depending on condition and optional equipment. More about BMW's GS series can be found at www.bmwmotorcycles.com.

KTM 990 Adventure All of the KTM dual sport bikes are capable performers, and they are more suited to advanced riders than lower-powered basic bikes like the KLR. The latest "Dakar" version of the KTM 990 Adventure boasts 115 hp compared to the 35 hp of the KLR. It has a six-speed transmission and a fuel capacity of 5.2 gallons. Like the bigger BMWs, the KTM 990 is not inexpensive. MSRP is around $15,000. The KTM website is www.ktm.com.

Standard Motorcycles

Standard motorcycles are the street bikes most similar to dual-sport bikes, in that they are basic, do-it-all machines with an upright seating position and little in the way of accessories, at least as delivered from the factory. For everyday transportation and utility, standards are great bikes. They are seen everywhere on the streets of less-developed nations, where many people ride motorcycles as their only means of transportation. Good examples of classic standard motorcycles are the venerable Triumph Bonneville, which has been in production from 1959 to the present in various forms, and the earlier Harley Davidson Sportster, which debuted in 1957 and was more of a standard than a cruiser in the early years. When Japanese motorcycles were first introduced into the United States in the late 1960s and 1970s, the majority of

Harley Davidson Sportster customized for dual-sport riding

them were standards in the small to medium sizes, such as the Honda CB series and the Kawasaki KZ series. Standard motorcycles are still offered today by most manufacturers, though they may look more aggressive and some are larger and more powerful than their predecessors.

Because they don't have fairings, windshields, plastic body panels, and other unnecessary cosmetic niceties, standard motorcycles are easy to work on and maintain. Everything is right there in the open—just a frame, an engine, two wheels, a gas tank, and a simple seat. Part of the appeal of the standard is this classic, stripped-down appearance and lack of distinctive styling common to other classes of motorcycles.

The standard riding position is as natural as possible. The handlebars are placed so that you don't have to reach far forward, with the shoulders in a line above the hips. Feet are naturally below you on foot pegs that keep them in a position for the best control while allowing you to stand if necessary to absorb the shock of hitting something in the road. Because of these ergonomics and the moderate displacement and power, most standards are ideal motorcycles for beginning riders to learn on. And for the more experienced, the clean slate of a naked bike is an ideal platform on which to build a custom bike for a specific purpose.

SOME STANDARD MOTORCYCLES EXAMPLES

Triumph Bonneville T100 The classic Triumph Bonneville is still available in its modern interpretation as a naked standard with an 856cc parallel-twin engine. Though the styling is right out of the '60s, the modern Bonneville is fuel-injected and features today's much-improved brakes and suspension. The current model has an MSRP of $8,800. Used models of the T100 version with mostly the same specifications go back to 2007 and can be found for as low as $5,000. The new Bonneville is featured on Triumph's website at www.triumph.co.uk.

Harley Davidson XR 1200   The XR 1200 is one of the latest of many variations of the Sportster, and this one is closer to a basic standard motorcycle than anything else offered by this American manufacturer. The seating position is upright, foot pegs and controls are in the mid-position, and exhaust pipes are high and upswept, unlike the low-slung Harley cruisers. Like the rest of the Sportster lineup, the XR 1200 is powered by the extremely reliable V-twin Evolution engine with its loads of low-end torque. Introduced into the U.S. in 2009, the current model has an MSRP of $11,800. All Harleys hold their value well, but used XR 1200s can be found for under $10,000. More information on the new XR 1200 can be found at www.harley-davidson.com.

Honda CB 750   The Honda CB 750 was one of the best of the Japanese standard motorcycles that swept the U.S. market back when it was introduced in the late 1960s. At that time, with its four-cylinder engine, it was considered a "superbike" and out-performed many motorcycles with larger displacement engines. The classic version of this model was manufactured until 1982 when it was replaced by the CB 750 Nighthawk version, which is also a standard, but with more modern styling. It's hard to say for sure what you would expect to pay for a good older CB 750. I owned a 1979 model in the mid-'90s and sold it for around $1,500. Clean examples of these are considered collectibles now and may be much pricier. The Nighthawk versions are more common and with some searching you can probably pick up a good one for $1,500 to $2,000.

Cruiser Motorcycles

This is the type of motorcycle that is most popular in the United States. Cruiser motorcycles have become an icon of American culture, with many styling cues and accoutrements derived from the horseback-riding cowboys of frontier legend. Cruiser riders tend to favor leather and chrome and most customize their bikes with add-on accessories. This style of motorcycle is defined by the relaxed riding position, often leaning back against a backrest with the feet extended on forward-control foot pegs or highway pegs. The more extreme examples, especially "choppers," feature tall handlebars called "ape hangers" and/or raked-out front ends that extend the wheelbase so much that they lose a lot of maneuverability at low speeds.

Because of the riding position and ergonomics of cruiser motorcycles, they are not designed for top-end performance or knee-dragging, high-speed cornering. Instead, they are best at what their name implies: cruising. This means they can comfortably eat up long distances at regular highway speeds. When set up with saddlebags and other luggage, or perhaps a tall sissy bar for lashing on a backpack, a cruiser can carry what you need in a bug-out situation if your route will be on pavement or well-maintained gravel.

Disadvantages of cruiser-style motorcycles as bug-out vehicles include the typically low ground clearance that is more about street styling than practicality, and all the added chrome bling found on most of them that will be hard to hide in the woods and may attract thieves in the city. The bigger ones are also heavy and too long to maneuver in any kind of real off-road riding, and often have minimal suspension systems that will jar your spine on bumpy terrain. Despite all this cruisers are everywhere and most are easy to work on and keep going.

HARLEY DAVIDSON MOTORCYCLES

Despite the premium price they command both new and used, in most parts of the country you will see more Harley Davidson motorcycles on the road than any other make. Harleys offer a few advantages worth considering when you're looking at motorcycles as bug-out vehicles. For one, because Harleys of all descriptions are everywhere, parts are easily obtained even in small towns and rural areas, unlike more exotic brands like BMW, Triumph, or KTM. One common criticism of Harleys is that they use primitive technology from an earlier era, which is partly true, but this can also be an advantage because the simple designs can be worked on without specialized knowledge or tools. Many parts can be fabricated in a home shop and because of this, you rarely see Harley Davidson motorcycles of any vintage retired to the junkyard.

They can be rebuilt over and over and for this reason could be the best choice in the aftermath of a seriously long-term grid-down event. Thanks to their basic electrical systems, they are already practically EMP-proof, and if you are really concerned about that you can get an older Harley with a kick-starter.

During the 1970s when the company was taken over by AMF, Harley Davidson products began to get a bad reputation as unreliable, oil-leaking machines and their popularity declined. Part of this decline was also due to the huge influx of Japanese motorcycles into the U.S. market, and these less expensive foreign bikes were readily accepted as they proved their reliability. But Harley Davidson made a big come-back in the mid-'80s and redesigned their power plants to make them more reliable than ever while still retaining the simplicity of the V-twin design they were famous for. These engines are tuned for low-end torque, which means you don't have to shift as often to accelerate or keep them in the power band. And of course they are also famous for their distinctive sound. There are many imitators, but if you are going to ride a V-twin cruiser, then Harley Davidson might as well be the first place you look. You can find used ones in great condition anywhere, often with low mileage, as many owners spend more time polishing the chrome and showing them off than actually riding.

One Harley Davidson model that is often overlooked by the riders of the bigger models but has potential as a bug-out motorcycle is the ubiquitous Sportster. The Sportster has been in continuous production since its introduction in 1957, and is still offered today in a variety of configurations with either an 833cc or 1200cc V-twin Evolution engine. Sportsters with this engine, which was introduced in 1986, are among the most bulletproof motorcycles you can buy and are easy to work on and cheap to purchase and maintain. I recently picked-up an 11-year-old XL 1200 Custom Sportster for less than the price of most used KLR 650s. It runs like a new machine and has had zero issues. Although not as lightweight as my KLR, at 540 lb., the Sportster is still small and nimble enough to be taken off-road to some extent and many owners have converted them to rugged adventure machines with knobby tires and taller suspensions. With these modifications the Sportster can be transformed into a powerful dual sport machine that gets great fuel economy and has loads of low-end torque.

SOME CRUISER-STYLE MOTORCYCLES EXAMPLES

Harley Davidson Sportster   The Sportster blurs the line between a cruiser and a standard, but most of the recent XL models other than the previously described XR 1200 are set up in a cruising configuration with forward controls and a low-slung seat and are usually decked out in chrome and glossy paint. They are also available in "blacked-out" versions such as the 883 Iron and the Nightster. Most of the Sportsters can be had with either an 883cc or a 1200cc engine. The 883 gets up to 60 mpg on the highway, and the 1200 averages close to 50 mpg. They range in price from a low of about $3,000 on the used market to over $11,000 new, depending on the size and model. Unless you are a competent mechanic, avoid the pre-1986 Ironhead versions of the Sportster. Read more about the modern Sportster and all current Harley Davidson models at www.harley-davidson.com.

Harley Davidson Dyna   The Harley Davidson Dyna family includes a wide range of models that use the Harley "big twin" engine but are still relatively lightweight and nimble compared to the company's heavier cruisers. Some of the Dyna models look just like a slightly larger Sportster and are widely considered to be the best-handling and best-performing Harleys of all. With their bigger frames and larger engines, they are better suited for carrying heavy loads, two-up riding, or long-distance days. They are more expensive than the Sportsters, both new and used, but you can sometimes find a good example from the 1990s for under $6,500, and later models for well under $10,000.

Touring Motorcycles

If covering long distances quickly and comfortably is important to you, then a touring motorcycle may be your best choice. Touring motorcycles (also sometimes referred to as "dressers" or "baggers") are typically large motorcycles with lots of factory luggage space built in, usually in the form of hard, lockable saddlebags mounted on the rear as well as an additional trunk or top box behind the passenger seat.

A touring motorcycle converted to a "trike" configuration

These motorcycles are designed for long-distance travel and are heavy for stability with a longer wheelbase for stretched-out, all-day comfort for the driver and passenger. Most touring motorcycles built today have large displacement engines designed for running at high speeds for hour after hour on the interstate. They are also fitted with higher-capacity gas tanks to extend their range between fuel stops on long trips. Touring bikes offer the best protection from the elements of any type of motorcycle, with large front fairings and windshields usually fitted as standard equipment. Other comfort features include heated grips and seats and accessory outlets for plugging in heated clothing. Most bikes in this class are equipped with stereo systems built into the dash behind the fairing, as well as other instrumentation not found on more basic machines. The seating position is usually upright as on a standard motorcycle, although some of the bikes in the sport touring category have a somewhat forward-leaning position.

The heavy weight of a touring motorcycle, which makes it so comfortable and stable on the highway, can be a disadvantage if you have to get it over or around obstacles or transport it in a pickup or trailer. Some touring motorcycles weigh as much as 850 to 900 pounds, making them unsuitable for going off-road except on well-maintained gravel or smooth, wide paths. If a bike that heavy falls over or gets stuck in mud or sand, it will be difficult or impossible for the rider to extricate it alone. Working on big touring motorcycles is much more difficult as well, partly because of the weight and bulk and partly because of all the extra parts like fairings, body side panels, and other covers and parts that have to be removed first to access the engine, battery, and other essential components. Fixing flats or changing tires will be harder and most components and parts will be more expensive. Because they are used for what they are designed for, most used touring bikes sold at low prices will have high mileage on them compared to other types of motorcycles that are ridden more casually. If you are buying new, expect to pay as much for a well-equipped touring bike as you would pay for an average new car.

TOURING MOTORCYCLES EXAMPLE

Honda Goldwing   The Honda Goldwing is the quintessential big touring motorcycle and has been continually refined and upgraded since the GL 1100 Interstate version was introduced in 1980. The latest version is the GL 1800, which has an 1832cc fuel-injected engine. Late-model Goldwings are loaded with technology, including antilock brakes, optional airbag, in-dash GPS, seat and grip heaters, and many other amenities not found on most motorcycles. The Goldwing was not produced in 2011, but a new model has been introduced for 2012. The 2010 model had an MSRP of $28,000, while used examples can be much more reasonable, starting at about $3,500 for a model from the 1980s. More information is available at Honda's website at power sports.honda.com.

Sport Bikes and Sport Tourers

Sport bikes (often referred to as "crotch rockets") excel at what they were designed for: flat-out performance. No other motorcycle can compete with these street-legal derivatives of pure racing machines when it comes to acceleration, top speed, and, in most cases, handling. If speed were your only consideration in getting out of Dodge, a sport bike would be ideal, as they are the fastest land vehicles an ordinary person can afford to own. Some are capable of exceeding 200 miles per hour in their stock form. But speed isn't everything, and these motorcycles call for a forward-leaning riding position that is not conducive to long hours in the saddle and don't offer much provision for carrying anything but the rider.

Sport touring motorcycles, on the other hand, offer much of the performance of pure sport bikes with practical advantages that include streamlined hard luggage and better all-around comfort. This type of motorcycle is often used for extreme long-distance riding at high speeds, such as the famous Iron Butt Rally in which riders check in at all four corners of the United States, riding well over a thousand miles per day, day after day. A sport touring motorcycle could work as an escape vehicle if your route will be on good roads and you plan to cover a lot of ground. Some, such as the Kawasaki Concours, can be loaded down to carry about as much gear as most of the other motorcycles in this chapter and have proven themselves reliable over long production runs.

SPORT TOURER EXAMPLE

Kawasaki ZG 1000 Concours   The Kawasaki Concours is a 1,000cc sport touring motorcycle with a huge (7.5 gallon) fuel tank that is capable of long-distance, high-speed touring with a full complement of gear. The ZG 1000 (first generation) Concours was in production from 1986 to 2006, and has since been replaced by the ZG 1400. The original Concours has always been an inexpensive touring machine compared to its competitors, but has long been popular because of its proven reliability and ease of maintenance. Good used examples can be found for as low as $2,000 for an older one, and $4,000 will buy a nice one in good condition. Don't be afraid of high mileage on these bikes, as they are meant to go the distance and will hold up to it. You can get all the specifications for the new ZG 1400 at www.kawasaki.com.

Trikes and Other Three-Wheeled Street Machines

Trikes (with two wheels in the back) and newer three-wheeled machines with two wheels in the front, like the Can-Am Spyder, are technically considered motorcycles and are legally registered as such. Kits to convert popular touring motorcycles like some of the Harleys and the Honda Goldwing to rear-wheeled trikes are available to those who just want something different or perhaps have a disability that prohibits them from safely handling a two-wheeler. The Can-Am Spyder is being marketed as a sporty alternative to a small car for commuters and others who might not consider a traditional motorcycle. Any of these three-wheeled vehicles can be set up with luggage systems and can serve as a bug-out vehicle in much the same way as a motorcycle, though they will lose some of the portability and concealment advantages of motorcycles due to their extra width and bulk.

BUG-OUT MOTORCYCLE CHECKLIST

MOTORCYCLE-SPECIFIC GEAR AND CLOTHING:

- ❏ Motorcycle helmet
- ❏ Face shield or protective eyewear
- ❏ Riding jacket
- ❏ Riding pants
- ❏ Raingear (if not incorporated into riding jacket and pants)
- ❏ Riding gloves
- ❏ Riding boots
- ❏ Foam earplugs (to cut wind noise)
- ❏ Electric vest and/or other items if in winter or cold climate
- ❏ Balaclava to wear under helmet in cold

SPARE PARTS:

- ❏ Spark plug(s)
- ❏ Fuses
- ❏ Bulbs for lights and signals
- ❏ 1 quart motor oil
- ❏ Chain lube (if chain drive)
- ❏ Inner tubes (if using tube tires)
- ❏ Tire plug kit (if using tubeless tires)
- ❏ Can of tire repair/inflator (e.g. Slime or Fix-A-Flat)

TOOLS AND ADDITIONAL EQUIPMENT:

- ❏ Factory-supplied tool kit (if any)
- ❏ Air pressure gauge
- ❏ 12-volt mini compressor or hand pump
- ❏ Tire spoons
- ❏ Small jack or compact jackstand (if bike has no center kickstand)
- ❏ Ratchet drive
- ❏ 6" extension for ratchet drive
- ❏ Socket wrenches to fit all bolt sizes, metric or standard, on bike
- ❏ Spark plug wrench
- ❏ Set of combination wrenches or crescent wrench
- ❏ Screwdriver with interchangeable bits
- ❏ Allen wrenches (metric or standard depending on bike)
- ❏ Torx wrenches or Torx bits for screwdriver (especially on Harleys)
- ❏ Vise Grips
- ❏ Needle-nose pliers
- ❏ Chain and padlock or brake disc lock
- ❏ Bungee net
- ❏ Bungee cords
- ❏ Spare ignition key
- ❏ Spare keys to panniers and other locks
- ❏ Cover or tarp for concealment and rain protection of bike and gear

3

BUG-OUT BOATS
Escape Watercraft—Power and Sail

Many types of boats, from the simplest canoes to ocean-crossing sailing yachts, can be used as bug-out vehicles. Canoes, kayaks, and other human-powered watercraft are examined in depth in Chapter Nine, while those boats that are large enough to serve as self-contained liveaboard vessels are the subject of Chapter Six. In keeping with the escape vehicle concept as covered in the previous two chapters on motor vehicles and motorcycles, I'm classifying escape watercraft as those boats that can offer a quick exit from a danger zone to a safe bug-out location. These boats will carry your bug-out gear and a varying amount of extra supplies, depending on the particular boat, but will not offer full-time shelter along the way, as larger vessels can. You will be living out of the boat, rather than in it, so boats in this category do not have cabins or other living accommodations, but they do vary widely in carrying capacity and types of propulsion. Some, like motorcycles, are only able to carry one or two people, while others could serve as escape vehicles for a small family. Most of the boats discussed here are the kinds of recreational boats people own for such purposes as fishing, water skiing, day sailing, or just getting out on the water for the sake of being there.

As escape vehicles, boats can offer you many advantages if you happen to live or work along the shores of navigable water. It's important to remember that as popular as recreational boating is, the vast majority of any given population still will not own or have access to a boat of any kind. This means that most people will remain shorebound and be forced to deal with crowds and traffic on land in a bug-out scenario, while those few who do have a boat can avoid many of these problems by taking to the waterways or open coast.

One of the best arguments for bugging out by water is that waterways can take you to places that simply cannot be reached by any other means, particularly islands, inaccessible swamps and marshes, and other areas that have no roads or even trails leading to them. In *Bug Out: The Complete Plan for Escaping a Catastrophic Disaster Before It's Too Late,* my guidebook to potential bug-out locations in the U.S., a substantial number of the best uninhabited areas I recommend are accessible only by boat. This is especially true in those areas without mountains or other large tracts of rugged land where road-building is difficult. Despite the heavy populations in many such areas, rivers run through them nearly unnoticed. Many coastal marshes and barrier islands are unknown to area residents who don't have their own boats.

Finally, another major advantage to bugging out by boat, especially in a situation that might require remaining away from population centers for a long term, is that your boat will give you access to additional natural resources. Many people planning to bug out may overlook this, but because you are traveling on the water and will be beside it even when you are stopped along the way, you have constant access to a supply of fish and other aquatic or marine life that can supplement your food supply. Living off the bounty of the sea or even a river or lake will be easier for most people than land-based hunting and gathering. If you are going to bug out by boat, it is certainly worthwhile to take the gear necessary to harvest this resource. Depending on whether you are traveling in fresh or salt water, consider the many options and include what will work best for your location. Such gear includes rod and reel (trolling and casting), artificial lures, drop hooks, hand lines and hooks, cast nets, crab nets, spearfishing gear, bowfishing gear, crab or lobster traps, and seine or gill nets. If you are skilled in the use of such equipment your small bug-out escape boat can allow you to remain independent in a remote location for an indefinite period of time.

Disadvantages of Watercraft as Escape Vehicles

Obviously, in order to incorporate a boat into your bug-out plan, you will need to be near navigable water to begin with, or be sure you can get to your boat and get the boat to your starting point in a SHTF scenario. If you live on or near the banks of a river, the shores of a sizeable lake that is in turn connected to other waterways, or the seashore, you are in the best position to take advantage of a boat as your escape vehicle. If, on the other hand, you have to trailer the boat to reach a launching point, or have to drive to a marina or storage yard where you keep the boat, you will still have to take all the considerations discussed in Chapter One into account. Pulling a large trailer behind a motor vehicle in evacuation traffic will add a lot of stress to an already stressful situation.

Other disadvantages of bugging out by boat include the fact that once you are committed to a boat there will be many places that you cannot go simply because there is no water route there. You will be confined to river courses and other waterways where there is deep enough water to carry the draft of the vessel you choose. If the route

you need to take is upstream, extra horsepower will be needed. If a sailing vessel is your choice, your route planning will need to take into account the prevailing wind patterns as well as currents, and you may not be able to travel at all in confined waters where there is little wind or no room to tack. Because of this, bugging out by water requires even better planning and more knowledge of navigation than most means of bugging out over land.

Confinement to waterways, especially restricted inland routes like rivers and canals, also exposes you to some of the same risks involved in travel by road with regard to those who might wish to take advantage of the situation. Rivers and other water routes have been favorite ambush sites since humans first took to the water in dugout canoes, and in a post-SHTF scenario it is feasible that you could be vulnerable to such an attack in some areas. But because cities and roads will offer easier access to many more targets, it's more likely that you can pass unnoticed along most waterways, especially if you travel at night in potentially dangerous areas.

The somewhat steep learning curve necessary for traveling by water can also be a disadvantage if you have no prior knowledge of boating. In addition to navigation skills, using watercraft effectively also requires knowledge of and practical experience in other aspects of seamanship, including boat handling, safety and emergency procedures, weather awareness, and maintenance and repair. Even in normal circumstances—never mind a post-SHTF scenario—boating can put you in situations where total self-sufficiency is required, as you may not be able to get outside help. Recreational boaters get in trouble all the time because they are not aware of this need for self-sufficiency. People who are interested in prepping and survival will find that boating offers a real-world opportunity to test their skills and utilize the same kind of gear and supplies that they may have in store for an emergency. If you have the navigation, seamanship, and emergency-management skills required for boating, you will likely be much better prepared to deal with problems than most of the population, whether you are bugging out on land or water.

Key Bug-Out Boat Considerations

Access to Navigable Water Bugging out by boat is an obvious choice if you happen to be lucky enough to have a waterfront home on the shores of navigable water. If this is the case, stepping aboard your boat and leaving the area could be as simple as driving the family car out of the garage is for most people, especially if your property has a dock and the boat is kept in the water or suspended in davits, ready for instant launch.

Even if you do not have direct access to water from your home, reaching navigable water with your boat may be easier than trying to leave a city by conventional routes overland. Driving to the water with a boat in tow or even walking to get to where your boat is stored on the waterfront could be faster than dealing with an evacuation traffic jam. This is especially true if you live in a coastal area and would have to cross long bridges over a bay or sound to travel inland. While everyone else is heading away from the water, you could be making your way to your boat with little resistance and preparing to make a quiet getaway afloat. If you live in an inland area, know the routes to the nearest boat ramp on a navigable river or lake and make sure your vehicle and trailer are ready to make the trip.

Trailering vs. Storage at a Marina If, like the majority of boaters, you do not live on the waterfront, you will generally have two choices regarding where to keep your boat: on a trailer at your home or stored at a marina or other storage facility. There are advantages and disadvantages to each approach.

If you keep your boat at home on a trailer, it's easier to stay on top of maintenance issues and it will be easier to pack it with your gear and supplies if you know you are going to have to use it to bug out. If you need to do your own modifications and other work on the boat, it's easier to find a spare hour or two at home than to drive somewhere with all your tools to do the job. You'll also be able to keep an eye on your boat and will know for sure that it is available and ready to go, without having to wonder if it has been stolen, vandalized, or damaged by a storm while out of sight at a marina. Unless you live in a neighborhood that prohibits things like boats on trailers, keeping your boat at home is also free, whereas monthly marina rates can be rather expensive.

The downsides of trailering your boat from home include the extra length and weight of the trailer behind your vehicle, which will be a liability in evacuation traffic, and the extra time it will take to get underway once you arrive at the launch ramp. A boat kept at a marina can be ready to go almost at a moment's notice, particularly if it is kept in the water in a slip. But most boats in the size range discussed here are not usually kept in the water by recreational boaters because of the extra cost of a wet slip and the need for anti-fouling bottom paint to prevent marine growth. If you can keep your boat on your own trailer in a secure lot at the marina, that could be the best option, allowing you to hook it to your vehicle and back it down the ramp when you get there. Avoid the new trend of dry-storage facilities where your boat is forklifted onto high racks along with many other boats until you request a launching. In a post-SHTF scenario, there will likely be no one there to do this for you and the forklifts or other machinery may not be working or available.

Motor vs. Sail Motorboats far outnumber sailing craft in almost all areas today, though recreational sailing is a huge industry and many varieties of sailboats are still being built and used practically everywhere there is enough open water and wind. The requirement for wind

Sea Pearl 21 camp-cruising sail/rowboat with convertible tent cabin

will determine whether a sailing craft could fit into your bug-out plans or not. In most cases, sailing will only be practical if you are in a coastal area or perhaps along the shores of some of the largest inland lakes. The advantages of sailboats of course include independence from a fuel supply and the ability to travel indefinitely, as long as there is wind. While most are slow compared to powerboats, they can still cover a lot of distance in the course of a day or several days. Sailboats are also silent, though they can hardly be called low profile because the mast and sails will be visible from a long distance in daylight hours. Consider also that even though sailboats are primarily designed for sailing, many in the sizes that make good escape watercraft are also fitted with an auxiliary outboard engine. This allows travel through calms and in windless restricted waterways such as canals and rivers.

If your primary bug-out route will include long-distance travel on rivers, a motorboat of some type is your best option. Because of the immense popularity of both freshwater and saltwater fishing, there are motorboat designs optimized for just about any size body of water you care to explore, from shallow streams to the open coast. Motorboat disadvantages include a finite range that depends on the amount of fuel you are carrying and the possibility of mechanical breakdown, which would leave many motorboat designs that are too big or heavy to paddle or row effectively useless for any kind of travel.

Monohull vs. Multihull   Within the category of sailboats, there is still the question of what type of hull you want. Conventional sailboats with one hull are typically referred to as "monohulls" to differentiate them from the other popular type of sailing craft called "multihulls." Multihull sailboats include a variety of catamarans (two equal-sized hulls), trimarans (a larger central hull with two smaller floats or "amas"), and outrigger designs such as "proas" that have one large and one small hull connected together by beams. Multihull sailboats are modern derivatives of the double canoes and outriggers that have been used for thousands of years by islanders in the Pacific and Indian Oceans. They get their stability by spreading their buoyancy across two or more hulls joined together to form a wide, raft-like platform. Because of this, they do not require heavy ballast to stand up to their sails in strong wind and so they can be built lighter, designed to skim over the surface of the water rather than plow through it like a monohull. As a result, most multihulls are capable of sailing at much faster speeds than monohulls.

The most common multihulls seen in coastal areas are the open-beach catamarans like Hobie Cats that have nothing but a fabric trampoline stretched between the hulls for a deck. Even these small catamarans can work as bug-out boats if you strap your gear down to them in waterproof dry bags, but there are many catamarans and trimarans better suited to the purpose that have built-in dry storage compartments. A great ex-

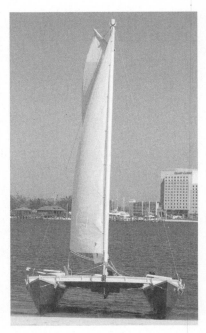

Wharram Tiki 21 beachcruising catamaran

ample of such a beachcruising catamaran was the Wharram Hitia 17 I built a few years ago. With two deep V-hulls fitted with watertight compartments and a solid deck in between large enough to pitch a tent on when anchored, it was an ideal bug-out boat for big bays, sounds, and barrier island chains such as those found along the Gulf and East Coasts of the U.S. The payload was adequate for two people and their gear. Larger catamarans can work in the same role for a family.

Types of Motors If you choose a motorboat in the size range I am considering here, it will almost invariably have a gasoline-powered outboard engine. In boats of this size range, outboard engines have many advantages over other types of engines, such as inboards. For one thing, most small boats will not have the space to install an inboard, and those that do will typically have it crammed into an inaccessible compartment where it is difficult to gain access for maintenance and repairs. Outboards also have the advantages of lighter weight and simplicity. In most cases the engine will simply be hung on the transom or on a transom bracket, requiring no complicated fittings such as shaft housings or through-hulls for cooling systems and other complexities of inboard engines.

Most outboards today, even in the smallest sizes, are four-stroke engines, meaning you don't have to pre-mix oil with the gasoline as is necessary with older two-stroke designs. Four-stroke engines typically run quieter than two-strokes, but they do have the disadvantage of having a lower power-to-weight ratio than the older designs. Electric outboards that are sufficiently powerful for many applications are also available today, but they should not even be considered for a bug-out boat. Without some way to recharge the deep-cycle battery or battery bank they require, electric motors will quickly become useless. Solar or wind charging systems will not have the capacity to keep up with the amperage demands of an outboard motor that is used for primary propulsion or even auxiliary propulsion on a sailboat.

Engine Size Another important consideration for outboard-powered motorboats is the engine size. For recreational purposes, such as sport fishing and water-skiing, it is common practice to mount huge outboard motors that cost far more than the hull itself and burn far more fuel than you would want to waste in a bug-out situation. While speed can be an asset in some scenarios, in most cases it would be more beneficial to have a motorboat set up for the longest possible range given the amount of fuel it can carry, rather than a shorter run at top speeds. If the engine is sized so that you can cruise at a reasonable pace at half-throttle, fuel consumption will be greatly reduced, engine noise will be reduced, and the ride will be comfortable and at a pace that will allow you to concentrate on navigation and looking for unexpected dangers.

Boat Maintenance and Repair It is essential to have on board the tools, parts, and materials to repair the hull and propulsion system of your bug-out boat, whether power or sail. This is even more critical than on land-based vehicles, as you may have a problem that leaves you stranded far from the possibility of getting any help from an outside source. Your two primary concerns while bugging out in a boat will be keeping the water out of the hull and keeping the boat moving.

Some issues, such as a hole in the hull, could be life-threatening if you are far from land. To avoid having to abandon your boat in a remote location, carry what you need to keep it going and know how to do so. The best way to learn about boat maintenance and repair is by doing it. If you buy an older boat and refit it or do some custom modifications to make your boat a better bug-out vehicle, you will learn valuable skills that will help you keep it going later on.

If you are relying on an outboard engine for propulsion, make sure you understand all the common causes of failure in outboards and know how to fix them. Carry spare spark plugs, fuel lines, fuel filters, starter cords, an impeller, and shear pins or a complete prop if it is the type that uses pressed-in bearings. Know how to disassemble and clean the carburetor and how to troubleshoot and fix fuel delivery, electrical, and cooling problems.

Sailboat rigs have lots of components that can fail as well. Make sure you have some fabric on hand to repair rips in the sails them-selves, as well as a heavy-duty needle and thread to repair damaged seams and attachment points in the sails. Carry spare hardware such as shackles, pins and blocks, and extra line to replace critical controls such as halyards and sheets, as well as wire, terminals, turnbuckles, and other components to repair the standing rigging.

Redundancy of Propulsion Systems   Although engine failure in a land vehicle such as a car or motorcycle can be a major problem, the failure of your engine on a boat can be a matter of life or death. On the ocean, you can be swept out to sea by wind or current; on a river, you can be pulled over dangerous rapids or into the path of barges or other vessels. A sailing vessel can likewise be disabled by a failure of the rig, particularly if the mast is broken and there is no way to jury-rig enough sail to keep the boat moving.

On any boat you should consider alternative or redundant propul-sion systems. At the minimum, any small boat, whether power or sail, should have paddles or oars on board. Oars will be more efficient for anything bigger than a canoe, but oarlocks will have to be fitted in advance to use oars effectively. Most fishermen operating outboard-powered boats in coastal waters have dual or multiple outboards fitted, not just for extra power, but in case one fails. Another common arrangement is a small "kicker" outboard of just a few horsepower mounted on a retractable bracket alongside the boat's main outboard. On sailboats, a small outboard mounted this way will give you two means of propulsion and a good safety net.

Modifications and Additional Equipment for Setting Up a Bug-Out Boat

Assemble the Extra Gear Required   Travel by boat will require you to bring extra gear that would otherwise not be needed for bugging out. Just as you must carry spare parts to keep an automobile or motorcycle running, you will need replacement parts and the tools to change them on any boat, whether power or sail. You will also need good foul-weather gear to stay dry in rough water conditions, and dry bags or boxes to protect your survival gear and supplies. You'll need emergency gear specific to the kinds of problems you could face while operating the boat, including fire extinguishers, a bailer, a bucket or bilge pump, flares and other signaling devices, and personal flotation devices for each person on board. Extra gear required simply to operate the boat will include anchors and mooring lines, compass or GPS, and paper or electronic charts.

Blend in to the Environment   If you are planning to bug out by river or into an inland swamp or lake, you can choose among the many types of small motorboats specifically designed for hunting and fishing that come from the factory with a dull green or even camouflage finish. This is a good thing if you want to be able to hide the boat at the water's edge or under overhanging branches and bushes, or perhaps in marsh grass. Try to avoid bright aluminum or flashy gelcoat finishes for bugging out in these areas. If your boat is too shiny or brightly colored, you can always paint it with flat, earth-tone colors to make it more inconspicuous. While no camouflage will completely hide a moving boat, the ability to hide it while you are away from it, perhaps hunting or engaged in other survival activities, is an important consideration. If you are traveling waterways at night, dark, non-reflective colors could hide your movements from anyone watching from a distance too great to hear your engine noise. Keep in mind that at low idling speeds, modern four-stroke outboards are extremely quiet and may not be heard beyond a short distance, particularly if there is wind, rain, or other noise to drown it out.

As already mentioned, sailboats on open water can be seen from a long distance, at least in daylight. There are still things you can do to hide, especially when the sails are furled or the mast is down while you are stopped. A dull gray color like the kind used by military vessels is much harder to see against a backdrop of water from any distance, especially from the air. Any non-reflective, earth-tone color is good for hiding a boat pulled up onto a beach or into a marsh. If you can pile on branches or other objects to break up the outline, most small boats pulled ashore cannot be recognized for what they are by anyone cruising past from a distance.

Create Organized Storage Space   Some of the small boats in this category come from the factory with good storage compartments for gear and equipment. Most can be improved on, however, and even the most basic boats can be modified with built-in waterproof storage compartments for your gear. If you are using an aluminum johnboat or some other aluminum boat, you can build such compartments out of wood and fiberglass and bolt or rivet them in place. If the hull is fiberglass, the job will be easier, as you can integrate the compartments directly into the structure, strengthening the hull in the process. Think in terms of the larger cruising boats, where there is a place for everything and everything is in its place. Having your gear and supplies well organized and secure will greatly reduce the stress of bugging out when you will have other things to worry about.

Be Prepared to Camp Afloat   Although the boats in this category are not designed to be self-contained cruisers, it's not a bad idea to be prepared to spend a night or two on board while on the move. Sometimes you simply will not be able to find a secure place to camp ashore, or, if you are in a large swamp or marsh, there may be no suitable high ground. If you can bivouac comfortably aboard the boat while it is tied up or anchored in such circumstances, this will reduce stress and allow you to focus on getting where you're going. All that's really needed is a flat area large enough to lie down on. In many small boats, there will not be enough room for this between seats and other fixed structures, so you may have to make filler sheets of plywood that can be fitted in place to span the gaps. Add a tarp to keep out rain and dew and mosquito netting for insect pests and you can turn most small boats into a floating campsite. Sailboats are even easier, because you can often use the boom or mast as part of the support to rig such a tarp, and some even come with purpose-made boom tents from the builder.

Escape Powerboats
for Protected Waters

If your bug-out plan will involve travel only on protected waters, you have a lot of flexibility in your choice of escape watercraft. Protected waters for this purpose are rivers, canals, bayous, small lakes, and bays that are not large enough or exposed to the wind enough to generate big waves. This takes away a big part of the worry of travel by boat. On protected waters your main concerns will be navigation and propulsion, rather than keeping out the sea and surviving storms. Protected water boats can be smaller, lighter, and cheaper than offshore-capable boats.

When it comes to boat design, there are two types of stability that have to be considered when building a hull for a given purpose: *initial* stability and *secondary* stability. Initial stability is a measure of how the boat feels in calm water and how much it dips or has a tendency to capsize when the occupants shift weight to one side or the other or move to the extreme ends. Secondary stability is the righting force of a good hull design that comes into play when the hull is leaned way over, virtually on the edge of capsizing, either by the shifting weight of the crew or wave action. Offshore boats need this secondary stability all the time, as big waves will continuously roll the boat from side to side and keep it anywhere but level. But for protected-water boats, initial stability is often more important and consequently such boats can be designed as wide, stable platforms that you can walk all around with little movement of the hull. Examples of this are flat-bottomed john-boats and pontoon deck boats that often feel as stable as a dock. Boats with high initial stability are favored by fishermen who use them in protected waters because it's easy to stand and cast and move around on the boat without worrying about it tipping over.

Because protected water boats do not need a deep-V section to provide wave-piercing ability and secondary stability, they can also be designed with much shallower draft than open-water boats. Flat-bottomed boats like johnboats can float in mere inches of water and can go aground or nose up to the bank without damage. Such boats excel in shallow creeks, swamps, and marsh areas with lots of sub-merged grass. This hull design, which spreads the load over a wide, flat surface, is also the best load carrier for a given size and will sink less as the weight is piled in than a comparably sized V-hull boat. This is the reason this basic flat-bottom design is also used in commercial barges that are designed for moving heavy loads through the water. Pontoon deck boats are also popular on inland lakes and rivers be-cause they provide a wide, stable platform from which to swim, fish, or have a party with lots of passengers on board. They are similar to catamarans in that they have a deck supported by two distinct hulls, but since they are designed to operate in relatively calm water, the hulls are really just tubular "floats" or pontoons that don't require a sophis-ticated hull design. They are cheap to build or buy compared to real power or sailing catamarans.

Used boats of the flat-bottomed, johnboat type are available almost everywhere in either aluminum or fiberglass, often for surprisingly low prices. You can find a complete boat, motor, and trailer in the used market for the price of a new high-end canoe or sea kayak. Sometimes you can also find older wooden vessels or well-built newer wooden hulls built by hobbyists. Building your own is relatively quick and sim-ple too if you can use basic tools and follow directions. Wooden hulls, especially of modern construction with epoxy and fiberglass laminated over a marine plywood core, are lighter in weight and usually have a better strength-to-weight ratio than either fiberglass or aluminum. This is especially true in flat-bottomed designs, where other materials require stiffeners to prevent them from flexing under loads. Also, a wooden hull constructed this way is quiet if you bump into something or drop something on it. This stealth aspect, which is favored by fishermen who don't want to spook their quarry, is naturally advantageous in a bug-out situation where you may need to drift or paddle down a stream or river undetected by those ashore.

SOME PROTECTED-WATER POWERBOAT EXAMPLES

Tracker Topper 1542   This riveted aluminum johnboat is a good example of a lightweight, low-cost, flat-bottomed skiff that can be carried on vehicle roof racks or in the back of a larger pickup without the need for a trailer, if desired. Though the hull weighs only 190 lb., it's a 15-foot boat with a 5-foot beam and a load capacity of 775 lb. The Tracker Topper 1542 is rated for up to 25 hp and would be very efficient with a modern four-stroke outboard for two or three persons and their gear bugging out on a smaller river or other protected water. This boat lists for $1,000 (hull only, without engine) and the Tracker lineup includes smaller models as well as a heavier welded-aluminum line in much larger sizes. Read more about the Tracker Topper at www.trackerboats.com.

Sun Tracker Bass Buggy 18   This is a pontoon barge–type boat in one of the smaller size ranges that could serve as a inland water escape boat with room for a family and their gear. At just under 20 feet long with an 8-foot-wide deck, the Bass Buggy 18 is rated to carry 1,775 lb., has a 42-gallon fuel tank, and can handle up to a 75 hp outboard. Though the layout is set up for fishing and seating up to eight people, it could be modified to work as a camping platform afloat if that function is needed. Total weight is just over 2,300 lb., making it easily trailerable. This model lists for a bit over $11,000 with a smaller 20 hp four-stroke outboard. Full specifications can be found at www.suntrackerboats.com.

Lund 2000 Alaskan   This is a roomy, 20-foot aluminum boat that can handle both protected waters and somewhat more exposed waters such as big, open rivers, lakes, and bays. It features a V-hull that is 20½ feet long with a beam of 7½ feet. There is a built-in 25-gallon fuel tank and the hull is rated for up to 125 hp on the transom. Most models offered by Lund are sturdy workhorse boats frequently seen on the big lakes and rivers of the north woods, especially in Canada and Alaska. This is a big, open boat with lots of flexible space for crew and gear. The base model that is steered by the outboard tiller weighs 1,105 lb., and with motor and trailer is within the towing capacity of most vehicles. This model lists new for $22,000 with the minimum recommended 60 hp four-stroke outboard. Older Lund boats of similar construction can be had for much less and are widely available on the used market. Check out the Lund website at www.lundboats.com.

Escape Powerboats for Open Waters

If you are willing to take to more exposed bodies of open water, your bug-out possibilities will be greatly expanded, especially if you live on or near the coast. The number of other people equipped to bug out on open water will be a much smaller percentage of those few in the population who own boats at all. But since recreational saltwater fishing is popular in these areas, there is a wide array of small, seaworthy powerboats to choose from. Some of these are best suited for use in the choppy conditions of bays and sounds, while others can venture offshore where encountering bigger seas is a possibility. Expect to pay substantially more for a seaworthy offshore powerboat than for a protected-waters boat of the same length, especially if you are buying new.

There are several key design differences between open-water powerboats and those intended for protected waters. First among these is the hull form. The wide, flat bottoms that make johnboats so useful in shallow, smooth waters would make for a teeth-jarring, pounding ride in a powerboat driven hard into choppy waves. What is needed for such conditions is a hull form that slices through the waves at the bow and then transitions further aft to a flatter mid and stern section to allow it to carry weight and get up on a plane at speed. The most common offshore powerboat hull is some variation of the V-hull form, in which the cross-section of the hull has some degree of a V-shape from the keel, or centerline, out to the edges of the hull bottom. The degree of this V is called "deadrise" and it varies according the boat's intended purpose. The V is almost always steeper at the bow and shallower near the stern, where the hull must carry the weight of a single or multiple engines. Hulls with deeper V-sections will cut through steep waves more easily, but will also roll more in a seaway and make for a wetter ride. Shallower V-sections have some of the attributes of flat-bottomed hulls, in that they can get up on a plane with less power, but they are less suitable for truly rough conditions.

Other offshore powerboat hull forms include variations of multi-chine, tri-hulled, and tunnel-hulled designs. Well-placed chines (essentially a fore and aft change in angle between sections of the hull) in a powerboat hull can greatly reduce the spray thrown over the bow and into the cockpit, as well as make for a smoother ride at high speed. Tri-hulled designs have a large V in the center of the hull and two smaller V-sections on either side. They roll less than single V-hulls when stopped, but the extra V-sections increase the total wetted surface at the bow and can make for a rough ride at speed. Tunnel-hulled powerboats reverse the shape of the central V-hull and instead have a hollowed out centerline where the propeller for the outboard is running in a protected location between the two sides. Tunnel hulls achieve most of the shallow draft of johnboats without the pounding of a big, flat hull, so they do well in shallow sounds and bays but are not designed for offshore sea conditions.

A more recent development in small offshore powerboat hull design is the power catamaran. Like sailing catamarans, power catamarans feature two distinct but identical hulls joined together with a central platform. Since they don't have to stand up to the pressure of a tall sailing rig, power catamarans typically have much closer hull spacing than sailing cats and the cockpit and decks often appear much the same as any other powerboat when viewed from above. Under the deck, however, they still have the gap between two narrow, deep-V hulls like their sailing counterparts. These two separate hulls can slice though big waves at higher speeds and with a much smoother ride than single-hulled boats. They are available in a range of sizes for use in all waters, including the open sea.

In addition to hull form, other features that improve a small power-boat's ability to handle rough water are partial decks to shed waves coming aboard and self-bailing cockpits that allow any water that does wash in to quickly drain away. A self-bailing cockpit design is essentially a seating and standing area from which the boat is operated that is *above* the waterline. The floor of this cockpit is sealed off from the lower parts of the hull that are below the waterline, and drains or "scuppers" that lead from this floor to openings in the hull or transom prevent the accumulation of water from waves washing in that would otherwise swamp the boat. In addition to this style of cockpit, many offshore boats also have built-in foam flotation sufficient to support the boat if it is swamped. Electric and manual bilge pumps should also be fitted to remove water that gets into the lower parts of the hull. Because of the pounding they take punching through waves at speed, offshore power-boats are also built to higher standards of construction, with stiffer hulls that won't flex or "oil-can" (deform) under pressure from waves. They are also generally fitted with sturdy cleats for mooring, anchoring, or towing, and decks should be of a non-skid surface for safe movement in rough conditions. Grab rails and other strong points to hang onto should also be incorporated into the design.

SOME OPEN-WATER POWERBOAT EXAMPLES

Panga Marine 18-Foot Skiff   This boat and the larger offerings by Panga Marine are based on the seaworthy skiffs commonly used by saltwater fishing guides in Latin America. The panga design features shallow draft combined with a deep, flaring bow to shed waves. The 18-foot skiff draws just six inches, with a beam of six feet and an unsinkable hull with built-in flotation. It's extremely capable in rough water for an open boat of this size and is light enough for easy trailering, and also small enough to negotiate rivers and other confined waterways. It can be purchased as a bare hull for about $8,000 and outfitted with a center console or other configurations; set up this way, with a 50 hp Honda outboard, it lists for around $17,500. Online in-

formation about the Panga Marine 18-Foot Skiff can be found at www
.pangamarine.com.

Boston Whaler 190 Montauk   This 19-foot center-console boat
with an 8-foot beam is built with the design features that have made the
Boston Whaler name famous for seaworthy small powerboats. A key
feature is the unsinkable hull construction, which the company used
to demonstrate by sawing a hull into two halves on the water. Center-
console Boston Whalers in this size range are frequently chosen by
marine law enforcement agencies for their rugged construction. The
190 Montauk is just one of many Boston Whalers that could serve well
as bug-out powerboat. Fully equipped, it goes for $40,000, but if you
don't have that kind of money to spend on an open boat, used Boston
Whalers of all sizes are easy to find and all are good boats. Boston
Whaler's website is www.bostonwhaler.com.

Caracal 180 Catamaran   This 18-foot power catamaran is a
versatile small powerboat capable of operating offshore and in a variety of shallow areas, with a hull draft of only nine inches. Weighing
1,200 lb. with a beam of eight feet, it is a stable platform designed to
slice through rough water efficiently and can run at the same speeds
with less horsepower than conventional boats of similar size. Its range
is 120 miles with its 30-gallon fuel tank and up to a 140 hp engine on
the transom. This boat is roughly in the $25,000 range and up, depend-
ing on the engine and other equipment. The company website is www
.twinveeboats.com.

Escape Sailboats

I'm not including separate categories for sailboats designed for protected vs. exposed waters because even the smallest sailboats are
by definition designed to operate in windy conditions, which implies
somewhat open water. Therefore, most small sailboats can at least
handle a chop, if not the big waves of true offshore waters. The main
criterion here is that the sailboats considered for this duty are suitable
for practical transportation under sail power and are not high-strung or
overcomplicated race boats that easily capsize in an unexpected gust.

For the most part, the sailboats I consider practical are those proven models that are already popular among people who like to venture out on weekend or longer boat camping trips in big bays, along the coasts, or among barrier islands. This style of sailboat travel is often called "beachcruising."

Beachcruisers don't tie up for the night in marinas like cruisers in bigger boats do. Instead, they either camp on the beach or sleep on board their anchored open boats under a boom tent or tarp rigged up for the purpose. These boats work well as escape watercraft because they are already well thought out when it comes to how gear and supplies will be carried and kept dry and are equipped for navigation and dealing with emergencies. Beachcruising boats are much shallower in draft than most bigger yachts, and many can go almost anywhere a canoe or kayak could venture, with some being small and lightweight enough to drag up on the beach at night or pull over shoals and sandbars.

Some small beachcruising boats have made impressive ocean voyages in the hands of adventurous sailors. The 18-foot open Drascombe Lugger was sailed most of the way around the world by a solo adventurer named Webb Chiles, and other open boats have crossed the Atlantic and the Pacific. Ocean crossings have been done on small catamarans and trimarans as well, all of these feats demonstrating that seaworthiness in a well-designed sailboat is not directly proportional to size. You would have to be tough to sail that far offshore in an open, exposed boat, but it's nice to know you *could* do it if you had to, and since the best boats of this type can handle offshore conditions, they are likely to get you to a destination closer to shore with ease.

FEATURES TO LOOK FOR IN AN ESCAPE SAILBOAT

Obviously, the first consideration in choosing a sailboat is stability. The sails that power the boat will also capsize it if it is not sufficiently stable to stand up to the wind. Sailboats get their stability from the design of the hull, ballast down low in the hull, or in the form of a weighted keel, or from a combination of these features. Lightweight multihulls like catamarans and trimarans do not use ballast, but rather rely on the wide stance of their raft-like platform to keep them upright. Most small monohull sailboats also rely heavily on this hull form stability, since heavy ballast or a fixed keel would make them much more difficult to trailer. Avoid racing-style hull forms that require you to shift the weight of the crew out to windward to keep the boat upright. You want to be able to relax and focus on where you are going instead of always worrying about capsizing.

Other important features are adequate flotation and a self-bailing cockpit. All open boats are more prone to swamping in big seas than decked boats with an enclosed cabin, but the best ones feature plenty of built-in flotation that keeps them from sinking even if they are filled. Boats with self-bailing cockpits keep any water coming on board above the waterline so it can quickly drain out through scuppers before it endangers the vessel. This flotation and self-bailing ability is also essential for recovering a capsized sailboat. Any small sailboat can be knocked down by a strong enough gust of wind, and you must be able to right it and quickly get rid of any water in the hull in order to get underway again.

Another feature to look for in this type of sailboat is the ability to go aground. This means that the hull will not be damaged if you pull it up onto the beach, so any appendages like rudders and centerboards should be retractable for this reason. This ability to venture into shoal areas will give you access to many remote areas surrounded by shallow waters where bigger vessels cannot go. Most of the best bug-out locations accessible by water are in such places, where a lack of natural harbors and deep-water channels has prevented development and left the area in a natural state. If you are going to bug out by small boat, these are exactly the kinds of places you want to be able to go, so don't restrict yourself with a deep-keeled boat.

SOME ESCAPE SAILBOAT EXAMPLES
Norseboat 17.5 Rowing and Sailing Cruiser   This is one of the few production sailboats available today that is purpose-designed for the kind of camp cruising described in this section. It features positive flotation, a draft of only nine inches with the board up, and berths for two

under a custom tent or the capacity to carry six people. The seaworthy hull design is derived from classic 19th-century fishing skiffs, and the traditional gaff rig is easily handled by a single person. It is designed as a capable rowing craft as well, eliminating the need for an auxiliary outboard. The standard model sells for about $19,000. More information about the Norseboat 17.5 can be found at www.norseboat.com.

Wayfarer Dinghy   If you can find one, this 16-foot open boat is one of the most seaworthy small craft around. It has been used for extensive offshore cruising and long open-water crossings, despite a weight of only 372 lb. The Wayfarer can carry 600 lb. of people and gear and has built-in watertight storage compartments fore and aft. This design has been built in wood and fiberglass for over 35 years, with some 9,000 hulls produced. They sometimes appear in classified listings for around $4,000 to $5,000 in good condition. An enthusiasts group that supports the Wayfarer Dinghy maintains an informative website at www.uswayfarer.org.

Hobie 21 Sport Cruiser   This 21-foot beach catamaran was specifically designed for camping aboard, unlike most of the more performance-oriented catamarans offered by Hobie. It came with an outboard motor mount, built-in cooler, and dry storage, and a custom tent was available to convert the entire trampoline/deck area into living quarters. This specialized Hobie model is no longer in production and sold for over $14,000 new, but used examples can be found for half that or less, depending on condition. Other, more general-purpose models like the Hobie 18 or Hobie Getaway can be customized to work as this type of escape sailboat as well, and are much easier to find. The Hobie Cat company website can be found at www.hobiecat.com.

Personal Watercraft (PWC)

Another category of conveyance on the water that some might consider as an escape vessel is the personal watercraft, such as the Jet Ski, See-Doo, and WaveRunner. For the most part, I don't consider these as viable options because they are designed more for playing on the water than real transportation and are too limited in carrying capacity compared to conventional boats. Some see them as the aquatic version of a motorcycle, and in many ways they are—providing high-speed fun for one, two, or on some models even three or four riders both in protected waters and on the ocean. I do know of people who use the larger variations of personal watercraft to carry camping gear and go on overnight trips to offshore barrier islands, so it *is* possible, if you pack well and keep your gear in dry bags or the built-in storage compartments some models feature, that you could bug out aboard one.

However, you should be aware that there have been quite a few cases of personal watercraft operators being swept out to sea when their engine failed and they were caught in wind or current. Though this can happen with any power boat without oars or sails for alternative propulsion, some personal watercraft are designed in such a way that you cannot even access the engine compartment while afloat, especially in deep water or in rough sea conditions. But if you are knowledgeable about this type of watercraft and have worked out a solution to its limitations, I wouldn't say that it's absolutely impossible to use one for bugging out, just that I personally wouldn't choose one for this purpose.

BUG-OUT BOAT CHECKLIST

BOATING SAFETY AND OTHER
BOAT-SPECIFIC GEAR:

- ❏ PFD (personal flotation device) for every person on board
- ❏ Safety harness and tether for every person if sailing offshore
- ❏ Flares and other Coast Guard–required signaling devices
- ❏ Fire extinguishers (two or more on vessels with electrical systems and/or engine or stove fuel)
- ❏ Bailer, bucket, or bilge pump for quickly removing water
- ❏ Paddle or oars for alternative propulsion in case of engine or sailing-rig failure
- ❏ Ground tackle (anchors and rodes) of adequate size and number for the boat size
- ❏ Mooring lines, bow painters, or other lines for securing the vessel to shore
- ❏ Waterproof foul-weather jacket and bib overalls

SPARE PARTS:

- ❏ Spark plug(s) for engine
- ❏ Fuel line for outboard engines
- ❏ Fuel filters
- ❏ Starter rope for outboard engines
- ❏ Prop and shear pins for prop shaft
- ❏ Water pump impeller
- ❏ Engine oil
- ❏ Lower-unit gear oil
- ❏ Line to replace essential running rigging
- ❏ Blocks, clevis pins, shackles, and other sailing hardware
- ❏ Wire rope, fittings, turnbuckles, etc. to repair or replace standing rigging

ESSENTIAL TOOLS AND
ADDITIONAL EQUIPMENT:

- ❑ Marine-grade sealant, epoxy, and other adhesives
- ❑ Fiberglass or other hull-repair materials (depending on construction)
- ❑ Sandpaper (for prepping areas to be patched)
- ❑ Duct tape
- ❑ Sail-patching materials (fabric, needle, and thread)
- ❑ Sail-repair tape (for quick emergency repairs)
- ❑ Wrenches, pliers, screwdrivers, and other mechanical tools to maintain engine and rigging components
- ❑ Hand saw, hacksaw, hand drill, rasp, tape measure, and other tools to effect hull repairs
- ❑ Gimbaled steering compass
- ❑ Quality hand-bearing compass
- ❑ Chart-enabled GPS with preloaded nautical charts of the region
- ❑ Paper charts or chartbooks covering the region
- ❑ Marine binoculars with bearing compass
- ❑ Handheld or fixed-mount VHF marine two-way radio
- ❑ Shortwave or SSB radio for receiving weather forecasts
- ❑ Dry bags or waterproof boxes for critical gear and supplies
- ❑ Rod and reel (for trolling and/or casting)
- ❑ Artificial lures and hooks, sinkers and floats for live bait
- ❑ Drop hooks, trot line, and hand lines
- ❑ Cast net, crab net, seine or gill net
- ❑ Crab or lobster traps, fish traps, and/or minnow traps
- ❑ Bowfishing rig, pole spear, or spear gun

Mask, fins, and snorkel for underwater hunting (if in clear waters)

Part II

Mobile Retreats

4

RECREATIONAL VEHICLES & OTHER MANUFACTURED MOBILE RETREATS

The concept of a mobile retreat is the next logical option to consider after looking at escape vehicles for both land and water. Mobile retreats combine two important aspects of bugging out: the vehicle that transports you, your family, and your gear; and the shelter you will need for a possible extended stay away from your home. This part of the book covers a broad range of mobile retreat options, but in this chapter I will look at the most obvious type: the manufactured units that are readily available as recreational vehicles. As with the passenger vehicles, motorcycles, and recreational boats mentioned in the previous three chapters, many people will already have some type of recreational vehicle on hand that can be pressed into service as a mobile retreat. If you do not already own one, given the staggering array of choices on the new and used market, you can likely find one of a size and type that fits into your bug-out plan and budget. And as with boats, motorcycles, and other nonessential recreational vehicles, you can enjoy using your mobile retreat for weekend and vacation getaways, whether you ever need it for bug-out purposes or not.

Recreational vehicles come in sizes and price ranges to fit almost every need. These vehicles are heavily promoted as lifestyle accessories and you will see them parked in backyards, driveways, and storage lots all over America. Some are used often for weekend getaways and summer vacations, while many others sit neglected year after year and can be picked up used for a fraction of the original price. The fact that so many of these units just sit in storage unused, combined with the huge depreciation of most new RVs after they are a few years old, means that it's a buyer's market for those looking at used models. If you have the slightest interest in acquiring such a vehicle you owe it to yourself to investigate the prices in the used market before writing off RVs as too expensive.

RV living is a full-time lifestyle for some people, especially retirees, and the manufacturers have met the demand to produce comfortable yet manageable vehicles designed to offer the creature comforts of home to people who are not necessarily the camping or outdoorsy type. Some of these comforts are overrated or unnecessary, as will be discussed in the sections that follow, but a self-contained RV can make for a well-organized and efficient mobile bug-out retreat that you can quickly and easily modify for the task with minimal extra effort and expense.

Disadvantages of Recreational Vehicles as Mobile Retreats

Factory-built RVs tend to be overpriced for the build quality that you get when new, unless you are willing and able to pay a premium for the products of the few top manufacturers or custom builders that exceed the average offerings. But be prepared for sticker shock if you are shopping new for the high-end makes. Despite these prices, cheap, lightweight construction that is designed to look good when new but not necessarily hold up over the long term is typical of the majority of recreational vehicles, whether of the pull-behind trailer or self-contained motorhome type. Ask anyone who has spent an extended time traveling and living in one and you will hear about the quality problems that include everything from leaky windows and hatches that cause rot, rust, and other water damage to a wide range of system breakdowns that run the gamut from electrical to plumbing, heating, and air-conditioning. If you are handy with tools and don't mind doing your own repairs and improvements, you can take advantage of good deals on used RVs with such problems that the original owners couldn't handle. But as will be discussed in the next chapter, if you have such skills, you could also put your energy into a do-it-yourself mobile retreat that you can control the quality of throughout the construction process.

The Huge Array of Choices

If you're new to RVs, you will most likely be bewildered by the confusing terminology used to describe all the different types available. While most people know the difference between a motor home and a travel trailer, there are many subcategories within these different types that you should become familiar with before deciding which one would work best for your needs. As with the previous chapters on escape vehicles, I have broken this chapter down into several sections. First is a list of the key considerations that will influence your choice of a manufactured RV and a discussion of the modifications and equipment that in general apply to all types. Following that is a description of each of the major categories of these vehicles, along with how each could fit into your bug-out plan and the disadvantages of each type that could influence your decision. Examples of each type are presented as well to give you some idea of what to look for and the price you might expect to pay.

Key Prefab Mobile Retreat Considerations

Size Just as with pickup trucks, SUVs, boats, and motorcycles, I would strongly discourage buying the biggest, most elaborate, or most expensive examples in any particular category of RVs, even if you can afford to do so. As with other categories of vehicles, many of the larger models are marketed as status symbols designed to appeal to the affluent or project an image of affluence and will not be as useful for the purpose of a bug-out vehicle as the smaller, more basic models.

All but the smallest mobile retreats have some inherent disadvantages when compared to the escape vehicles discussed in the previous section. Larger vehicles will be difficult to maneuver in heavy evacuation traffic and limited in their ability to go around obstacles or travel rough roads or off-road, and will consume more fuel for the same distance traveled. Large, expensive-looking RVs also go against the concept of blending in that I covered in the discussions of escape vehicles and could look like easy and irresistible targets to looters, who will perceive them as storehouses of goods and equipment.

For all these reasons, I recommend basing your size choice on your *minimum* requirements, rather than what might be nice to have. First of all, this means dedicated sleeping and personal storage space for each person who will be aboard, whether you are going solo or with family or friends. This is a requirement that you should never try to skimp on, especially if you are preparing for a possible long-term stay in your mobile retreat. Beware of manufacturers' claims that a particular model "sleeps six" or "sleeps eight" or other such exaggerations, because they are usually referring to the maximum number that can be crammed in for weekend trips, not long-term accommodation. The other minimum requirements include space and equipment for self-contained cooking and washing and enough storage capacity to carry your essential gear, as well as an adequate food and water supply. With these guidelines in mind, a single person and perhaps a couple can function fine in some of the smallest types of RVs, such as pop-up campers, truck campers, or conversion vans. Families will need more space, with the exact amount depending on the number of children and their ages, as well as special needs such as provisions for disabled or elderly adults.

Trailer or Motorhome? The first and most obvious difference when you begin looking at the types of RVs available is that some are pull-behind trailers designed to be towed by another motor vehicle and some are self-contained motorhomes with the living quarters built onto the same chassis that houses the engine and driver's cabin. Deciding between these two completely different concepts is one of those hard choices so common in picking out equipment in that it is a compromise with advantages and disadvantages whichever way you decide to go.

If you choose a trailer-type RV that must be towed behind another vehicle, then that vehicle will have to be large enough and powerful enough to pull the trailer in any conditions and on every kind of terrain you expect to travel. This means that unless you choose one of the smallest kinds of trailers, like pop-ups or mini-campers, your tow vehicle will likely have to be a full-sized pickup or SUV that will get poor fuel economy whether burdened with the RV or disconnected from it. Pulling this kind of RV with a tow vehicle also means that you will have to disconnect and leave the RV somewhere to use the vehicle separately for other tasks. Also, the living accommodations of the RV will be inaccessible to the driver and passengers of the tow vehicle while you're on the road.

Motorhomes are self-contained RVs that are built on a van, truck, or bus chassis so that the driver's cabin is within the unit at the forward end, eliminating the need for a separate vehicle altogether. But with a larger RV, short trips and errands are still a burden because of the overall size and difficulty of maneuvering in traffic, so most recreational motorhome owners tow a small runabout vehicle behind them in much the way yachts and other large boats carry a dinghy or tender. Depending on the size of the motorhome, this auxiliary vehicle can range in size from a full-sized SUV or passenger car to a compact crossover car or perhaps even one or more motorcycles or bicycles.

Using the auxiliary vehicle will still require you to leave the motorhome behind, just as with an RV trailer, but if you chose a smaller one it will be less wasteful of fuel than driving around in a larger tow vehicle or the bulky motorhome itself.

The final choice between these two types often comes down to personal tastes, as well as where you might expect to bug out to with your mobile retreat and how much you might expect to use the tow or auxiliary vehicle for other tasks during your stay. If you plan to travel far off the beaten path on rough roads and a smaller unit meets your size requirements, then a truck camper on a 4WD pickup or light pop-up camper trailer towed behind such a pickup or 4WD SUV will probably be the best choice, since with such a setup you can get your mobile retreat into really remote areas. If the number of people going with you dictates a larger unit, it may be easier and less stressful to drive a motorhome than to pull a large, heavy trailer with all the associated problems that entails.

Off-Grid Functionality   A key difference in using RVs as bug out vehicles vs. the recreational uses that they were intended for is that you will have to think in terms of being totally off the power grid without access to running water, pump-out stations, and other amenities. The typical RV owner plans weekend trips and vacations around parks and developed campgrounds where electrical and plumbing hookups provide all the comforts of a modern home. But although most owners don't make use of it, most RVs do have some off-grid functionality by design, at least for short-term excursions. Most of the functions available while plugged in can be used in remote campsites as well; this includes lighting and low-power electrical devices like radios, televisions, and fans, but not microwaves, washers and dryers, or air conditioners unless a powerful generator is running. Basic plumbing systems using storage and holding tanks allow the use of water faucets and toilets, and cooking stoves using fuels like propane or butane allow the cooking of hot meals.

The key to extending the time period that your RV can function off the grid is simplicity of systems. Recreational RVing appeals to many because they like the idea of going camping with all the comforts of home. But the more home-like comforts you and your family are willing to give up or compromise on, the better off you will be when it comes to power management, recharging systems, and fuel, water, and waste storage. Living this way won't be as rough as camping out of a bug-out bag or in a primitive bug-out shelter such as those discussed in the last section of this book, but it won't be luxury vacation living either.

Electrical Systems The popularity of modern RVs (and the self-contained cruising boats that are the subject of Chapter Six) has led to the development of well-engineered 12-volt DC electrical equipment and systems that can provide most of the conveniences off the grid that you are used to with a 110-volt AC system at home. The exceptions to this are high-powered devices that draw a lot of current, like air conditioning systems, washers and dryers, electric stoves and ovens, etc. While it is possible to power such appliances off the grid using a gasoline or diesel generator, this won't be practical for a bug-out stay of any duration because of the fuel consumption. Aside from such power-hungry equipment, there are many devices such as computers and rechargeable electric tools that have their own built-in batteries but are designed to be plugged into an AC outlet for recharging. Power inverters that convert 12-volt DC power to 110-volt AC work well for recharging such equipment, and can also run many AC devices directly as long as they are within the power rating (measured in watts) of the inverter.

Most of the basic electrical equipment needed in a mobile retreat will not require an inverter to convert DC to AC, as 12-volt versions of many appliances are standard in the RV industry. Lighting, in particular, has benefited from new technologies such as the widespread use of LED (light-emitting diode) clusters to replace standard incandescent bulbs. LED lighting draws a fraction of the electrical current needed to run conventional bulbs, allowing you to use interior lights for reading and other tasks much more freely, without worrying about depleting the house battery bank.

The house battery (or ideally, a bank of batteries connected in parallel) is the heart of any off-grid 12-volt DC electrical system. These batteries are the deep-cycle storage type, designed to be able to withstand many cycles of complete draining and recharging without damage. Storage capacity is measured in terms of ampere-hours, and your daily energy budget for all the electrical devices in your mobile retreat can be calculated from the number of amps each device draws when in use and the estimated amount of time it will be needed each day. Each of these devices will be helping to deplete the stored energy of the batteries when in use, so of course you must have a way of replenishing this energy. Forget about the 30- or 50-amp power connection that practically all RVs feature for plugging into at campgrounds or for charging at home between trips. Your options will be limited to an engine-driven alternator, a generator, or alternative power sources such as solar panels or wind generators.

While charging from an alternator driven by the vehicle's engine (or the tow vehicle in the case of a trailer) can work while you are on the move, running the engine to charge batteries once you are set up in a remote location is not as efficient as using a small, separate generator powered by gasoline, diesel, or propane. Such a generator, when used for battery charging and not for running high-powered devices as discussed above, can be a viable option if you are conservative in your power use. A better alternative for serious long-term living off the grid in an RV is an array of solar panels mounted on the roof that can be redirected to the correct angle for maximum exposure to the sun throughout the day. Small wind generators such as those used on boats can also be used on RVs once you get where you are going, and if you are in a windy area they can produce much more charging current than solar panels.

Water and Sewer Systems Just as with electrical systems, most RVs are set up with water and sewer systems that allow at least short-term off-the-grid use. The freshwater supply for drinking, cooking, and washing needs will obviously be one of your top priorities in a bug-out scenario, and you must keep that supply uncontaminated and accessible. When operating in the self-contained mode, water faucets on RVs are supplied by 12-volt pumps in the water lines from the storage tanks. You should also have a manual pump option or other means of accessing this stored water in the event of a failure of the pump or 12-volt system. Manual hand- or foot-operated water pumps have the added advantage of not wasting your valuable water supply because someone forgets to turn the faucet off. In a bug-out situation, your RV's built-in water tanks will not hold enough water for your needs and should be supplemented with extra jerry cans or one-gallon jugs stowed in any available space. As with any method of bugging out, even with a large mobile retreat, you will also need to think about how you will resupply your water when your tanks are dry and how you will purify locally available sources for your drinking needs.

Recreational users of RVs depend on the built-in holding tanks for gray water and waste to take care of their sewage disposal needs, pumping out the tanks at a convenient pump-out station when they leave developed campgrounds. For longer-term use, dealing with holding tanks will become more than an inconvenience, and you may have to find alternate solutions—like using a latrine dug nearby—rather than allowing these tanks to fill up.

Cooking Facilities   Larger RVs come equipped with kitchens (or galleys) that mimic those of modern homes as closely as possible, featuring range tops with multiple burners and an oven, a microwave, a refrigerator and freezer, and lots of cabinet and counter space. While all this is nice to have, all you really need is a space to prepare food and a simple stovetop burner to cook on. The stove will most likely be a gas range supplied by one or more refillable propane cylinders mounted outside the RV or in purpose-designed vented compartments. These stoves are efficient and you can easily carry a supply of fuel that will last several weeks if you use it only for cooking and not for running heating, refrigeration, or hot water systems. In good weather, you can save stove fuel by doing at least some of your cooking outside over a fire. Backup cooking solutions can include portable gas or propane stoves such as those used for tent camping and backpacking.

Additional Equipment and Spares   As with any motor vehicle, you should carry the tools and spare parts you need to maintain the mobility of the vehicle, and this includes things like spare tires for RV trailers and commonly needed engine parts for motorhomes. You should also carry a wide range of spares to maintain your electrical, recharging, plumbing, and cooking systems. The actual checklist will depend on the complexity of your particular RV, but you can start by making of a list of everything that is vital to the function of the unit and purchasing spares for components that commonly need replacement. This will include such things as circuit breakers and fuses, battery terminals and cables, bulbs, alternator belts, valves, hoses and pump diaphragms, propane gas fittings and hoses, stove burner components, and so on. The complement of tools needed to replace or repair all these added systems will be more extensive than a simple motor vehicle tool kit, and with larger RVs will need to include most of the tools needed for home maintenance as well. 18-volt rechargeable power tools are a viable option on an RV with a functioning 12-volt electrical system and inverter, and a few select tools of this type, particularly a reversible drill and perhaps a jigsaw or small circular saw, will make many tasks easier.

In addition to maintaining these onboard systems, you should have the equipment needed to survive comfortably in the event that none of them function. This will include a separate stove (as already discussed), alternative lighting like flashlights and portable lanterns, a water purification system, warm sleeping bags and alternative shelter in case you have to abandon the RV, and plenty of reliable firestarters such as waterproof matches, butane lighters, and magnesium firestarters.

Safety and Security

Fire safety is an important consideration in any enclosed structure, even more so in an RV with a 12-volt electrical system and cooking stove. Fire extinguishers should be mounted in easily accessible and visible locations throughout the unit; a smoke detector and a carbon monoxide detector should also be installed in living spaces. With the extra storage space available compared to a smaller escape vehicle or other methods of bugging out, you can also find room in your mobile retreat for a much more extensive first aid kit and extra first aid supplies.

Security is always a concern as well, whether in a mobile retreat or at home. Except for tent trailers with their fabric and screen enclosures, just about any kind of RV will give you more sense of security when sleeping at night than you would feel sleeping out in the open or in a tent. Though the doors on many RVs are flimsy and could be broken into easily, at least there are doors, and any intruder trying to enter at night will have to make a lot of noise. With the 12-volt electrical system you can also install alarm systems and motion-activated exterior lighting—which is a good idea, because insulated inside your vehicle you may not hear someone approaching the area as easily as you would if you were in a tent.

Needless to say, you should have weapons to defend yourself and your family in the event you are attacked while in your mobile retreat. When choosing firearms for this role, consider the close quarters inside a vehicle and the likelihood that over-penetration will be an issue with most weapons. It's imperative to have a plan in case of such an event so everyone will know what to do to avoid confusion and getting in the line of fire. Handguns are usually quicker to get into action in such confined spaces, but shotguns are also good in situations where you won't have time to take careful aim.

Truck Campers

Truck campers use drop-in units to convert a pickup truck bed into a self-contained camper unit. Most are designed to fit one-ton or ¾-ton pickups. They range from a basic shell that covers the bed, with a roofline in line with the truck cabin's roof, to large units that are much wider and taller than the vehicle and extend additional accommodation space over the top of the truck's cabin. Though more compact than other RVs, the truck camper concept has some advantages that could make it good for many bug-out vehicle needs. Because there is no trailer involved, the overall length is greatly reduced, making the truck camper more maneuverable in traffic jams and on rugged, poorly maintained roads. Because you can choose the camper unit to fit your truck and not the other way around, you can use the pickup that best suits your needs for other purposes and remove the camper unit when it is not needed. Unlike most motor homes, your truck can have 4WD and high ground clearance, making it even more suitable for accessing remote bug-out locations.

The typical truck camper that extends over the cab of the vehicle is designed to sleep four people, with a dinette table in the central area that converts to a bed, as well as an overhead single bunk and a double or queen-sized bed over the cab. Like many travel trailers, some also have slide-out sections to expand living space even more. Despite the number of possible bunks, two people or perhaps a couple with a small child would probably be the maximum number that could use one of these units as a mobile retreat for an extended time period.

TRUCK CAMPER EXAMPLE

Northstar Laredo SC   This is a roomy hard-shell truck camper that is 7 feet wide by 15 feet, 2 inches long (including the cab-over section in which a 60″ x 80″ bed is fitted). It has standing headroom in the main section over the bed of the pickup and in this area there is a small galley, a separate toilet, and a dinette that converts to another single bed. Dry weight is 1,800 lb., and the Northstar Laredo SC has an MSRP of around $18,000. Manufacturer's info is available at www.northstarcampers.com.

Pop-Up or Folding Campers

Pop-up or folding campers are the smallest class of trailer RVs and are popular for their light weight and low profile when folded, which makes them suitable for use with a wider range of vehicles than heavy travel trailers. Some pop-up campers are small enough to tow behind passenger cars and other small vehicles, ranging in weight from about 1,500 to 4,000 pounds. Yet, when unfolded and set up, they can offer surprisingly comfortable accommodations compared to tent camping or other small options like truck campers or camper vans. A typical unit will feature comfortable seating, a table, a stove and kitchen work surfaces, toilets, and showers.

Because of their small size when folded, pop-up campers may be the best option for urban or suburban dwellers who would have difficulty finding a place to keep a larger RV or other type of mobile retreat. But because they must be folded to travel, storage space for extra gear and supplies will be minimal and camping this way may not offer many advantages over tent camping from an escape vehicle. In fact, pop-up campers are also called tent trailers because a large part of the structure is flexible fabric material similar to a tent that allows the unit to be expanded. Because of this, they do not offer as much of a feeling of security as sleeping inside a hard-shelled unit with locking doors.

POP-UP CAMPER EXAMPLES

Jayco Jay Series Sport   Jayco manufactures a wide range of pop-up campers and travel trailers. The Jay Series Sport line includes a range of pop-ups on the small end of the spectrum. The Sport 10, for example, weighs only 1,385 lb. empty and when folded for travel measures 13½ feet long by 5 feet high. Yet, when set up for camping, it expands to almost 20 feet long and features a large bed on each end, a dinette, counter space for a stove, and storage cabinets in the main compartment. The Jay Series Sport pop-up campers start at an MSRP of $5,800 and the Jayco website is at www.jayco.com.

4x4 Tent Trailers   This company manufactures a line of pop-up tent campers specifically designed to go practically anywhere an off-road 4x4 vehicle can tow them. Built to handle abuse, these trailers feature heavy-duty axles rated for 3,000 lb. They have a dry weight of 900 lb. and a storage capacity of over 43 cubic feet and convert to a basic shelter with a tent on an elevated platform in under 5 minutes. Options include a 12-volt electrical system, water system, propane cook top, hi-lift jack,

4x4 tent trailer

bike rack, and extra storage. The 4x4 Tent Trailer starts at $1,495. More information is available at www.overlandtrailers.com.

Camper Trailers

The camper trailer or travel trailer is perhaps the most popular type of large RV among recreational users, particularly weekend and vacation users who don't live in their RVs full time. Because they do not incorporate an engine, drive train, and all the other parts and components that make up a self-contained vehicle, large travel trailers are less expensive than comparably sized motorhomes; but because of their larger size in comparison with pop-up campers and truck campers, they can offer much of the comfort of a motorhome. Unlike pop-up trailers, they are towed ready to use, so things inside do not have to be packed or organized to move to another location, though many travel trailers do feature slide-out living quarters to expand their interior space as well as roll-out awnings that must be put away before towing.

Standard travel trailers are designed to be towed behind a pickup or SUV by means of a receiver hitch attached to the frame of the tow vehicle. "Fifth wheel" trailers use a different system that involves a special hitch mounted on the truck bed. Because of the way the fifth wheel hitch pivots and the way much of the bulk of the trailer is carried forward over the truck bed, fifth wheel RV trailers feature an extended overhead section that rides above the passenger cab of the tow truck, further increasing accommodations without an increase in overall length.

Toy hauler and horse trailer RVs are yet another type of travel trailer that splits the living accommodations in the trailer with auxiliary vehicle storage compartments or livestock transport compartments. This type of trailer could be of particular interest to those whose bug-out plans include utilizing additional means of transport, either operating out of a base camp with the RV or proceeding on into more remote or rugged territory with a secondary vehicle or on horseback. Toy haulers can accommodate most any type of motorcycle, ATV, or personal watercraft, and horse trailers can carry one or more horses as well as saddles and other gear. The living quarters of these trailers can be as well-appointed as any other type of RV.

CAMPER TRAILER EXAMPLES

Airstream Classic Limited 30 The distinctive styling and bright aluminum exteriors of Airstream travel trailers may not help you blend in, but hiding any 30-foot travel trailer is not going to be easy. Airstream trailers are notable for their high-quality construction, which puts them in a different class than the cheap and flimsy travel trailers offered by many manufacturers. An Airstream trailer can last a lifetime and many older models are popular as restoration projects. The Classic Limited series offers first-rate accommodations. The 30-foot version weighs 7,285 lb., is just under the 8½-foot maximum legal width limit, and has an exterior height of 8 feet. A queen bed and cabinets occupy the rear end and a dinette and lounge area converts to additional bunk space. There is a full galley, a private toilet area, and a shower, in addition to lots of storage space. New Airstreams are not inexpensive, and the MSRP for this model is about $91,000. But because of their quality construction and popularity, they hold their value well. You can find out more at www.airstream.com.

Coachmen Chaparral 355RLTS Mid-Profile Fifth Wheel This line of fifth wheel travel trailers is designed to combine good maneuverability with an aerodynamic profile for easier highway travel. The 355RLTS is the largest in the series and could be a good choice if you need a lot of living space and cargo-carrying capacity. At almost 38½ feet long and just over 12½ feet high, it offers a voluminous accommodation plan that includes a queen bed, slide-out rooms with expanded seating and convertible bunks, and an overhead loft area with another large bed. Total unloaded weight is almost 10,500 lb. and there is capacity to carry an additional 3,500 lb. You will need a serious truck to pull a trailer like this, and almost $50,000 to purchase a new one at MSRP. The manufacturer's website is www.coachmenrv.com.

Jayco Octane ZX Toy Hauler At just under 29 feet overall, this toy hauler RV trailer weighs 6,500 lb. unloaded and features a cargo bay that is 11 feet, 7 inches long. A retractable 7-foot-long metal ramp makes loading and unloading motorcycles, ATVs, and other backup vehicles easy. This model features lots of foldaway bunk space and a large queen bed over the rear living area. There's a galley, toilet, and shower as well as plenty of cabinet space. MSRP starts at around $30,000; the website is at www.jayco.com.

Motorhomes

The RV industry categorizes motorhomes into three distinct classes. Class A includes the largest and most luxurious of all RVs: those that are built on a bus chassis or a specially designed chassis that resembles a bus and is of a similar size. Class A motorhomes often approach the maximum legal limits for the height, width, length, and weight of a noncommercial vehicle, ranging from about 21 to 40 feet long. A luxury Class A motorhome will contain a full-sized kitchen, private bathrooms, and every amenity known to the RV industry. While some are advertised as being able to sleep 10 people, RV builders are the same as yacht builders in exaggerating these numbers, which are only suitable for occasional weekend use. But a big Class A motorhome can certainly accommodate the average family in comfort. Average MSRP in this class is $81,000, but many of them cost several hundred thousand dollars.

Class B motorhomes are at the other end of the size spectrum from Class A and are also called camper vans because they are usually built on conventional passenger van frames, but with modifications like raised roofs to add extra interior space. Most are between 16 and 21 feet long and are designed to sleep four people. They usually feature a compact kitchen and basic bathroom facilities. Class B motorhomes average around $43,000, but specialized models like the 4WD Sportsmobile described below can be nearly double that amount.

Class C motorhomes are built on standard truck frames and can range from 20 to 32 feet long. They can be as luxurious as Class A motorhomes on a smaller scale and for a lower total cost, generally averaging just under $50,000 MSRP. These are the motorhomes most people think of when they think of vacation RV camping, and they are well-represented by the established builders such as Winnebago.

SOME MOTORHOME EXAMPLES IN EACH CLASS

Itasca Ellipse 40BD This is an example of a big Class A motorhome that comes with a 400 hp Cummins turbocharged 8.9-liter diesel engine and a price tag to match its size and luxurious accommodations. At just over 40½ feet long, it has the space to serve as a long-term or semi-permanent mobile bug-out retreat. You wouldn't be able to take such a big vehicle far off the beaten path, but wherever you take it, there would be room inside for your family and all the supplies and gear you need. Of course it comes with all the amenities and an 8,000-watt Cummins Onan diesel generator to keep everything running. Base MSRP is $301,245. You can get the full details at www.goitasca.com.

Sportsmobile 4WD Camper Van This highly customized camper van fits into the Class B category, but could be in a class of its own. Designed to go places ordinary Class B motorhomes would not be able to venture, these rugged vehicles could serve as a ready-

The 4WD Sportsmobile Camper Van

made BOV solution for many people who do not need a larger mobile retreat. Billed by Sportsmobile as the "ultimate adventure vehicle," this 4WD van—an example of which is featured on the cover of this book—was designed to combine off-road capability and backcountry camping with in-town maneuverability and decent open-road fuel economy. This particular model is based on the Ford E350 1-ton cargo van and is powered by a 6-liter turbodiesel V8. It has a beefed-up suspension with room for oversized wheels and tires and a custom-built front axle and front sway bar. The 4WD system features a heavy-duty transfer case and manual shift dual-mode 4WD and 2WD. The 4WD camper version of this van starts at $61,000 and ranges up to more than $70,000 depending on options included. Find out more at www .sportsmobile.com.

Winnebago Aspect 28B   This streamlined Winnebago motorhome is an example of a Class C type that is built on a gasoline-powered Ford E450 chassis. Overall length is just under 30 feet and height is 10½ feet. It features slide-outs for the queen bed and a U-shaped dinette to expand available living space. Like all Winnebago motorhomes, its interior is well appointed and overall build quality is good. MSRP for the Aspect 28B starts at $88,255, and the Winnebago website is at www .winnebagoind.com.

5

DIY MOBILE RETREATS

The DIY (do-it-yourself) mobile retreat is an appealing alternative in setting up a self-contained bug-out vehicle because you can customize it to your particular needs based on the number of people and amount of stuff you need to carry, as well as the environment in which you will be operating. DIY mobile retreats can be built onto many readily available platforms, including pickup trucks and flatbed work trucks, as well as open or enclosed cargo and utility trailers. Many existing vehicles with lots of enclosed space such as vans, buses, and commercial box trucks can also be converted into custom DIY mobile retreats. Building a DIY mobile retreat can be a fun and interesting project whether you need it for bugging out or not, and when you're done you can use it for weekend or vacation getaways in the same way you would use a manufactured RV.

As mentioned in the previous chapter, lightweight, flimsy construction is the norm rather than the exception in factory-built RVs. Most of the utilitarian work vehicles like vans, buses, and box trucks that you might convert yourself will be better built to begin with, and when you modify them to include living quarters, your add-ons can be more substantial as well. Instead of cheap fake-wood veneer over particleboard and other cost-cutting materials that RV manufacturers use, you can use real plywood and lumber and have a better structure at a lower cost. Parts you can't build—such as stoves, sinks, and other fixtures—can be purchased from RV suppliers, or better yet, marine supply dealers who sell higher-quality fixtures built for liveaboard boats. The accommodations inside a DIY mobile retreat can be as spartan or as luxurious as you care to make them.

Another advantage of DIY mobile retreats is that they can be disguised to not look like what they are. This is especially true of converted vans, box trucks, and other common vehicles that are normally used for hauling cargo. Some people who practice the alternative, low-cost lifestyle of living in their vehicles put this advantage to good use by parking in plain sight along streets, in store and other business parking lots, or even among the parked vehicles at apartment complexes or college campuses. In a bug-out situation you may be able to keep a low profile in such a vehicle, even while moving, because it doesn't look unusual. When stopped, it may appear to anyone passing by to be just a parked or abandoned work vehicle rather than an occupied and well-stocked mobile retreat.

Disadvantages of DIY Mobile Retreats

Disadvantages of the DIY type of mobile retreat of course include the time and effort it will take to do the building or conversion. If you are not handy with tools or willing to learn the skills needed to do this work, hiring someone to help or to do it for you could cost more than buying a ready-made RV. Even if you can do all your own work, some types of DIY mobile retreats can be expensive and labor-intensive to build, particularly if you are building from scratch, as in the case of a camper trailer or house truck built from plans. New construction of anything almost always costs more than buying a used fixer-upper, so, before you begin, it's important to assess your needs carefully to be sure the DIY option is right for you. If the project is too big you may lose enthusiasm for the effort it takes or run out of funds to complete it.

If you are not willing to take the time to do quality work or spend the money for quality components and parts, you might end up with a converted vehicle that is inferior to an old fixer-upper RV. A poorly made home-built mobile retreat can endanger the users with inadequate ventilation, faulty electrical wiring, or improper use of portable stoves and fuels. There are books on outfitting RVs and boats and lots of online resources for specific, detailed information on all such systems that go into home-built RVs and retreats, so if you are going to invest time and money in building one, you should also be willing invest the time to do your research.

Key DIY Mobile Retreat Considerations

Enough Space for Comfortable Sleeping   You can sleep in practically any vehicle in a pinch, and on long road trips I have spent many a night sleeping in the reclined driver's seat of a sports car or sedan, curled up across the bench seat of a pickup, or stretched out in my sleeping bag in the open bed in back. But for a bug-out vehicle to be truly considered a mobile retreat, it should have designated bunk space available for every person who will be on board. This means, at minimum, flat spaces wide enough and long enough to comfortably accommodate each person without requiring body contortions. Most vans have enough space for full-length bunks behind the driver and front passenger seats if any additional seats in the rear are first removed. Buses have plenty of interior space but the passenger seats that come in them will not be long enough for adults to stretch out on, and some or all will have to be removed so proper bunks can be built. If you are building bunk spaces into a converted vehicle, or a structure on a trailer or the back of a truck, consider that the minimum dimensions recommended for adults are 6½ feet long by 24 inches wide. This will give most people enough room to fully stretch out, roll over, and otherwise move around without hitting walls or bulkheads. If possible, it is also best to have comfortable sitting headroom over each bunk, so the occupant can get in and out without hitting a shelf or cabinet overhead.

Bunks can be fitted with custom-made upholstered cushions like those found in RVs and yachts, or you can use camping-style mattresses with sheets, blankets, or sleeping bags. There are many excellent air mattresses and self-inflating camping mattresses available today that are comfortable enough for everyday, long-term use, so bedding does not have to be elaborate or expensive.

Built-In Storage for Everything Organization and storage are important parts of setting up a small mobile retreat. Space will be at a premium in any such structure, and how you utilize that space can make a huge difference in the size of the retreat you need for yourself and your family and how much you can carry in the way of gear and supplies. To see the possibilities, it's helpful to look at how some of the manufactured RVs are designed and how they make use of hidden spaces that would simply be wasted in a house. Examples include seats and bunks that have lids you can lift to access storage space under them, and shelves and cabinets in places such as the dead space in corners where walls meet ceilings and other such out-of-the-way places. Yacht designers make even better use of available space when designing liveaboard boats, as the streamlined space of a cruising boat leaves a lot less interior room available compared to a boxy RV of the same length. You can find many ingenious ideas for maximizing the use of available interior space in boatbuilding and boat improvement how-to books like Ferenc Mate's *The Finely Fitted Yacht.*

Ventilation and Other Comfort Considerations Adequate ventilation will be a top concern in converting many smaller vehicles such as vans and box trucks to DIY mobile retreats. Cargo vans usually have few if any windows in the rear area, and even some passenger vans may have windows that do not open. Such vehicles are designed around air conditioning, which will not be available when you are stopped for the night and is not practical anyway in a situation where you must conserve your fuel. Passenger vans and buses that do have opening windows will not have insect screening on them, so in most areas you will have to add this. Box trucks and other vehicles designed only for hauling cargo will not have any windows at all and so they will have to be installed, just as you will have to install functional ventilation in any structure you build yourself, such as a house truck.

Residential-style windows such as those you can buy at a building supply store can work for home-built structures, but are far from ideal. Most are too big and too fragile for this use; the glass they are made with is easily broken and when broken fragments into large, danger-ous shards. You should look instead at windows, hatches, and portlights designed for RVs or for boats. The best of these will have strong lenses of cast acrylic or Lexan bedded with waterproof sealant into an anod-ized aluminum or plastic frame. Most will also have built-in, remov-able insect screening. Smoked lenses are better than clear, as they reduce the heat inside a small space by blocking much of the sunlight. The opening type of window or portlight should be designed so that it seals watertight when closed and can be opened to various degrees between closed and fully open. In addition to these manufactured win-dows that open, you can purchase or make additional fixed windows and skylights to let in more light and to allow better visibility. DIY fixed windows can be cut from Lexan or cast acrylic and fit over the open-ings you cut in the structure with a bedding of waterproof adhesive sealant such as DOW 795, which is so strong it is used to install large windows in skyscrapers without fasteners or frames.

As with cruising boats, opening hatches installed into the roof of a DIY mobile retreat can be more effective than vertical side windows at letting in a cooling breeze and keeping the interior fresh. Such hatches also let in a lot of ambient light, even through smoked lenses. The best system for a good airflow is two or more of these rooftop hatches along with several opening ports or windows in the sides.

Despite the effectiveness of opening windows and hatches, it's still nearly essential to install 12-volt electric fans in the interior of your mobile retreat, particularly in locations where they can blow over the bunk areas. If it's hot outside and there is no breeze, you won't get air-flow no matter how many openings you have and fans can make all the difference in making it possible for you to sleep.

12-Volt Electrical Systems and Power Management Any mobile retreat should be set up for self-contained, off-the-grid liv-ing and have provisions for operating that way for extended periods of time. You will want a basic electrical system in even the simplest DIY mobile retreats, as there will be a need for lighting and comfort-enhancing equipment like the 12-volt fans mentioned above. It's not a good idea to use the vehicle's one and only starter battery for this purpose, even in small vehicles such as converted vans. You need to keep the starter battery separate from the house battery or bank of house batteries so that you can depend on the starter battery having a full charge when you need to start the engine. The house batteries should be deep-cycle storage batteries, as these are designed to be able to withstand multiple cycles of draining and recharging without damage, unlike starter batteries.

Ideally, you want to be able to recharge the house battery bank without having to run the vehicle's engine, and this will entail using a small gasoline or diesel generator, an array of solar panels, or perhaps a wind generator of the type used on the liveaboard boats described in the next chapter. Gas or diesel generators have the disadvantage of being noisy and requiring extra fuel, but they also are generally the fastest and most reliable way to recharge batteries. Solar or wind power makes you more independent of the grid for extended periods of time and works well as long as you are operating in areas exposed to either bright sunlight or a strong breeze. Redundancy of systems is a good thing here, and the best solution of all is to have all three available to be used as conditions dictate.

Water and Plumbing Systems　Water and plumbing systems in a DIY mobile retreat can be as simple or elaborate as you care to make them. An adequate supply of drinking water is, of course, a top priority, and how you store and gain access to that water depends on whether you are of the primitive camping or luxury RV living mindset, or somewhere in between. The simplest solution is a supply of one-gallon jugs or larger jerry cans sized anywhere from three to about seven gallons. These can be secured in any available location inside or outside the mobile retreat and used as needed, then refilled when a water source is available. The advantage of this system is that it separates your water into more than one container, helping to prevent contamination or loss of the entire supply if you should refill with some bad water or damage a container. Jerry cans can be almost as convenient as water on tap if you get the type with the removable spigot in the cap and have a countertop or other space where the one in use can be secured with the valve accessible.

If you want a more RV-like setup, you can purchase or build fixed water tanks that go into otherwise dead space within the mobile retreat and are plumbed to one or more sinks with faucets. Plumbing should be of flexible plastic water hose and the pump to get the water from the tank to the spigot can be either a hand- or foot-operated manual pump or a 12-volt DC pump that is connected by a circuit to the house batteries. In general, a fixed system like this makes more sense on board a large mobile retreat used by a family, while the jerry-can system may be all you need as an individual or couple in a smaller vehicle like a converted van.

If you have access to enough water, washing and bathing can be accomplished easily enough with the flexible plastic bladder-type solar showers commonly used on boats. A five-gallon shower bag like this, made of black material to absorb heat rapidly, will get as hot as you can stand it if you place it in the sun on the dash of the vehicle while driving or on the roof when stopped. If you are in a remote area, the easiest way to use it is to hang it outside, but if your mobile retreat is large enough and you have a family on board and need the privacy, you could build in a shower stall and either use the portable solar shower inside, or set up a permanently mounted black plastic tank on the roof plumbed to a gravity-fed shower head.

The need for a toilet inside a mobile retreat can be addressed with one of the many types of portable toilets that are made for campers and boaters. These units have a small holding tank attached beneath the seat and bowl part that can be removed for emptying. Smells are kept in control by the seals on the tank and a small amount of chemical treatment that is added after each time it is emptied. In a remote area you could empty the tank in a latrine or not use the toilet inside at all. However, having a toilet inside that can be used in bad weather and while on the move is convenient, if not absolutely necessary. As with other aspects of mobile retreat living, your needs will depend on your desired comfort level and whether or not you are used to roughing it. The toilet can be permanently installed with an electric or manually flushed unit connected to a built-in holding tank if you have the space and enough people in your group to warrant the added expense and complication.

Onboard Cooking Facilities   No mobile retreat can be considered truly self-contained unless it has provisions for preparing real meals inside. To do this, at minimum you will need a single-burner camp stove and enough counter space to set it up and to prepare the food you intend to cook. The simplest solution is to use a backpacking-type stove, but you have to be careful about the design and type of fuel because of the fire hazard of using such a stove indoors. Adequate ventilation is also essential when using any type of open flame burner in an enclosed space. Avoid the kind of stoves that use pressurized white gas, as these can flare up and get out of control in a hurry, as well as spill burning fuel if they are inadvertently knocked over. Portable stoves that attach to sealed canisters of propane or butane are safer, and some of these are designed to be used inside RVs and boats. Alcohol is another safe onboard cooking fuel that is particularly popular on boats because of safety concerns. On the other hand, alcohol stoves are a bit slower than propane to bring water to a boil, and the denatured alcohol used for fuel is more expensive.

If more than one or two people will be using the retreat, the galley will become a more important feature and a larger stove with an oven may be called for. You can purchase these from RV or marine suppliers. Most cooking units of this type will be fueled by propane, supplied through a hose and regulator from one or more large refillable tanks. This type of propane tank should be mounted outside the enclosed living quarters or in a well-ventilated locker built onto the exterior so that any leaks will not lead to a potentially explosive buildup of invisible propane.

As mentioned in the previous chapter, many modern RVs have propane or electric refrigeration to keep perishable foods cold or frozen. While this is easy for weekending or vacation camping, it will likely not be feasible for a longer-term bug-out situation where you will need to reserve any available propane for cooking. There are small 12-volt DC coolers that serve adequately as mini-refrigerators and I have used them successfully on boats, but if you use one for extended periods of time you will need adequate charging capacity from a solar array or a wind generator to keep from draining the house batteries.

As mentioned above under water systems, you can build in a sink with a faucet plumbed to your water tanks if you want the convenience of a conventional kitchen-like setup for washing dishes and preparing meals. But if simplicity is more to your liking, a simple two- or three-gallon bucket placed under the spigot of a jerry can will work fine for dishwashing chores and can be simply dumped outside when you're done.

Security and Escape Hatches Any mobile retreat that you are going to stay in should have provisions for locking the entrances from the inside while still allowing adequate ventilation. Some vehicles designed to haul cargo will have to be modified for this, as they are designed to lock from the outside. Deadbolts and other simple latch systems can serve the purpose as long as they are strong and solidly mounted to sturdy doors and surrounding casings or frames. If you are building from scratch, you have many more options available for fortifying your entrances.

Alternative escape hatches are something else to consider and may be worth incorporating into your design. Such hatches can be as simple as ventilation hatches on the roof of the vehicle's living quarters. As with boats, such hatches should be a minimum of 16 by 16 inches square to allow an average adult to exit them. Hidden escape hatches can also be built into the floor of your DIY mobile retreat, allowing you and your family to exit quickly and hopefully unseen in the event of some circumstance that prevents you from using one of the other entranceways.

Construction Materials and Methods for Building from Scratch If you intend to build your structure from scratch rather than converting an existing enclosed vehicle, there are several approaches you can take depending the amount of time, money, and skill you have. In the sections on specific types of DIY mobile retreats to follow, you will see that the possibilities range from the funky house truck built of ordinary building materials to the finely fitted home-built travel trailer or truck camper built from detailed plans.

Whatever construction method you decide on, keep in mind that a mobile retreat is just that—mobile—and that it will be subjected to stresses that ordinary fixed structures do not have to endure. These include the vibrations and hard bumps of driving over rough roads and the constant near-hurricane-force winds that result from moving down the highway at 65–70 mph. You cannot just nail a house-like structure together, tack shingles on the roof, and expect it to survive long. Better methods of joinery and fastening are required, but can still be simple, quick, and cheap.

The fastest method of assembling such a structure out of ordinary house-framing lumber is to use an electric drill driver and self-starting deck screws that are coated to prevent corrosion. These screws have long been my favorite fasteners for quick assemblies, as they have much greater holding power than nails and can be removed easily if you make a mistake in aligning parts and need to start over. Screws are much better than nails for any structure that will be in motion and are less likely to work their way loose. For even better rigidity, use lap joints or plywood gussets and reinforce all screwed wood joints with wood glue or epoxy. Once you have a framework, the exterior of the structure can be sheathed with plywood or exterior siding, or individual lapped planks of a durable species like cedar or cypress. If you use plywood it should be exterior or marine grade, and the outside surfaces should be well painted to seal them against water intrusion. The roof can be made of aluminum or steel panels screwed down the way metal roofs are in house construction.

A better but more expensive building method using plywood is the composite method used to build modern wooden boats. In this type of construction, all exterior surfaces of the plywood are faired smooth and sheathed with one or more layers of fiberglass cloth laminated over the wood with epoxy resin. A structure built this way will be lightweight, rigid, and extremely durable as long as the outer skin is protected with paint or UV-inhibiting varnish to prevent sun degradation. The roof and sides can be built the same way with no need for a different roof material.

If you have the skills and tools to weld, you can build the framework out of steel or aluminum and cover it with a sheathing of wood or aluminum sheet metal like that used by the prefab RV builders. Other possible construction materials include solid fiberglass shells hand-laid in a mold and foam-cored fiberglass panels joined together with epoxy fillets and fiberglass taped seams.

Converted Passenger and Cargo Vans

As with prefab RVs and liveaboard boats, it's better to pick the smallest vehicle that will meet your needs as a mobile retreat rather than the biggest you can afford. Smallness has many advantages other than cost, including ease of driving in congested traffic, ease of hiding in an urban or backcountry environment, and better fuel economy. For a single person or a couple, almost any van can be converted into a comfortable mobile retreat. I have spent months at a time traveling this way, once as a couple in a GMC Safari minivan, which is about as small a vehicle as will work well for two people in this role. With the rear seats removed and a raised plywood platform for a bed in the back with cubbyholes for storage underneath, there was plenty of room for all our gear and supplies. Cooking was usually done outside, which is

Even a small mobile retreat can carry backup vehicles like kayaks and bikes.

easier in a van this size, but a galley could be built in as long as you provided adequate ventilation. A large solar shower bag kept on the dash during the day provided plenty of hot water for washing up when hung from the overhanging canoe racks while in camp. With this small van, we were able to explore remote Forest Service and BLM gravel roads all over the southwestern U.S., camping far off the beaten path away from anyone. An advantage of this size van is that the used market is full of good examples at very reasonable prices. Vans don't have the cool factor of SUVs and nicer pickups, and consequently there is not as much demand for older ones, except as work vehicles.

With a full-sized van, it's possible to build a completely self-contained bug-out vehicle with sleeping, cooking, and storage capacity for two people and perhaps a small child or two. Fifteen-passenger vans, like their cargo-carrying equivalents, have a lot of empty space in the rear when the extra seats are removed.

An interesting option for those who are interested in using vans as bug-out mobile retreats is the availability of 4WD conversions of many popular models. This work is done by a few shops that will professionally convert the new van you choose for around $10,000 to $14,000 (excluding the price of the van). You could then modify the 4WD van using the same principles as any of the other conversions in this chapter to meet your mobile retreat requirements. Of course, custom-built 4WD camper vans like the Sportsmobile mentioned in the previous chapter can be purchased ready to go, but because the market is so specialized for this type of vehicle the prices are high.

SOME EXAMPLES OF VANS YOU MIGHT CONSIDER CONVERTING

Chevy Astro/GMC Safari   The popular Astro/Safari series of vans is a good choice if you are looking for a van on the smaller end of the spectrum to convert to a mobile retreat. They have a good reliability record and, unlike most minivans with their streamlined exteriors and car-like interiors, the Astro or Safari van has a decent amount of space inside to work with. These vans were in production from 1985 until 2005 and were offered in both cargo and passenger versions with varying levels of trim. Beginning in 1990 they were available in all-wheel drive. The area behind the driver and front passenger seats is large enough for a fixed bunk with storage underneath, and with some design ingenuity, a portable toilet and foldaway galley could be fitted as well. Because of the large numbers of these vans in circulation, you can easily find a clean example in good running condition for under $5,000.

Clydesdale 4WD Van Conversions Sportsman Light Truck and Offroad in Kamloops, British Colombia builds rugged 4WD Ford van conversions starting with the new van platform of your choice. The Clydesdales are not ready-built campers like the Sportsmobile, but come with many available options to optimize them for off-road use, including heavy-duty solid front axles and independent front suspension. Other options include dual rear wheels, dual suspension front or rear, skid plates, and winch kits. More information is available at www .sportsman4x4.com.

Converted Buses

Just as Class A RV manufacturers use a bus chassis to build the finest luxury RVs, an older bus can provide a platform with nearly endless possibilities for mobile retreat conversion. Most buses are heavy-duty vehicles with strong diesel engines and standard transmissions. If you have a need for such a large bug-out vehicle but lack the funds to purchase even a used Class A RV in good condition, a DIY bus conversion may be just the thing. I've seen some amazing accommodations built into old school buses bought for little or nothing at auction. All it takes is creativity and a willingness to do the work, which in this case will likely become a large project. With all those rows of seats removed, the interior of an average-sized bus offers a lot of real estate for building living quarters, storage spaces, and even workshop space. You could even set up such a bus as a permanent dwelling for a family if need be, and as a mobile retreat, it could carry enough supplies to survive independently for extended periods of time.

BUYING A USED SCHOOL BUS

Many of the used school buses you might find for sale are built by the Bluebird Corporation, which has been around since 1932. You can sometimes find great deals on used school buses sold at auction by school districts that are upgrading or simply have policies requiring them to get rid of vehicles over a certain age or mileage. It's not uncommon to be able to purchase such a bus in good condition with a diesel engine for as little as $5,000 to $10,000 when it might have cost $70,000 or more new. The important thing when buying an older bus to use as your platform for a large mobile retreat is to inspect it for body and frame rust, as rust can ruin your investment. You should also make sure that all the major drive components (engine, transmission, steering, hydraulic lines, brakes, etc.) are in order. You could end up spending a lot more than you paid just for repairs if you are not sure about this. Try to find a bus that comes with fleet service records to get an idea of how well it's been maintained.

Box Trucks

Older commercial box trucks of the kind used to deliver everything from snack foods to medical supplies can often be bought well used for next to nothing. These trucks are bigger than vans and the cargo area usually has a much higher ceiling, opening up more possibilities for bunks and built-in storage. Some of these trucks also have diesel engines, and if they have been maintained as part of a company fleet, can have a long service life. I've seen such trucks converted into everything from RVs to mobile woodworking shops. Making one into a custom BOV could be a fun and interesting project. The biggest disadvantage may be the size and bulk of such a vehicle. While smaller than a converted bus, it will still be awkward to maneuver on anything other than a good road.

COMMERCIAL BOX TRUCK EXAMPLE

Used U-Haul 17-Foot Ford Box Truck   Rental companies like U-Haul and Enterprise sell off their older inventory at low prices. A common model is the 17-foot box truck built on the Ford E350 chassis, which has a 6.8-liter gas engine with 265 hp and a towing capacity of 7,500 lb. The cargo capacity is 849 cubic feet, with inside dimensions of just over 14 feet long on the floor and 7½ feet wide. A cab-over extension increases the total inside length to 16', 8". This much empty space provides plenty of possibility for building in accommodations. The only access to the cargo area is a rear roll-up door, but this could be modified and a side door, windows, and hatches could be installed as well. As a basic platform, such box trucks are cheap, with U-Haul advertising the 17-footer starting at $4,295.

House Trucks and Homebuilt Truck Campers

House trucks are not commonly seen today, but were once popular in places like Northern California, especially in the '60s and '70s. The typical house truck has infinitely more character than any manufactured RV and the possibilities for creativity in building one are nearly limitless. The idea most builders have in mind is to make them look as much like miniature conventional houses as possible, with no real resemblance to the truck campers that are the closest prefab equivalents. Instead, a house truck looks more like a gypsy caravan than anything you would normally see at your local KOA campground. Some house truck builders favor steep rooflines and fancy carved trimwork, while others go for a more rustic and rugged cabin in the woods look.

DIY truck camper on a flatbed work truck

A boat carpenter friend of mine who lived in a large house truck back in the 1980s recently built a smaller one that is more like an oversized truck camper to fit on the flatbed of his Ford F350 work truck. This structure was built with simple 2x4 framing and cypress plank siding, and with a standard window-unit air conditioner powered by a generator mounted outside and several bunks built inside, it provided comfortable accommodations for his work crew en route to a boat-building job across the country. It was even removed from the truck for use as a portable office on the job site. Such a structure could serve as a mobile bug-out retreat en route to your bug-out location and then be removed and used as a fixed retreat.

If you are not into the somewhat eccentric look of the self-designed truck camper that uses ordinary house-building methods, you can purchase plans for more conventional truck campers that use wood, aluminum, or composite construction to achieve a final result that is similar to the prefab truck campers you can buy. Glen-L RV is one supplier of such plans.

SOME RESOURCES FOR INSPIRATION TO DESIGN YOUR OWN HOUSE TRUCK

House trucks are so far out of the mainstream that you will have to do some searching to find much information on them. As already mentioned, most are owner-designed, so finding building plans is difficult. Some books on the subject, such as the classic *Roll Your Own* by Jodi Pallidini, are long out of print but can be found used. Another resource is *Some Turtles Have Nice Shells* by Roger D. Beck. This book is an encyclopedia of house trucks and house buses, with hundreds of photos of these creations for your inspiration; more information is available at www.housetrucks.com. Another informative website on the topic is www.mrsharkey.com, which features lots of photos of examples and some informative articles. For more ideas on homebuilt house trucks, a search of the web will turn up photos and blogs that owners have written about their experiences.

Commercial Homebuilt Truck Camper Plans

Glen-L RV Cascade   Glen-L RV offers complete building plans for a line of truck campers ranging from about 13 to 16 feet in overall length. These designs have a dated style reminiscent of the 1960s or '70s, but are fully functional and can be fitted with modern equipment and conveniences to improve them. The Cascade has a double bed over the cab and 9 feet of floor space in the main living area with room for a dinette that converts to another double bunk, as well as a galley and enclosed toilet compartment. It weighs 1,400 lb. and is designed to fit a ¾-ton or larger pickup truck. The building plans and patterns package is $54.00, and the company website is www.glen-l.com/campers.

HOME-BUILT CAMPER TRAILERS

House trucks are certainly not the only type of DIY mobile retreat that can be built from scratch. Some ambitious backyard builders aim to build RVs that look as good as or even better than the offerings of the factory builders, and plans providers like Glen-L RV Plans support them by offering professionally drawn, detailed building instructions. This type of DIY RV builder, like the backyard boatbuilder, wants something that can be customized for their specific needs and/or believes they can build to a quality standard that is higher than a mass-produced unit. As with building a boat, the cost can be stretched out over time, allowing you to pay as you go and end up with the RV you want free and clear of a monthly payment.

Building one of these elaborate travel trailers will be a time-consuming and expensive project if you are trying to emulate the amenities and level of finish of a prefab model. For those who want a quicker, easier, and cheaper solution, there is also the option of approaching this kind of build on a trailer in the same way the house truck builders do it with truck beds. You can start with practically any type of trailer, but particularly useful are the flatbed utility trailers used by contractors to haul lumber and materials or by homeowners to haul their lawnmowers, ATVs, and other toys from place to place. Open utility trailers can be had in a wide range of sizes, with single- or double-axle configurations depending on the load rating for which they are intended. A trailer of this type is a clean slate for designing and building practically any kind of structure you want for your mobile retreat. Instead of the time-consuming construction methods used to build a conventional-looking trailer, you can assemble your structure with regular house-framing lumber and plywood. It can be permanently attached to the bed of the trailer or designed to be hoisted or winched on or off when necessary.

EXAMPLE OF A PROFESSIONALLY DESIGNED TRAVEL TRAILER FOR HOME BUILDING

Glen-L RV Plans Niagra The Niagra model is one of several in a series of travel trailer plans offered by Glen-L. It is designed to be

RV AND DIY MOBILE RETREAT CHECKLIST

The spare parts, tools, and additional equipment in the checklist at the end of Chapter One (page 94) should be carried on your RV or DIY mobile retreat as with any motor vehicle. The checklist that follows covers some additional items needed for larger vehicles and for self-contained living in the vehicle. Adjust it as needed for your particular mobile retreat.

TOOLS AND SPARE PARTS:
- ❏ Spare wheels and tires for trailers
- ❏ Hydraulic jack sized for the vehicle or trailer
- ❏ Leveling blocks, boards, and chocks
- ❏ Multimeter for testing electric circuits
- ❏ Spare fuses, breakers, and electrical wiring
- ❏ Crimp-on wire terminals
- ❏ Soldering iron and solder
- ❏ Electrical tape
- ❏ Wire strippers/crimp tool
- ❏ 18-volt electric drill/driver with assortment of bits

- ❏ 18-volt jigsaw and blades
- ❏ 18-volt circular saw
- ❏ Tape measure and combination square
- ❏ Handsaw for cutting wood
- ❏ Hacksaw for cutting metal
- ❏ Files, chisels, and assorted hammers
- ❏ Assorted fasteners for repairing or rebuilding DIY structures
- ❏ Rivet tool and assorted aluminum rivets
- ❏ Assorted hose clamps
- ❏ Spare flexible water/drain/sewer hose for all fixtures
- ❏ Silicone sealant

covered with an exterior aluminum skin and if carefully constructed, will be comparable to the best older factory travel trailers, as like the other Glen-L RV plans, the styling dates back to the 1960s and '70s and looks a bit plain by modern standards. The Niagra is 20 feet long and just under 8 feet wide with a dry weight of 3,500 lb. This is a travel trailer that could accommodate two adults and their supplies and possibly two children as well for shorter stays. The plans for the interior layout show a large dinette that converts to a double bed, as well as a spacious bathroom with toilet and enclosed shower. A galley is located in the middle, opposite the dinette. This DIY travel trailer is designed to be equipped and set up in much the same way as its manufactured equivalents. The price for the plans is $60.00. More info is available at www.glen-l.com/campers.

- ❐ J-B Weld cold weld
- ❐ Other assorted glues
- ❐ Fire extinguishers mounted in living/cooking areas
- ❐ Spare burners and other stove components
- ❐ Spare components for propane bottle connections

GEAR AND SUPPLIES FOR VEHICLE CAMPING/LIVING:
- ❐ Sleeping bags/blankets/sheets
- ❐ Inflatable or custom-fitted mattresses
- ❐ Insect repellent and pest-control spray
- ❐ Battery-powered lanterns and flashlights
- ❐ Battery-powered fans
- ❐ Holding tank/portable toilet chemicals
- ❐ Sewer hose and fittings (if using built-in holding tank)
- ❐ Adequate supply of tissue

- ❐ Bathroom and kitchen cleaning solutions or sprays
- ❐ Buckets, mop or rags, broom and dustpan, small Shop-Vac
- ❐ Supply of stove fuel
- ❐ Cookware and utensils
- ❐ Plates, bowls, cups, and food storage containers
- ❐ Dishwashing soap
- ❐ Aluminum foil
- ❐ Ziploc plastic bags
- ❐ Extra jerry cans of fresh water
- ❐ Water purification filter or chemical treatment
- ❐ Solar shower (if no built-in shower)
- ❐ Bath soap, shampoo, and other toiletries
- ❐ First aid kit (can be much larger than escape vehicle kit)

6

LIVEABOARD BOATS

Liveaboard boats are among the best options for comfortable mobile retreats and have most of the advantages specific to boats that were already discussed in Chapter Three. The liveaboard lifestyle is a popular alternative in many waterfront areas and is often less expensive and less complicated than life ashore. Larger vessels, both power and sail, that are designed as cruisers to be taken on extended trips have self-contained onboard living quarters that include provisions for sleeping, cooking, eating, and waste management. Those who live full-time on such boats generally fall into two categories: the cruisers who move north and south along the coast or among islands following the seasons, and the marina liveaboards who work regular jobs ashore and use their boats as floating apartments, rarely taking them out of the slip.

In considering a larger boat as a mobile retreat, you want to first be sure the vessel you have in mind is a real cruiser and not a "dock queen" incapable of traveling and operating away from shore power and other land-based amenities. And while the term "liveaboard" implies permanent residency afloat, this does not have to be the case at all. Many people who are not so committed to the lifestyle that they want to give up their shore-based homes still keep cruising boats docked at a marina or stored in a boatyard for use when they can get away to cruise. Some of the boats in this category may be too small to live aboard full-time anyway, unless you are young and single and don't mind putting up with a lot of discomfort. The key requirement in making a boat a mobile retreat, is that just like the RVs, vans, buses and other land-based mobile retreats discussed in the previous two chapters, the boat needs to serve as both transportation and moveable shelter. It should be able to get you out of a danger zone while carrying everything you and your crew need to live off the grid for a reasonable period of time after bugging out.

Liveaboard Cruising Is Not Just for the Wealthy

If you're new to the idea of cruising-sized boats, you may have the mistaken impression that such vessels are the domain of the idle rich, but not all large and capable boats are gold-plated yachts. When you start investigating what is out there in the used boat market, particularly in the current economy, it will shock you how much boat you can buy for the cost of many of the other bug-out vehicles in this book. If you are not familiar with this market, you may be surprised to find that you can buy an older liveaboard bluewater sailing vessel capable of taking you and your family anywhere in the world for the cost of an average new SUV or pickup. If you're really handy with tools and know something of boats, you can buy one for less. I personally bought one such boat for $5,000 and, with a few modifications and improvements that cost just a few thousand more, lived aboard and sailed it all over the Gulf of Mexico for years. This is not to say you can't spend a whole lot more money on a boat of this type. If you read the advertisements in the yachting and sailing magazines, you would have the impression that you couldn't leave the shore without a vessel costing as much as or many times more than your house. Depending on your resources, you may wish to spend a small fortune on the vessel that best meets your requirements. But my point is that no one should discount this kind of boat because they mistakenly believe that it is beyond their means.

The other option for obtaining such a vessel is to build it yourself, as many have done or are in the process of doing as you read this. There are almost limitless options for DIY backyard boatbuilding plans, many designed for first-time builders with little or no experience. I've been building boats myself, both as a hobby and professionally, for some 15 years. I'm currently building a 26-foot sailing catamaran to use for my own bug-out and adventure travel purposes. More about that particular vessel will follow in this chapter's section on sailboats. Modern construction methods—with adhesives and sealants like epoxy resin and protective sheathing and structural laminates like fiberglass, Kevlar, and carbon fiber—have made DIY boatbuilding a viable means of obtaining a high-quality cruising vessel that can last your lifetime and beyond. If you don't have a large sum of cash available to plunk down on a good used boat, then building at home is a way to get the boat and pay for it over time. Instead of taking out a loan and making payments to a bank with interest, you buy the materials little by little as you need them and invest your own "sweat equity" until, before you know it, you have the vessel you want, paid for free and clear. The other advantage of the DIY option is that *you* control the quality of the construction from start to finish. You will know every plank, screw, and nail that goes into it and by knowing your boat so intimately, you will easily be able to maintain and repair it when necessary.

Disadvantages of Liveaboard Boats

Like every other kind of bug-out vehicle in this book, liveaboard boats come with their own set of disadvantages that you should consider before deciding this is the best option for you. The size that enables them to be self-contained is a problem in itself, as you won't easily be able to trailer such a boat home to the suburbs to keep it when you are not using it or to do the maintenance that will be necessary. The most capable cruising boats usually spend practically all their useful life in the water tied to a dock, mooring, or anchor. If you are one of those who prefers to live aboard full time, this is not a problem—as they say, "home is where the boat is," and whatever docking or mooring fees you are paying are probably a lot less than rent or a mortgage ashore. But if the boat is not your residence, you will be paying to keep it somewhere month after month, year after year, whether you are using it or not. How much you will pay depends a lot on the region you live in, as popular cruising areas like Southern California and south

Florida are much more expensive than someplace like the northern Gulf coast or most inland navigable waterways. You can avoid this expense, of course, if you are living and cruising aboard the boat full-time as many people do. Anchoring out is still free in most places and under U.S. maritime law any vessel underway has the right to anchor while navigating. It is only when you try to stay for extended periods of time in certain coastal municipalities that you run into problems with local authorities. In a bug-out situation, you'll be headed for remote areas away from towns anyway.

Another disadvantage of cruising boats related to their larger size is the difficulty of hiding them. You can't drag such a boat up on the beach or into the marsh grass as you can a smaller one, so once you embark on a bug-out voyage, you will essentially be tied down to the vessel for security reasons, unless you're willing to risk leaving it unattended. This same difficulty of hiding your cruising boat puts you at risk of a personal attack as well, as a large boat that looters assume is probably loaded with useful provisions could be quite an enticing target if they think they can outnumber or outgun the crew. Although you will be able to anchor the boat in remote locations far from the reach of land-based thieves and robbers, don't discount the possibility that some of these opportunists will take to the water in their own boats looking for easy prey. Have a plan to defend your vessel and keep a watch when in areas where you feel threatened. If you plan well and know your area of operation, you will likely be able to remain out of reach of those who would do you harm. As a last resort or deliberate plan, you can leave land behind entirely and bug out to the open sea if you have chosen a bluewater-capable boat.

Key Considerations Regarding Liveaboard Boats

Power or Sail? Just as with the smaller escape watercraft discussed in Chapter Three, the two primary propulsion systems you will have to decide between when choosing a cruising boat as your mobile retreat are internal combustion engines (using gasoline or diesel fuel) or sails to harness the wind. As with smaller boats, the choice between sailing and motoring will often be determined by your area of operation and your planned bug-out destination. There are many thousands of miles of inland waterways in the U.S. that are more suitable for motor cruising than sailing, and if you plan to use these routes you will need an engine, even if it is just an auxiliary engine on a sailing vessel.

The good thing about motor-powered cruising boats compared to small runabouts is that true cruising motor yachts utilize displacement-type hulls rather than planing hulls. They don't need an overpowered, fuel-guzzling engine to push them at high speeds, but rather are designed to cruise at slow to moderate speeds over long periods of time, the best ones sipping fuel at a reasonable rate. Cruising boats of this type will feature large fuel tanks and are designed to travel long distances without resupply. The useful range can be from a few hundred miles to two thousand or more, depending on the size and type of vessel. A disadvantage of this is that when it is time to fill the high-capacity tanks of such a vessel, you'll feel the hurt in your pocketbook. And in a long-term post-SHTF scenario, your motor-only vessel will be dead in the water when you do eventually exhaust the large supply of fuel you are carrying.

A sailing cruiser, on the other hand, can operate indefinitely in such a scenario and, if it is a bluewater design, can take you anywhere you want to go along the open coast or across the horizon to distant landfalls. Few motor cruisers can do the kind of offshore voyaging that even modest sailboats can accomplish with ease. This is primarily because of the range limitations determined by the amount of fuel a motor vessel can carry, but there are also design elements that make small sailboats more seaworthy and more comfortable in rough open-sea conditions. While you may see more motor yachts and cruisers in inland waterways and along protected coastal routes like the Intracoastal Waterway, if you go to remote island groups that can only be reached by crossing lots of open water, the sailboats will greatly outnumber the occasional private motor yacht that has arrived there on its own hull. If your bug-out route planning includes any offshore passages, a sailboat is the logical choice. Even for coastal and inland cruising, a sailboat with a reliable auxiliary engine offers the best of both worlds. If you are a skilled sailor and use the engine only when there is no alternative, you can make a small supply of fuel last over a long period of time. Many recreational sailors cover thousands of miles over a season while burning only a few gallons of fuel to enter the occasional tricky harbor.

Bluewater vs. Brownwater Cruising The terms "bluewater cruising" and "bluewater boat" are often used to differentiate offshore-capable cruising boats from those designed for coastal or inshore work. To the uninitiated, the differences will probably not be readily apparent. One common misconception is that larger size equals greater seaworthiness. This can be true given two different-sized boats of equal design and construction, but is not true across the board. Bluewater boats are designed from the keel up to withstand whatever the ocean throws at them, with the idea in mind that they will be operated far from land where running for shelter in the nearest harbor is not an option. Coastal or inshore boats, however, do not have to meet such rigorous standards, as it is assumed they will not be taken out in gales or other dangerous conditions.

Naturally, if a bluewater boat is good enough for the open ocean, it will be safer to operate near shore as well, but sometimes the accommodation plan for such a boat will be more limited than in boats designed for gentler waters. Offshore boats tend to have small cabins relative to their overall size. They will have small deck openings for greater strength in these weak areas. This means the hatches will be smaller, ventilation may not be as good, and the companionways leading from the deck to the cabin below may not be as convenient to pass in and out of.

Boats designed for protected-water cruising, on the other hand, can have larger, more spacious cabins. The extreme example of this is the houseboat, which does not even look like a boat at all. Houseboats are designed to be floating homes and to look and feel as much like a shoreside house as possible. The type of cruising that these inshore boats do best is sometimes called "brownwater cruising." Keep in mind that there are vast areas of this kind of water in North America as well as elsewhere. This term can include rivers, man-made canals, bayous, marshes, bays, and sounds. The bug-out options available among all these waterways are many, and you could feasibly live aboard and cruise such waters for a lifetime without ever needing to go offshore to explore new territory.

Going International If you decide that a bluewater cruising boat is right for you, then you will have options that few others in a bug-out scenario will be able to think about. One of these is to simply sail away, leaving the entire country or continent behind to evacuate to a more peaceful part of the globe, since it's hard to imagine a worldwide SHTF scenario that will affect the most remote coastal and island areas that could only be reached by boat. Chances are you could find a place to wait out the storm or start over if it got so bad where you came from that returning was not an option.

In normal times, international cruising is still one of the most care-free, inexpensive, and uncomplicated ways to see the world. The boat that takes you there is your home, so you don't have to worry about accommodations when you arrive. However, paperwork and bureaucracy are facts of modern life, and to enter other countries aboard your boat you will need documentation proving that you own the vessel, as well as your passport, and, in some countries, proof of insurance. Bugging out with firearms will also be problematic, as many countries will not allow you to bring them in or will require you to surrender them for storage by customs until you are ready to leave. Carrying weapons on the high seas in international waters is not a problem though, and many recreational cruisers are well armed and put up with the inconvenience of checking in their firearms for the security of having them aboard while underway.

How Big Does It Need to Be? In most cases, a bigger boat means more comfort, storage space, and carrying capacity, but also more initial cost to buy or build and more time and money to keep up with the maintenance. As with an RV, the number of people you will need to accommodate is a good starting point in trying to decide how big a boat you need. Many boat brochures (like RV advertising blurbs) describe boat accommodations by the number of people the vessel "will sleep." This is misleading and usually exaggerated, because they are referring to occasional weekend overnight cruises, not long-term living aboard. While a 25-footer may sleep five or six people, it will not have adequate storage space for that many to live aboard for an uncertain amount of time in a bug-out scenario. But a single person, a couple, or a family with one or two small children could do fine on some cruising vessels under 30 feet. I was able to live comfortably enough on my Grampian 26 sailboat with two other people for a few months, both while underway and while docked at a marina. One important consideration is that everyone on board should have their own personal space. If you have to move a lot of stuff every day just to clear some bunk space for one of your crew members, you need a bigger boat with more dedicated bunks.

As for seaworthiness, size does not have as much bearing on this as many think. Many well-designed sailboats in the 20–25 foot range have crossed oceans and circumnavigated the globe, and not just as publicity stunts. The smallest cruiser that will meet your needs has a lot of advantages, especially when it comes to ongoing maintenance costs and the replacement costs of systems such as sails, rigging, engines, and other components. Smaller vessels can also be more manageable in storms and typical offshore conditions, as the sails will be smaller and forces generated will be lighter. But as far as comfort goes, a large vessel will almost always have a gentler motion at sea and will keep the crew drier and less exposed to the elements. If you have the experience and seamanship skills to handle a larger vessel, it can reward you with these benefits and much more storage capacity for extended voyages without resupply. With proper planning, a 40-foot sailboat can carry six months' worth of supplies for a family of four.

Draft and Mast Height A major limitation of some large liveaboard boats is the amount of "draft," or depth of the hull below the waterline, which determines how many inches or feet of water they need to float without going aground on the bottom. The majority of sailboats, in particular, are limited in draft because of the deep underwater ballasted keel that is used to counteract the force of the wind in the sails and keep the hull upright. A typical 30-foot sailboat with a fixed keel will draw 5 feet, a 40-footer may draw 6 feet or more, and

DIY wood-epoxy composite 45-foot shallow-draft sailboat designed by Reuel Parker

even a 26-footer may draw 4 feet. Offshore, this is not a problem, but even 4 feet of draft severely limits where you can go in many bays, sounds, and rivers and around barrier islands.

Yacht designers have addressed this problem in many ways, including retractable keels or centerboards, twin bilge keels that angle out instead of straight down, and flat-bottom designs like the Sharpie that carry most of their ballast inside rather than outside the hull. Large multihulls such as catamarans and trimarans are also designed with shallow draft in mind. If your area of operation involves shoal waters and estuaries, it would pay to investigate these options, as you can get a large liveaboard cruiser of one of these types that draws 2 feet or less. Personally, I would never consider any vessel drawing more than 4 feet and my catamaran under construction draws only 18 inches. Motor yachts and houseboats generally draw less than monohull sailboats by design, so finding one to meet your water depth requirements will not be as hard.

Mast height, or "air draft," is another consideration for sailboats as bug-out vehicles if you plan to operate in rivers, canals, or on the Intracoastal Waterway system. Fixed bridges that span such waterways will determine your maximum mast height even in normal times. Along the Intracoastal Waterway, all such bridges have to be at least 50 feet high. But after a SHTF situation, you cannot assume that opening drawbridges, which are even more numerous than high fixed bridges, will be in operation. Many of these opening drawbridges are less than 30 feet high, which is too low for even the smallest liveaboard sailboats to pass under with the mast up. If such waterways are in your bug-out plan, you can modify your vessel's mast so that it can be easily raised and lowered while underway by means of a "tabernacle" pivot attachment at the base and a gin pole or A-frame and block and tackle arrangement for raising and lowering. This is a good setup for any bug-out sailboat because it also allows you to perform masthead maintenance and inspection without having to climb the mast.

Hull Construction When you start looking at larger vessels, as opposed to the kinds of boats covered in Chapter Three, the most common hull construction materials you will find are fiberglass, wood, and steel. Aluminum is less common because using this material for a larger boat is too expensive in most cases. You might also encounter ferro-cement hulls, which were popular among amateur builders a few decades ago but are mostly of suspect quality and should be avoided unless the construction was well documented.

Fiberglass is the most common of these materials, especially in production boats, as it is the most cost-effective material for manufacturers producing large numbers of a particular design to sell at a profit. As a result, new fiberglass boats can be sold at lower prices than one-off or semi-custom vessels of wood or steel. The used market is flooded with low-cost examples of fiberglass hulls dating back to the 1950s, when this material was introduced. Fiberglass hulls require less maintenance than other materials, but should not be completely neglected, as they can develop blisters below the waterline that can lead to delamination of the layers comprising the hull skin. Fiberglass is also susceptible to hairline cracks in decks and cabin structures that can lead to water intrusion from rain and dew in these areas. At minimum, a fiberglass boat needs to be hauled out of the water on a regular basis for a bottom cleaning and a fresh coat of anti-fouling paint. While fiberglass hulls can be incredibly strong and stiff, the construction quality and strength varies from manufacturer to manufacturer and according to the boat's intended purpose. Some fiberglass hulls can be easily holed or otherwise damaged in a collision or impact with something solid. Others are so thin that they can flex or "oilcan" in rough seas, causing structural failure that can lead to disaster. If you are choosing a fiberglass hull for offshore use, make sure it was built for that purpose.

Wood is the traditional boat construction material and is still a viable choice today despite the more modern options available. Wooden hulls are still being built in both the traditional plank-on-frame manner and using various new methods of laminated construction, such as cold-molding, which incorporates high-tech materials like epoxy resins and protective sheathings of fiberglass, Kevlar, and other fabrics. Many wooden hulls are also designed to be built from plywood using various assembly methods and modern adhesives, and high-tech marine plywood allows for some of the highest strength-to-weight ratios of any material other than expensive exotics like carbon fiber. Traditionally planked wooden hulls require the most maintenance to ensure that they do not leak or rot, but if such as boat is built properly and maintained properly throughout its service life, it can easily outlast the owner. The biggest disadvantage of wooden hulls is that well-built ones are expensive propositions if ordered from a professional. Well-maintained older examples will command a high price as well, especially if they are of a classic design. An advantage, however, is that many wooden boat designs can be home-built by the amateur boatbuilder, allowing you customize them to your particular needs and maintain quality control throughout the process.

Steel is the material of choice for practically all commercial work vessels such as tugs and larger fishing craft, as well as for military craft of all sizes up through the largest ships. Steel pleasure boats are not as common, but they can be found in the used market or can be special-ordered or owner-built by those who have welding skills. There are several well-known yacht designers that offer home building plans and even pre-cut kits for steel vessels. Steel is often the material of choice for adventurous sailors planning to go to remote, high-latitude destinations such as Arctic waters where ice is a possibility and holing a hull would be much more serious than in more populated regions. A sturdy steel-hulled vessel could be the ultimate bug-out boat as long as it was maintained and painted to prevent rust. The potential for rust is the biggest disadvantage of steel, as it will destroy a neglected hull inside and out in short order.

Electrical and Charging Systems   Like land-based RVs and other mobile retreats, a cruising-sized boat will have more equipment that requires 12-volt electricity than a small escape vessel. Lighting, fans, and navigation instruments can all be run off a 12-volt electrical system built around deep-cycle storage batteries. How you recharge these batteries will be determined largely by the type of vessel you have. A motor yacht fitted with an inboard diesel can easily keep its house batteries charged with an alternator that runs whenever the engine is in use. Most outboard engines in the sizes used on cruising boats also come equipped with 12-volt alternators, though their output capacity will be much smaller than the alternators typically fitted on inboard engines.

On a sailboat, you will have to look at alternative charging systems since your engine and its alternator will in most cases be much smaller, and you will be under power only a small percentage of your moving time. There is a also the consideration on both sail and motor cruisers of keeping the system charged when you are anchored for extended periods of time. You could run the engine at idle for a couple of hours a day, but this is a waste of fuel that would certainly not be viable in a bug-out situation where you may not be able to obtain more. A better alternative is a charging system augmented by solar panels or a wind generator. Because of the popularity of cruising off the grid for extended periods of time, marine solar panel arrays and wind generators are highly refined and many boats run entirely off one or the other, or even a combination of the two. Solar charging works well on boats because out on the open water, panels are much more exposed to the sun throughout the day than they would be on most houses. Likewise, wind generators work well because there is almost always a breeze out on the water, especially on the ocean. A third alternative for sailboats is a water generator, which is a towed device that has a small prop that spins as it is dragged behind the boat, generating electricity from the water in much the same way a wind generator works in the air.

Another consideration regarding the electrical systems on boats is safety. Fire is obviously a more serious problem on a boat than on any other type of mobile retreat. A fire far from land that cannot be contained can have you abandoning ship in a life raft or even swimming in your PFD within minutes. While some onboard fires are caused by gasoline, diesel, or cooking fuels stored on board, the most common cause is an improperly wired and fused 12-volt electrical system. All onboard wiring should be sized to carry more than the calculated load required by each device, as wire that is too small can burn through and start a fire. Every circuit should be protected by a fuse or circuit breaker of the correct size, and all wiring should be routed so that it is protected from sharp objects, chafe, and other potential damage, and is organized and easy to inspect and troubleshoot.

Water Supply If your bug-out plans only include freshwater cruising, then your water supply considerations will be simpler, as you will only have to be concerned with purifying the freshwater that surrounds you. This can be done using any of a variety of filters or chemical purification systems or a combination both. The best place to collect water for converting to drinking water is from small feeder streams or other cleaner sources if you are traveling along major river systems that may have high levels of chemical contaminants.

Saltwater cruising, on the other hand, will require much better planning and more water storage capacity to meet the needs of the crew between resupplies, especially on long voyages. Most cruising boats have built-in water storage that includes freshwater tanks and a plumbing system to get the water to the galley sink and other fixtures. But unless the boat has been designed for serious voyaging, the amount of storage will likely be inadequate and will have to be supplemented by owner-installed additional tanks or jerry cans stowed aboard. The minimum recommendation for extended voyages is one half gallon of water per day per person on board, but you will be much more comfortable if you double that amount to one gallon per day.

The freshwater supply onboard can also be replenished while underway or anchored by means of rainwater catchment systems and desalination systems. Rain catchment systems can be as simple as a tarp or awning with a bucket under the low edge, or they can be fitted with flexible hoses to drain the rain directly into the vessel's storage tanks. It's surprising how much water you can collect from even a brief shower with a large surface like this. Some boats are even designed so that water from the decks can be drained directly into the tanks—after waiting long enough to wash off any salt residue or debris, of course. Reverse osmosis desalination systems can be purchased from marine suppliers or custom-built from available components. The smaller ones are hand-operated and are more suitable for emergency situations such as being stranded in a life raft. For everyday use, a 12-volt desalination system can be large enough to supply all your crew's drinking, cooking, and washing needs. But the filters are the weak link and the most expensive part of reverse osmosis systems. If you plan on using this method to make drinking water over an extended period of time, you will need to invest in an adequate supply of filters as well as other components that need periodic replacement.

Waste Disposal Unlike camping on land, where you can dig a latrine or simple hole for human waste, on a liveaboard boat you will have to have some sort of toilet to use while underway. The simplest arrangement is a five-gallon plastic bucket, which can be fitted with a toilet seat/lid made for the purpose and is often used by crews of racing sailboats who don't want the weight of a marine head on their vessel. This works fine offshore, as the bucket can be simply dumped over the side, which is legal beyond certain established distance limits. It could also be used inshore in a bug-out situation where enforcing waste disposal laws will be the last thing on anyone's mind, but a better option is a portable marine toilet with a removable holding tank that can store at least a few day's waste. This holding tank can later be emptied ashore in a hole or emptied over the side when far offshore. Built-in marine toilets should have a manual pump to transfer waste to a holding tank and a bypass valve leading to a seacock below the waterline for pumping waste overboard when offshore. Pumping out at a marina pump-out station will likely not be an option post-SHTF.

Onboard Cooking   Cooking on a liveaboard boat, particularly a vessel that is underway offshore in rough conditions, presents a set of unique problems not found in other mobile retreats. The first consideration here is safety, because just like a faulty electrical system, a stove and its fuel can be the cause of an onboard fire, or even an explosion in the case of more volatile fuels like propane. Propane is the most commonly used stove fuel aboard cruising boats because of its low cost, high heat output, and convenience, but it is also one of the most dangerous fuels if not properly stored and properly connected to the stove. Since it is heavier than air, any leaking propane inside a boat cabin can settle in the bilges and ignite with the slightest spark. For this reason, many marine stoves use either non-pressurized alcohol or kerosene for fuel, though the latter is becoming less common.

The other safety consideration for cooking on a moving boat is that pots and pans and their boiling contents can be tossed around the cabin in rough conditions if they are not secured to the stovetop or if the stove top itself is not mounted on a gimbaled system that allows it to swing with the motion. All properly outfitted galleys should have gimbaled stoves with pot clamps or retaining rails around the burners. Even on boats used for river cruising or inland waterways, the wakes from passing ships and other large vessels can roll a boat enough to dump pots off the stove.

Security and Defense   As with any other mobile or fixed retreat, you have to be prepared to defend your liveaboard boat from attackers who would take it or what you have on board. Firearms are obviously the first choice, but there is no one weapon that is best for all situations. Ideally, you would want a hard-hitting rifle that fires a large-caliber round that could disable an attacking boat by penetrating the hull or engine from a distance if you knew the approaching crew's intentions in advance. At closer ranges, such as when the attackers are already alongside or on board, a shotgun would likely improve your chances of hitting your target, particularly if there is a lot of wave action and vessel movement. Down below in your bunk at night, a handgun offers the best maneuverability in the confines of the cabin. When using a firearm of any kind on board a boat, you have to be aware of stray rounds or over-penetration of rounds that could damage your own hull or vital systems or hit other members of your crew.

As mentioned before, if you are traveling internationally, firearms may not be an option, depending on where you are going. Distress flares fired from a 12-gauge flare pistol can be a good alternative at close range, and dummy flares for these pistols with a real pistol cartridge such as a .357 Magnum encased in them can also be purchased for vessel defense. Other alternatives that might pass through foreign customs include spearguns for underwater fishing and powerheads or "bang-sticks" for divers' defense against sharks, which fire a rifle round or shotgun shell when jabbed into a target. Beyond these weapons, you can keep a machete or other large knife close at hand. For early warnings when you are asleep, you can rig an alarm on deck, keep a watchdog, or do as the first solo circumnavigator, Joshua Slocum, did when anchored off Tierra del Fuego in the days when it was still inhabited by wild Indians. Each night before going to bed, he would sprinkle large tacks all over the decks, and was once awakened by howls of pain followed by large splashes as barefoot intruders tried to board his boat in the darkness.

Deep-draft family cruising sailboat

Liveaboard Sailboats

Cruising-sized sailboats vary tremendously in design and in build quality. The most common production models range in length from about 25 to 50 feet. Generally, you can find a design within this range that will work for you whether you are single-handing or sailing as a couple or a family. There is little reason to buy new unless you just have plenty of money and want to spend it. When new, well-built boats from reputable manufacturers at the larger end of this size range can cost hundreds of thousands of dollars or more and rarely come from the builder outfitted with everything you will need to cruise or live aboard. Used models will sell for a fraction of the price and often come well equipped by the previous owners.

The most common sailboats you will find for sale new or used are monohull cruisers, both those of the traditional full-keel heavy-displacement design and those with fin keels and hulls derived from modern racing yachts. Monohulls are less expensive to build new than cruising-sized catamarans and trimarans, and since they have always been more mainstream, they far outnumber multihulls in the used boat market. In boats of this size range, each type has advantages and disadvantages. Small monohulls under 30 feet have much more interior living space than similarly sized multihulls, but the multihulls have a lot more deck space. Monohulls with a heavy external keel can survive being knocked down and rolled over by big waves, but can sink if water fills the cabin before the boat recovers. Big multihulls are almost impossible to turn upright if they capsize, but since they do not carry ballast, they rarely sink and can float upright or inverted indefinitely. Monohulls have a deeper draft unless they use a retractable keel or centerboard, while many multihulls, even in the larger sizes, can be sailed right up to the beach and easily pushed off if they run aground. Multihulls can attain much higher speeds under sail than ballasted monohulls. The choice between these different hull types will come down to which of these tradeoffs matters more to you, which will be largely determined by where you intend to take the boat and the size of your crew.

SOME SAILBOAT EXAMPLES

Grampian 26   I'm including the Grampian 26 as an example of a small, low-cost cruising sailboat because, as already mentioned, I owned and sailed one for six years in a variety of conditions and it never let me down. The Grampian 26 is one of many older fiberglass family weekenders or cruisers built in the 1960s and '70s but no longer in production today. With a beam of 8.5 feet and 6 feet of standing headroom in the cabin, it is a roomy boat for its 5,600 lb. displacement, and while not as heavily built as some boats of that era, it is sturdy enough that at least one has crossed the Atlantic Ocean. Some Grampian 26s came with inboard gas or diesel engines, but most have an outboard mounted on a cutout in the transom. Mine had a Honda 9.9 hp four-stroke that provided plenty of power when needed. I bought it in 1999 for $5,000 and sailed it home from Florida to Mississippi with little additional work or expenditure. You can find them in various states of repair from well under $5,000 to more than $12,000. The Grampian 26 is a bargain for a single person or a couple. You'll find lots of information on these boats as well as classified listings of Grampian boats for sale at the at grampianowners.com.

The author's Grampian 26 sailboat, owned from 1999 to 2005

Tayana 37 Cutter The Tayana 37 is a solidly built bluewater voy-aging boat suitable for a couple or small family intent on open-water voyaging in relative comfort and safety. Displacing 22,500 lb. with 7,340 lb. of ballast in a long, traditional keel, with a cutaway forefoot, the double-ended Tayana 37 is the kind of boat that can weather most any storm encountered offshore. But with a draft of 5' 8'', its ability to enter remote places near shore is somewhat limited. The Tayana 37 is fitted with an inboard diesel auxiliary with 90 gallons of fuel capacity in built-in tanks. Since its introduction in 1975, this bluewater sailing yacht has been immensely popular among adventurous sailors who embrace the voyaging lifestyle, and examples can be found in anchor-ages around the world. Prices on the used market range from $55,000 to $115,000, and the company website is www.tayanaworld.com.

Wharram Catamarans If you like multihulls and are handy enough to build your own, you can choose one of the excellent James Wharram–designed catamarans from 21 to over 60 feet in length to meet the needs of any reasonably sized crew. Wharram catamarans are renowned worldwide for their seaworthiness and ease of construc-tion. They are based on the design of the ancient Polynesian double canoes and incorporate conservative sail plans with proven canoe-

DIY Tiki 30 catamaran designed by James Wharram

The author's Wharram Tiki 26 catamaran under construction

form hulls that feature symmetrical ends and plenty of flare to provide lift in rough seas. A Wharram Tiki 21 catamaran still holds the record for the smallest catamaran to circumnavigate the globe. I am currently in the final stages of building my own Wharram Tiki 26, a catamaran big enough to cross oceans safely, yet small enough enter shallow rivers and to disassemble and trailer anywhere. This is my ultimate bug-out sailboat for one or two people, but if you have a family, one of the larger Wharram cats will be a better choice. You can build an ocean-going Wharram catamaran for anywhere between about $15,000 and $200,000, depending on the size you choose and the level of finish and outfitting you desire. You can also let Boatsmith, Inc., Wharram's authorized U.S. builder, do the work for you. Find out more at www.wharram .com or www.boatsmithfl.com.

Liveaboard Cruising Motor Yachts

As already mentioned in the comparison between power- and sail-boats, most long-distance motor yachts differ from small runabouts in that they have heavy displacement hulls and engines designed to run at low rpm, pushing the vessel along at hull speed hour after hour, day after day with a reasonable fuel consumption rate. Depending on the underbody shape of the hull, hull speed can be exceeded with more powerful engines, but for maximum fuel economy, the rule of thumb is that about 1.4 times the square root of waterline length equals optimum hull speed in knots. Therefore a 40-foot trawler type motor yacht with a 32-foot waterline would travel farthest on the available fuel in its tanks if it does not exceed about 9 knots.

Fuel conservation will be a primary concern if you use a motor yacht for any type of bug-out situation. While many big powerboats like sportfishing yachts that come with luxurious interior accommodations have the hull design and power to get up on a plane and run at high speed, the amount of fuel they burn is measured in gallons per hour rather than miles per gallon. This could be okay for a quick get-out-of-Dodge escape, but cruising at a more sedate pace will allow you more options over the long run if you're not able to obtain more fuel.

The best engine for this kind of service is the inboard diesel, which is designed for constant running and requires little maintenance. Diesel is safer to store on board than large quantities of gasoline and could possibly be supplemented with biodiesel in a long-term SHTF scenario. Some older motor yachts you find on the used market may have inboard gasoline engines. If you choose one of these, the safest route is to repower the vessel with diesel, but if you decide to run an inboard gas engine, it should be properly installed, well vented, and equipped with safety measures such as a bilge blower to remove gas fumes from down below before any electrical switches are turned on.

There are also small motorcruisers designed for outboard power, usually equipped with one or two four-stroke outboards of an appropriate size to propel the vessel at hull speed. The C-Dory discussed below is one such outboard-powered cruiser. If a smaller vessel meets your requirements, this type of boat has some advantages, as the entire engine can be easily removed for service and repairs do not require a skilled diesel mechanic.

SOME CRUISING MOTOR YACHT EXAMPLES

C-Dory   The C-Dory 25 is an example of small motorcruiser powered by outboard engines rather than an inboard diesel. At 25½ feet long with an 8½-foot beam, this compact cruiser features a large cockpit and full standing headroom in a hull that weighs under 4,000 lb. and can be trailered. With a hull draft of 12 inches, this could be a good brownwater bug-out vessel for traveling rivers and estuaries too shallow for larger yachts. Built-in fuel tanks carry 100 gallons and with the recommended twin 90 hp outboards, the C-Dory 25 can cruise at 10–12 mph while averaging 5 mpg. MSRP for a new C-Dory 25 is around $71,000, depending on engines and equipment. The C-Dory line can be found at www.c-dory.com.

Parker Marine Enterprises Commuter 36 If you prefer to build your own version of an efficient shallow-draft motor cruiser that can be outfitted with either a small inboard diesel or one or two four-stroke outboards in a well, Reuel Parker's Commuter 36, as well as his smaller and larger variations in the Commuter line, are well worth a look. This boat is built with the cold-molded plywood and epoxy technique and displaces 6,000 lb. with a hull draft of just 8½ inches. Like Parker's range of sailing sharpie designs, this motor yacht is designed specifically for the shallows and flats of south Florida and the Bahamas, with the ability to cross open water in good weather. The plans sell for $650.00 on Parker's website, www.parker-marine.com, where you can also buy several books he has written on the subject on the subject of boatbuilding and design.

Diesel Duck 38 Yacht designer George Buehler has done for the home motor yacht builder what James Wharram did for multihull

Commuter 36 shallow-draft motor cruiser designed by Reuel Parker

sailors: designed a range of rugged cruising powerboats for low-cost amateur construction that have traditional lines and inherent seaworthiness in their hull forms. He offers a range of sizes in his Diesel Duck series, with one of the most popular being the 38-footer, a cruiser capable of serving as a full-time liveaboard home for a couple or a family with small children. Plans are available for either steel or wood construction. The Diesel Duck 38 displaces 32,600 lb., with a draft of 4' 9'' and a beam of 12' 9''. An inboard diesel of 50 to 80 hp is enough to push this vessel at a reasonable cruising speed and 700 gallons of fuel carried in the tanks can give you a range of thousands of miles depending on your speed and whether you are bucking wind or current. Plans are available from the designer for $2,895, while the cost to build can vary greatly depending on materials, construction method, and outfitting. The designer's website is www.georgebuehler.com.

Liveaboard Houseboats and Shanty Boats

The final category of liveaboard boats includes both houseboats of the manufactured, recreational variety and an assortment of DIY floating retreats or camps, sometimes referred to as "shanty boats." This category can include virtually anything that floats and can be lived aboard. Some houseboats are designed and built to be used as actual boats and are capable of cruising from place to place under their own power, while others are mostly built to stay in one place, tied to a dock or moored to a riverbank, perhaps built offsite and then towed to the mooring location by another boat.

Nothing can beat a houseboat for sheer volume of interior accommodations relative to overall size. Because they are not designed with seaworthiness or efficiency of motion through the water in mind, houseboats resemble houses ashore more than they resemble true cruising boats. They are essentially built on a wide, flat deck that is supported by either a barge-like, flat-bottomed hull, or two or more pontoons connected together in a raft-like structure. Houseboats typically feature vertical cabin walls and square corners, unlike the more complex curved and rounded deckhouse structures of cruising boats.

Because of this simplicity of design, houseboats lend themselves to amateur construction better than any other type of liveaboard boat. Many are nailed together with ordinary lumberyard building materials and fitted with standard home windows, doors, and interior fixtures. True shanty boats can be an eclectic mix of funky materials and design, including combinations of floating platforms with old buses, camper trailers, or other types of vehicles fastened to the deck to provide accommodations.

Houseboats are popular on inland lakes, along rivers, and in swamp and marsh areas. If your bug-out plans do not require you to travel long distances on the water, a houseboat could be a viable option. A shanty boat or similar floating retreat can also serve as a fixed retreat that you can bug out to using a smaller boat such as those described in Chapter Three.

SOME HOUSEBOAT EXAMPLES

Myacht 3510   The Myacht 3510 is a typical production houseboat that, although no longer being manufactured, is widely available on the used market. Built on aluminum pontoons, this 35-footer has a 10-foot beam and a roomy cabin with six berths and an enclosed head and shower. A typical used example with a 90 hp outboard and auxiliary generator goes for about $45,000.

Glen-L Marine Mark Twain Series DIY Houseboat Plans   Many people build their own shanty boats or rustic houseboats without any sort of plans. If you want something more refined, however, there are a number of real boat designers who offer houseboat plans that allow you to build a floating mobile retreat to rival anything you can buy. Glen-L Marine offers a number of houseboat designs, including the Mark Twain series, that are built on easily constructed pontoons for catamaran-like stability and low resistance moving through the water. This series is available in lengths from 28 to 40 feet, depending on the number of people you need to accommodate. The above-deck structures can be built with ordinary house-building materials and customized to your tastes and needs. Plans are available at www.glen-l.com, with prices ranging from $152 to $182.

LIVEABOARD CRUISING BOAT CHECKLIST

The items included in the Boating Safety and Boat-Specific Gear Checklist should be taken aboard any vessel, large or small. The additional items listed here address the added requirements of cruising and living aboard a larger boat, as well as the extra gear and supplies to you'll need if you are venturing far offshore.

ADDITIONAL SAFETY
GEAR FOR LARGER BOATS
VENTURING OFFSHORE:
- ❏ Certified life raft of adequate size for each crew member
- ❏ Safety harnesses and tethers for each crew member
- ❏ Man overboard pole and horseshoe buoy with tether
- ❏ Personal battery-powered strobe lights for man-overboard location
- ❏ Abandon-ship grab bag with life raft survival essentials
- ❏ 406 MHz satellite EPIRB (emergency position indicating radio beacon)
- ❏ Fixed-mount VHF radio with external antennae for extended range
- ❏ SSB radio receiver or transceiver for weather reports
- ❏ Barometer
- ❏ Hand bearing compass and backup handheld GPS
- ❏ Radar reflector
- ❏ Emergency water desalinator and freshwater still
- ❏ Sea anchor and/or drogue for slowing boat speed in storms

- ❏ Oversized main anchor and rode, plus at least two additional anchors and rodes
- ❏ Manual and electric bilge pumps
- ❏ Emergency plugs for all through-hull fittings
- ❏ Fire extinguishers in all enclosed compartments
- ❏ Smoke detectors in cabin areas
- ❏ Carbon monoxide detector

TOOLS AND SPARE PARTS
FOR LARGER BOATS:
- ❏ Fuel filters
- ❏ Diesel fuel biocide
- ❏ Spare prop and shaft packing material
- ❏ Spare water impeller
- ❏ Emergency steering tiller
- ❏ Spare stove components
- ❏ Electrical wiring, connectors, fuses, etc.
- ❏ Soldering iron and solder
- ❏ Electrical tape
- ❏ Spare alternator and spare belts
- ❏ Rigging wire and terminals
- ❏ Shackles, pins, turnbuckles, and other sailing hardware
- ❏ Suitable patch materials to repair hull damage

Part III

Alternative & Backup Vehicles

7

OFF-ROAD MOTORCYCLES, ATVS, & SNOWMOBILES

The motorized vehicles discussed in this chapter fall into the backup or alternative vehicle category; they are not commonly used as everyday conveyances but instead are mostly intended for recreational or sporting activities rather than serious transportation. But these are machines powered by internal combustion engines that could be viable alternatives for overland travel in a SHTF situation, including everything from small off-road motorcycles and ATVs to snowmobiles. In this chapter I'll present the pros and cons of each category just as I did with the larger vehicles in the preceding chapters, as well as outline the key things you need to take into consideration when choosing and outfitting this type of vehicle.

Backup Transportation or Alternative Vehicle?

Alternative vehicles offer something different from the usual choices. They are generally lighter, more versatile in many cases, and usually better suited for rough roads, cross-country or all-terrain travel, or, in the case of snowmobiles, winter travel. But even if you are not interested in this type of machine as an alternative means of transportation, you may want to think about considering one of them as a backup vehicle. The concept of the backup vehicle is all about redundancy of equipment, which is a good idea in any aspect of survival preparation, as you can't count on all your gear to work as it should at all times. Carrying or towing a backup vehicle is a form of insurance in the event the main vehicle breaks down, gets stuck, or comes to an impassable obstacle. Backup and alternative vehicles can also be a vital part of your plan to proceed into more remote country after you reach the limits of travel in a larger vehicle. Likewise, they can be excellent in the role of runabout vehicles for personal transportation if you are bugging out in a larger, land-based mobile retreat such as a prefab RV or DIY retreat and want to keep it set up in place once you reach your bug-out location.

If this type of vehicle appeals to you as either an alternative or a backup, there has never been a better time to shop for one. The recreational and utility market for such machines has led to the development of many new and exciting choices in any category you may find of interest.

Disadvantages of Specialized Machines as Bug-Out Vehicles

Obviously, one of the main disadvantages of using any of the machines described in this chapter as bug-out vehicles is that most are designed for specialized purposes and therefore lack versatility if you are thinking of them as alternative rather than backup vehicles. For example, while some of the largest ATVs can perform many of the tasks that small pickup trucks are normally used for, the small pickup truck is usually a better all-around choice because it can also operate at highway speeds on any type of road while the ATV cannot. The big, soft tires that make ATVs so capable off-road, especially in mud and deep sand, are a liability on hard pavement where they can make the machine dangerously unstable in hard turns and sudden stops. Considering that the price of many of these ATVs is well over $10,000, it may be wiser financially to purchase a nice used example of almost any type of pickup or SUV for less money.

Other machines in this class have the same disadvantages when it comes to versatility. While a small and lightweight but powerful two-stroke dirt bike can go many places off-road that would be too challenging for a big dual-sport motorcycle, the dual-sport bike is able to easily travel roadways at sustained highway speeds that would be hard on the dirt bike with its smaller-displacement engine. Other obvious examples include the fact that while snowmobiles may be the only motor vehicle that can get you deep into the backcountry in winter, when the snow melts they will be useless.

As backup rather than alternative vehicles, all of the internal-combustion machines in this chapter have the disadvantage of also requiring their own supply of fuel, engine oil, and spare parts, and will need regular maintenance to ensure they are reliable. Even with this maintenance, like any vehicle with an engine, they are subject to mechanical problems and breakdowns. Engine-powered alternative vehicles will also be heavier and bulkier than bicycles, for instance, and may require a trailer to carry them depending on what you are using for your primary vehicle. In light of these disadvantages, it is wise to weigh your particular situation and see if it would not be better to use some other backup transportation that does not require an engine, possibly a bicycle or human-powered boat, which will be discussed in the next two chapters.

Key Considerations Regarding Off-Road Motorcycles, ATVs, and Snowmobiles

Two-Stroke vs. Four-Stroke Engines When looking at different types of small off-road vehicles, you may be confused by some of the terminology, such as the different engine types. When it comes to engines, one difference you will see is that some of these machines use two-stroke engines and others use four-strokes. The bigger the engine and the newer the model, the more likely it will be a four-stroke. But many small dirt bikes and ATVs still use two-stroke engines, which require more maintenance than four-strokes but also produce more power in a lighter-weight package. The difference is that in a two-stroke engine the cylinder fires every time the piston moves up and down once, while in a four-stroke the piston has to move up and down twice to make power. This means that the two-stroke can deliver more power with the same-sized cylinder, which translates in the real world to more power per pound. The main reason two stroke engines require more maintenance is that they run hotter since they fire so much more frequently, meaning that if they are run hard, you will have to do a top-end rebuild much sooner than you would on a comparable four-stroke. But the upside of this more frequent rebuild interval is that these engines are super simple to work on.

Unlike a four-stroke engine, where the oil is poured directly into the crankcase through an oil fill opening, most two-stroke engines require you to manually pre-mix the gasoline with two-stroke engine oil that lubricates the engine when it is running. This can be a minor hassle, as the mixing ratios must be measured exactly according to the owner's manual of your machine. If you don't get this right, performance can suffer, but if you use the small pre-measured containers of two-stroke oil that are available most anywhere engine oil is sold, it is not much more complicated than pumping gasoline directly into a fuel tank.

Four-stroke engines have cleaner emissions and better fuel economy than two-strokes, which often put out a lot of smoky exhaust, especially if the pre-mixed oil and gas ratio is not just right. Many types of two-stroke engines have been banned from certain national parks because of this, and new government regulations are leaning heavily on the manufacturers of these kinds of machines to abandon the two-stroke engine in favor of the cleaner-burning four-stroke design. One example of this is in the outboard boat motor industry, which has now switched almost completely to four-stroke technology, producing engines that get almost double the fuel economy of older two-strokes of the same horsepower.

Water Crossings on ATVs and Off-Road Motorcycles   Most ATVs and dirt bikes are quite capable of crossing mud holes and puddles, small streams, and even big, shallow rivers. Recreational riders of these machines enjoy the challenge of water crossings and like to test the limits of their vehicles deliberately. But in a bug-out situation where you are depending on your ride to get you where you're going, you'll want to be more careful with it and make sure you don't get water in the engine, or that if you do, you know how to get it out before attempting to restart it. The exhaust pipes, carburetors, and air boxes of these machines are located as high as possible so that they can be taken across water within reason, but you must know where the air intake waterline is and be sure you don't get into a situation where it becomes submerged. Water cannot be compressed by the piston of an engine and the pressure will build up until it finds somewhere to go, destroying the engine. It's well worth taking the time to wade across any water obstacle first before attempting to ride through it if you are unsure of the depth or bottom composition.

Water can get in not only if you misjudge the depth of a crossing or fall through thin ice in the winter, but also if you go too fast and splash it into the air box. It only takes a little to do the damage, so you must know how to get it out. Follow these steps to make sure you get all the water out:

1. Drain the fuel tank, fuel lines, and oil.
2. Remove and clean the carburetor, take the spark plug(s) out of the cylinders, and turn the motor over to force the water inside to come out.
3. Add some oil and turn it over again with the plug(s) still out if water can still be seen in it, drain the oil. Repeat until no water is visible in the oil.
4. Refill the oil, reinstall the plug(s), add fuel, and start it if you can. If it does start, run it a few minutes, then shut it off and drain the oil and change the filter one more time. Run it again and if no milky color shows in the oil to indicate water, it's good to go.

ATV Accessories: Racks, Winches, and Trailers   Most types of ATVs, whether they are open four-wheeler quads or side-by-side UTVs, can be made more useful with factory-installed or owner-added accessories. Cargo racks are practically essential and can be fitted front and rear on most quads and on the roof of large, partially enclosed UTVs. These racks give you a large platform to lash on backpacks and other gear when you are bugging out, and later after you reach your destination, can be used to haul firewood, water containers, large animals such as deer after a hunt, or anything else you need to move. If this rack space is not enough, you can greatly increase an ATV's load-carrying ability by towing a trailer behind it. Rugged off-road cargo trailers are available in many sizes and in single or tandem axle configurations to work with just about any ATV you may have. Some of these have huge cargo capacities and even feature dump bodies to make unloading easy. Depending on the towing capacity of the ATV or UTV, you can move a lot of stuff at one time with this type of trailer, doing practically the work of a pickup truck, as some of these trailers have a load rating of several thousand pounds.

Another essential accessory you should consider installing if your ATV doesn't already have one is an electric winch. A winch can make all the difference in getting out of difficult situations, such as being stuck in deep mud. ATV and UTV 12-volt DC winches are available in a range of capacities, from around 1,500 lb. to 4,500 lb. or more. In addition to an electric winch, you should also carry a manual come-along as a back-up, and, if traveling with more than one ATV, a towing strap.

Safe Riding Techniques and Safety Gear for ATVs and Dirt Bikes Recreational and competition dirt bike riders know that spills are much more likely in the kind of riding they do—including wheelies, jumps, fast slides, and other maneuvers—than on street bikes, so they dress accordingly in protective gear such as heavy boots, shin and knee guards, chest protectors, and so on. That kind of gear won't

be practical in a bug-out situation, though, and if you are using a dirt bike for this purpose, you must ride much more conservatively and try to avoid crashing at all cost. There is simply too much potential for serious bodily injury, which could be disastrous in a SHTF scenario where medical attention may not be avail-

A quad ATV with front and rear luggage racks

able. There is also too much risk of disabling damage to your bike or the gear you have strapped to it to attempt unnecessary stunts. Instead, think of your dirt bike as a means of transportation rather than a fun toy and ride it accordingly.

Riding an ATV, especially the open quad type, can be as dangerous as riding a motorcycle. Because it is much larger and heavier, there is also the potential for it to flip over on you on steep climbs or descents or in high-speed cornering. Many people are seriously injured or killed this way while riding ATVs. Whether you are bugging out off-road on two wheels or four or more, you should wear a helmet, eye protection, gloves, boots, and long sleeves and pants, not only in case of a spill, but to protect your body when bashing along through overgrown brush and briars and under overhanging limbs.

Essential Equipment, Tools, and Spare Parts for ATVs and Dirt Bikes

As with any other type of motor vehicle used for bugging out, you will have to carry what you need to be self-sufficient when it comes to maintenance and common repairs. Most motorcycles and ATVs come with a manufacturer's toolkit that will get you through many jobs, but you should supplement this with a few quality wrenches, a ratchet and sockets to fit the hardware on your machine, and any other tools that may be lacking in the supplied kit. A tire repair kit (for tubeless tires) or spare tubes and a patch kit (for tube tires) are essential, as is a 12-volt mini-compressor and pressure gauge. It's also a good idea to carry a can or two of Slime or Fix-A-Flat for a quick fix to get you going when there isn't time to do a proper repair. As mentioned above in relation to water crossings, you will have to drain your oil and change the filter if you inadvertently flood your engine, so if there is a chance of this happening, carry spare filters and enough oil to refill it after draining. Other essentials include duct tape and electrical tape, zip ties, and extra fuel strapped to the racks in jerry cans if you need a longer range.

Snowmobile Equipment and Survival Gear Even more than ATVs or dirt bikes, snowmobiles are a lot like small, open powerboats, in that they can quickly whisk you many miles from safety deep into a hostile environment and then fail, leaving you stranded with no easy means of getting out or getting help. Recreational users of these machines frequently find themselves in life-or-death survival scenarios because they ride off deep into a winter wilderness without adequate gear, supplies, or knowledge and get stuck in ice or snow or stranded by mechanical failure. Obviously, if it's cold enough for there to be adequate snow cover to operate such a machine, nighttime temperatures are going to plummet to hypothermia-inducing levels and finding food or walking far will be difficult, if not impossible.

Of course, it goes without saying that if your survival plan includes bugging out on a snowmobile, you will be better prepared than the average weekend rider, and your bug-out gear will already include everything you would need in a winter survival situation or for an extended wilderness stay in the environment you are traveling through. But in your planning you should allow for all contingencies, including what you will do if you have to abandon the machine completely. This means having a backup means of travel, which in this case will be either snowshoes or cross-country skis and a backpack to carry your essential gear.

Carry what you need for basic repairs, including the toolkit that comes with the machine and any extra tools to make common repairs. Spares should include a belt, spark plugs, and an ignition key, along with duct tape, wire, and extra nuts, bolts, and other fasteners. You should also carry a manual come-along and tow rope and a folding shovel to aid in freeing a stuck machine. Keep a close watch on your fuel supply, of course, and carry as much extra fuel as you will need to get to your destination with plenty of reserve.

Safe Snowmobile Travel Aside from the possibility of getting stranded along the way far from your starting point or bug-out retreat, travel by snowmobile has other inherent dangers that you should be aware of and take precautions to avoid. These dangers include obstacles hidden in the snow, thin ice over water, and the possibility of getting caught in an avalanche. Most of these hazards can be avoided by simply slowing down and increasing your awareness, which is a good idea with any mode of bug-out transportation. High speed will reduce your ability to recognize threats and the amount of time you have to react to them. Slow down and stop to scout if in doubt about a frozen water crossing or other obstacle. Avoid avalanches by staying off long, open, and steep slopes; try to travel in timbered areas and along ridges where the snow tends to be anchored. Above all, dress properly for the cold, taking into consideration the extra wind-chill factor you'll be subjected to at speed. A snowmobile suit or other outer shell that is wind- and waterproof over heat-retentive and moisture-wicking layers will help prevent hypothermia.

Dirt Bikes and Small Dual Sport Motorcycles

Most of the motorcycles in this category have a single-cylinder two- or four-stroke engine of under 500cc and in some cases under 250cc. One of the main advantages that small dirt bikes and small dual-sports have compared to larger, more highway-capable motorcycles is their light weight and high power-to-weight ratio. Most weigh less than 300 lb., which makes them much lighter than full-sized dual-sport bikes. This is what makes this kind of bike fun to ride and has led to the popularity of sports such as motocross racing, and it is also the key reason such bikes can ride far off the pavement into terrain no other motorcycle can handle. Dirt bikes can climb up seemingly impossible slopes and power up to a wheelie to clear obstacles such as fallen logs if the rider is skilled. If the bike is dropped, as will frequently happen in this kind of riding, it will be easy to pick up. It will also be easier to pull out of deep mud or sand or otherwise manhandle around impassable obstacles.

If you want light weight but not a pure dirt bike, small dual-sport motorcycles with 125 to 250cc engines are widely available as beginner bikes or for riders who are not tall enough for full-sized 650cc or larger bikes in this class. Despite the fact that few people do extensive highway riding on small dual-sport motorcycles in the U.S.—mainly because of the high-speed traffic and long distances between cities typical here—in other countries motorcycles under 250cc are commonly used for everyday transportation and work. Most of these bikes have plenty of power for city and back road riding; it is only in high top-end speed and the ability to cruise at 70 mph for hours on end that they are lacking. In a bug-out situation, that may not be important at all, and the small bike's ability to jump curbs, cross ditches and sidewalks, and go cross-country may be more important, as the freeways leading out of your city may be gridlocked in an evacuation.

You can certainly rig up a system of racks and panniers for practically any motorcycle with some ingenuity, and many people have done long-distance adventure touring on small dual-sports like the Kawasaki KLR 250 and the Suzuki DR 200. If you can travel long-distance on a bicycle, as will be discussed in the next chapter, then it stands to reason that you can do so on any size motorcycle, moped, or scooter; it's all just a matter of adjusting your expectations of speed and distance traveled per day. If you are looking at dirt bikes rather than dual-sport models in this size range, keep in mind that even though they are not technically street-legal motorcycles, "Enduro" dirt bikes come with headlights, brake and tail lights, and street-legal mufflers, while "MX" bikes do not. Most Enduros have four-stroke engines while many MX bikes still use lighter, more powerful two-strokes.

ENDURO DIRT BIKE EXAMPLE

KTM 450 EXC Six Days Edition   This powerful KTM Enduro is designed for cross-country racing in the grueling International Six Days Enduro competition, but could serve well as an off-road bug-out bike that could get you into rougher country than most motorcycles. It features a 449.3cc, four-stroke, liquid-cooled engine and six-speed transmission, and both an electric starter and a kick-starter. At a dry weight of just 251 lb., it has an incredible power-to-weight ratio and, like most KTM models, is designed for performance. The fuel tank, at just 2.5l gallons, will limit your range; but if you're using it as a backup vehicle once you get to the end of the pavement, the places it could take you might be so remote you wouldn't need to travel farther than this limited range. MSRP is around $7,800, and more information is available from KTM at www.ktm.com.

SMALL DUAL-SPORT EXAMPLE

Kawasaki KLR 250/KLX 250   The Kawasaki KLR 250 is a lighter-weight, smaller version of the venerable KLR 650 dual-sport motor-cycle described in Chapter Three. Like the bigger 650cc version, the KLR 250 is street-legal, but with a fully fueled weight of just 314 lb., it is more agile off-road and easier to load and unload from a truck if used as a backup vehicle. It also has a kick-starter instead of the electric starter of the 650. The fuel economy, at about 65 mpg, is better than the larger 650, but the tank is smaller at 2.9 gallons. It cruises the highway just fine at 55 mph or perhaps a bit faster. The KLR 250 was in production from 1984 to 2005, then was replaced by the KLX 250S, which is still in production. The KLX features better suspension and ground clearance than the older KLR, but has a smaller fuel tank, mak-ing it more dirt-oriented than dual-purpose. MSRP for a new KLX 250S is approximately $5,000. Used examples of either model can be found for well under $3,000 and you might find a good-running KLR 250 for $1,500 or even less.

ATVs and Side-by-Side UTVs

The ATV industry has exploded in the last two decades or so and new models and new types of these vehicles are being introduced so fast and with so much new terminology that the uninitiated buyer will likely be totally baffled by all the available offerings. The ear-liest examples of these machines were three-wheeler models with balloon tires that were marketed mainly as fun alternatives to small motorcycles but proved to be quite dangerous to ride because they tend to roll over easily, particularly in high-speed turning maneuvers. Open four-wheeler models soon replaced these three-wheelers, with the earliest versions still having quite small engines until users started figuring out that they had the potential to do a lot besides just recreational mud riding. As hunters started using four-wheelers (or "quads") to ride to their deer stands and to carry out their game af-ter successful hunts, the industry began offering larger versions with add-ons like racks to tie down a deer carcass and mounts to carry a rifle or shotgun in a scabbard or hard case. Quad ATVs began to be offered with 4WD and powerful electric winches, allowing them to go practically anywhere off-road.

As these vehicles got bigger and people figured out still more ways to use them, another class of even larger ATVs called "side-by-sides" was developed, allowing comfortable bench seating or side-by-side bucket seats instead of a motorcycle-like seat that has to be straddled by the driver and passenger. Unlike open quads, these machines are built on a golf cart–like chassis complete with a roof and integrated roll cage. Some of these side-by-sides are almost as big as small pickup trucks and come in four- and six-wheel configurations. Some manufacturers simply call their products "side-by-sides" and some use the term "UTV" (Utility Terrain Vehicle, or just Utility Vehicle), but confusingly, UTV is also used to describe some of the more utilitarian heavy-duty open quad four-wheelers. Other terms used for some of these vehicles are RUV (Recreational Utility Vehicle) and MUV (Multi-Use Vehicle).

UTVs are quite capable of serious work and for many tasks can take the place of a pickup, a tractor, or even a horse or mule. They are becoming increasingly common on farms and ranches everywhere, as well as in certain types of fieldwork such as construction, land surveying, law enforcement, and emergency services. These side-by-side UTVs are much bigger and heavier than quad ATVs and are typically fitted with engines up to about 800cc in displacement. A UTV is usually equipped to pull trailers and is outfitted with a large cargo bed in the rear; some can even function as mini-dump trucks. With their semi-enclosed driver and passenger compartments, and even amenities such as heaters in some models, UTVs ride much more like a real vehicle than a four-wheeled version of a motorcycle, especially in inclement weather.

One of the drawbacks of these larger side-by-side UTVs is that many of them lack the performance of the smaller open quads because of a poorer power-to-weight ratio. Often using the same engines and drive trains as the smaller ATVs, they lack the get-up-and-go of the lighter machines, and the taller and wider chassis limits their ability to go into really rugged terrain or cross obstacles and makes getting one unstuck a bigger deal than it would be with a small quad. Transporting a large UTV as a backup vehicle will also be more difficult than most small four-wheelers, which can easily fit in even a small pickup bed. Large UTVs and the bigger quads are also surprisingly expensive when purchased new, as seen in the examples below. You can, however, find great deals in the used market, especially each year at the end of hunting season when many owners are starting to think about fishing boats for the coming spring.

FOUR-WHEELER OR QUAD EXAMPLE

Suzuki KingQuad 750AXi This is a big quad ATV with a fuel-injected, liquid-cooled 722cc engine that is bigger than those of most larger side-by-sides and strong enough to power over obstacles and reach top speeds of up to 70 mph. It features a differential lock system for 4WD traction and handlebar-mounted push-button controls for switching between 2WD and 4WD modes. Front and rear cargo racks are standard and fuel capacity is 4.6 gallons. This machine has a 12-volt electrical system powered by an 18-amp generator to run the powerful halogen headlights, plus tail and brake lights and a handlebar-mounted auxiliary light. Weighing in at 655

A helmet and protective clothing are a good idea on any ATV.

lb. and right at 4 feet wide by 7 feet long, the KingQuad 750AXi is big for this type of ATV, but still much more compact than most side-by-sides and for a machine this powerful and capable. It's also quite a bit less expensive, with a 2011 model carrying an MSRP of $8,199 for the base model or $9,049 with added power steering. The website for all Suzuki motorcycles and ATVs is www.suzukicycles.com.

SIDE-BY-SIDE UTV EXAMPLE

Arctic Cat Prowler HDX 700 This powerful side-by-side UTV is designed to be able to carry three passengers plus a 1,000 lb. payload in the rear cargo bed. This huge rear dump bed can be transformed to a flatbed for even more versatility by taking off the removable side panels. If that's not enough, there is storage for another 25 lb. under the hood and a trailer-towing capacity of 1,500 lb. The "700" in its name comes from the 695cc four-stroke, liquid-cooled, fuel-injected engine. The HDX 700 drive train offers 2WD, 4WD, and electric differential locking. Like most UTVs in this class that are popular with hunters, it is available in an optional camouflage color scheme that will aid you in keeping it hidden in a bug-out scenario. Still, it's a big machine to hide or transport as a backup vehicle, at almost 11 feet long and 5 feet wide and weighing in at 1,336 lb., not counting the gasoline needed to fill its large (8.2 gallon) tank. Suggested MSRP in Advantage Timber Camouflage is $13,799. More information from the manufacturer is available at www.arcticcat.com.

Snowmobiles

Snowmobiles are among the most specialized types of bug-out vehicles because they are useful only in certain regions and even there only in the colder seasons. Bugging out into a winter wilderness in deep snow cover is a serious undertaking that should only be considered by those with experience in such an environment. Most likely, if you are traveling in such conditions, it will be to reach a bug-out retreat shelter such as a remote cabin that you have prepared in advance with stocked supplies and additional equipment. A snowmobile can be an excellent choice of vehicle in such a scenario, getting you there much faster than hiking in with snowshoes or skiing cross-country with a backpack. Snowmobiles are also easier for most people to keep and maintain than other means of snow travel, such using as a team of dogs to pull a sled.

Like ATVs and UTVs, there are many different types of snowmobiles designed for specific purposes from work and utility to touring, sport

and racing, and mountain riding. In looking at snowmobiles for bug-out transportation, you'll probably find a touring or utility model to be best suited for serious travel where load-carrying capability is a concern. Touring snowmobiles come in one-person and two-up seating configurations just like motorcycles, and usually have larger windshields, as well as side mirrors. They are designed to cover long distances in comfort, with a longer track length to cushion the ride and add stability. Electric start and a reverse gear are standard, which is not the case with some entry-level snowmobiles.

Snowmobiles designed for work are longer, heavier, and wider than recreational models. These are serious vehicles that can carry a lot of equipment and also tow sleds in the same way ATVs can tow trailers if more capacity is needed.

UTILITY SNOWMOBILE EXAMPLE

Polaris Widetrak LX   In production since 1999, this classic Polaris utility snowmobile is a solid example of a basic work sled that has a large rear cargo area along with seating for one or two persons, depending on how the adjustable backrest on the long seat is set. It utilizes a 488cc, liquid-cooled, two-stroke engine, which is less common today when most of these machines are four-strokes. This particular engine has proven extremely reliable over the years and produces ample power for the machine's intended purpose. The large-capacity fuel tank holds 11 gallons. The Polaris Widetrak LX is 43½ inches wide by 10½ feet long, weighs 613 lb., and runs on a 20-inch wide, high-flotation track. In addition to the rear cargo rack, there is a wide storage area under the seat, and it can pull a sled if more space is needed. MSRP for this model starts at $8,799. You can find out more at www .polarisindustries.com.

DIRT BIKE, ATV, AND SNOWMOBILE CHECKLIST

SAFETY GEAR FOR RIDING:
- ❏ Helmet
- ❏ Gloves
- ❏ Eye protection
- ❏ Long pants
- ❏ Long sleeves or jacket
- ❏ Boots
- ❏ Rain/wind-protective outer shell
- ❏ Inner layers for warmth in cold weather

DIRT BIKE AND ATV TOOLS AND SPARE PARTS:
- ❏ Manufacturer-supplied toolkit
- ❏ Additional wrenches, sockets, ratchet drive, etc., for your machine
- ❏ Air pressure gauge
- ❏ 12-volt inflator and/or hand pump
- ❏ Tire and tube repair kit
- ❏ Spare tubes if using tube-type tires
- ❏ Slime or Fix-A-Flat tire repair
- ❏ Change of oil and spare filter (in case of submersion)

- ❏ Spare spark plug(s)
- ❏ Spare fuel filter
- ❏ Spare belt (if machine has one)
- ❏ Chain lube (dirt bikes)
- ❏ Multitool
- ❏ Tow strap, come-along, and/or 12-volt winch
- ❏ Duct tape
- ❏ Electrical tape
- ❏ Cable ties
- ❏ Wire

SNOWMOBILE-SPECIFIC TOOLS AND SPARES:
- ❏ Folding saw or axe
- ❏ Folding shovel
- ❏ Tow strap or rope
- ❏ Come-along
- ❏ Pry bar
- ❏ Spare belt
- ❏ Spare spark plugs
- ❏ Manufacturer' toolkit
- ❏ Spare nuts and bolts specific to machine
- ❏ Duct tape
- ❏ Baling wire

8

BICYCLES AS
BUG-OUT VEHICLES

Bicycles could be the ultimate land-based vehicles in the event of a long-term grid-down scenario where fuel for motorized machines would be difficult or impossible to obtain. Bicycles are the most efficient means of land transportation ever devised in terms of the energy input required to make them go. Modern light-weight bicycles with multiple gears allow long-distance human-powered travel at a pace that can cover a lot of miles over the course of a few hours or days. Those who enjoy riding bicycles for recreation, fitness, or competition are well familiar with the appeal of riding and the many benefits it offers. If you choose a good-quality bicycle and do enough riding in advance to get yourself in shape, the distance you can travel given enough time is unlimited. With no fuel tanks to fill other than the rider's stomach, which will have to be filled whether they're riding or not, bicycles offer a type of flexibility that no other vehicle can match. Those who don't ride or haven't been on a bicycle since childhood may tend to dismiss them as serious bug-out trans-portation and in doing so overlook what could be the best option in some situations.

Because there is no internal combustion engine involved, bicycles are simple, dependable machines that require little maintenance or ongoing expense to keep them in working order. The lack of an en-gine means that they are quiet in operation, which could be a survival advantage in a bug-out situation, especially if you travel past danger zones at night, when you can pass by camps and occupied residences unheard and unseen. As long as the bike is in good repair with no bearing noises, squeaks, or rattles, it will be virtually silent from even a short distance away. Riding on smooth trails or paths in the back-country, you won't spook nearby game or alert other people in the area to your presence.

Low initial and ongoing cost is another advantage to using bicy-cles as bug-out transportation. Although high-end models of certain types of bicycles can be shockingly expensive, compared to any other kind of vehicle, the average bicycle is about the cheapest transporta-tion available other than walking. Since quality bicycles will stand a lot more use than most owners ever put them to, it is often possible to obtain a top-of-the-line machine with plenty of useful life left in it on the used market.

Bicycles are also great secondary or auxiliary bug-out vehicles because they are so lightweight, relatively compact, and can easily be disassembled to even smaller packages if necessary. A bicycle can be stored just about anywhere and, unlike even small ATVs and small motorcycles, can be carried inside or on the roof racks of the smallest cars or aboard many types of boats. For liveaboard boaters in par-ticular, they are a great addition to have on board, as they can provide land transportation that you would not otherwise have when you reach distant shores.

Disadvantages of Bicycles as Bug-Out Vehicles

One of the disadvantages of a bicycle, of course, is that you have to pedal it to make it go. If you are in poor physical condition or have an injury that makes this difficult, then covering long distances by bicycle may not be feasible, and even the most athletic person is subject to fatigue and the effects of exposure to heat, humidity, or extreme cold. Building endurance for riding so that you can make the most of a bi-cycle as a bug-out vehicle is discussed in the "key considerations" section of this chapter.

Another disadvantage of the bicycle is that while it is incredibly efficient and fast compared to walking, it is slow compared to any type of motor vehicle, and people accustomed to high-speed travel will have to adjust to a traveling pace that may average somewhere around 10 to 18 mph, again depending on rider conditioning, weight of the load carried, and the terrain. If you have to travel a few hundred miles to get to your bug-out location, your trip will be measured in days instead of hours. This pace means that you will have to be able to carry adequate food and water for your journey and be prepared to camp along the way when you need rest.

Another disadvantage of bicycles is the variety of dangers involved in riding, which include everything from the risk of being hit by larger motor vehicles to vulnerability to an attack because of your limited top speed. These dangers, of course, vary by the particular situation. Riding on the edge of roads used by high-speed motor vehicles is dangerous at any time, but in the kind of bug-out scenario where bicycles would likely be needed, motor vehicles might be inoperable because of a shortage of fuel or damage to electrical components after an EMP-type event. In other situations, such as mass evacuations after a disaster, there may be so much vehicle traffic that it is gridlocked or moving at a crawl, allowing a bicyclist to move faster.

The kind of situation where a bicyclist might be in the most danger is on the open road, where it will be impossible to outrun aggressors in motor vehicles bent on attack. In such a situation, those in vehicles could take out a cyclist with thrown objects or even the vehicle itself. Even in normal times cyclists are sometimes the victims of road rage, and the everyday commuting cyclist who rides in city traffic knows that the key to survival on a bike is constant vigilance and the ability to react quickly and take evasive action. In the heavier traffic of a mass evacuation, drivers may not be as much of a threat as gangs of attackers on foot who could cut off a bicyclist trying to slip between all the cars. The best defense is to stay aware and look ahead for potential escape routes. This risk of this kind of attack can be reduced somewhat by traveling in groups if possible or avoiding well-used roads.

Key Considerations for Bicycles as Bug-Out Vehicles

Bicycles Can Operate On Roads or Off-Road Any bicycle can be ridden both on roads and off-road, with the more rugged mountain bikes able to go places practically no other wheeled vehicle can go if pedaled by a strong rider. In the city, they offer many advantages over cars in their ability to weave through traffic, splitting lanes and squeezing through gridlocked traffic because of their narrow width. Like dual-purpose motorcycles, many bicycles can easily negotiate road shoulders and sidewalks, jump curbs, cross medians, and thread their way through alleys and other places four-wheeled vehicles cannot go. Off the pavement, bicycles with suitable tires can handle gravel roads, dirt or rocky trails, and some sand and mud. In some places, such as deserts, they can be ridden cross-country where there is no trail.

Bicycles Can Be Carried over Obstacles In discussing the kind of terrain that off-road bicycles like mountain bikes can negotiate, it should be remembered that there really are no limitations to where a lightweight bicycle can go, because the rider can simply pick it up and carry it over or around impassable obstacles. These can include fallen logs; steep bluffs, ditches or ravines; creeks, swamps, deep mud or sand; or man-made obstacles like fences, barricades, or rubble. Many such obstacles will require only a short carry of the bicycle before it can be ridden again. While a bike with loaded panniers and other gear strapped on may be a burden to carry for any distance, it will still be much easier to carry than any type of motorized vehicle, even the smallest dirt bikes. The gear can always be removed and carried in a

separate trip if necessary, just as you would portage a loaded canoe between lakes. You can also walk beside the loaded bicycle and push it through deep sand or mud, or up hills too steep to ride.

Training, Fitness, and Technique for Long-Distance Bicycling   The importance of fitness cannot be overestimated if you intend to cover any distance on a bicycle at a reasonable pace, particularly if you will be carrying a full complement of bug-out gear and supplies. Even those who are in great shape from running or other workout routines will find it necessary to spend some training time on a bike if they are not accustomed to the strains it puts on specific muscles, as well as the pain it can cause to contact points where the body meets the machine, specifically the hands, feet, and rear end.

I've enjoyed taking long rides since well before I started driving, and because I've been riding on and off most of my life, it doesn't take too long for me to get back in shape for it after periods of not riding. Even so, the first two or three rides after a long break in training can be painful and hard to complete. Everyone is different in regards to their fitness level, but I find that if I do two or three rides a week of 20 to 30 miles, after about a month's time I'm comfortably back to where I can average 50- to 80-mile days on a touring bike. Serious bike tourists and competitive cyclists can easily do 100 miles per day or more, even in hills or mountains. It all depends on your level of commitment and how much time you have to train. You don't have to ride every day to maintain a base level of riding fitness, but the more miles you put in per week, the better. If you've spent all your spare time on the couch and expect to bug out on a bike loaded with 40 to 60 lb. of gear, you will certainly find it to be an unpleasant experience, to say the least.

Wind and hills are a bicycle rider's two worst enemies when it comes to making progress. Even if you haven't ridden since childhood, you probably remember having to stand up on the pedals or get off and push to get up a steep hill. Modern bicycles are designed to overcome the difficulties of riding uphill with a wide range of low gearing that allows you to keep your seat while pedaling, as well as lightweight construction. You'll feel every extra pound while struggling up a long grade, and considering the weight of gear you'll have to carry in addition to the bike, it pays to buy a bicycle that is lightweight to begin with. Two additional things that can help you level out the hills in your path—a proper spin technique and a means of securing your feet to the pedals, will be discussed below.

Strong headwinds can be as brutal as steep hills, especially out on open roads if you have to battle them all day. This is why most road and touring bicycles have drop-style handlebars that allow you to get your head and shoulders lower and decrease the frontal area that the wind can push against. While beginning riders may perceive an upright riding position to be more comfortable, riding upright will be exhausting in strong headwinds. Carrying luggage will increase your windage as well as your weight, so it's important to choose streamlined bags and other gear instead of haphazardly tying stuff on so that it sticks out everywhere.

Riding technique is just as important as fitness to maintaining a good pace hour after hour. One basic principle many new riders and returning adult riders don't understand is that of developing a spin rather than pushing the pedals slowly. This means that when you're riding a multi-speed bike, you should always shift gears to match the terrain so that you are not mashing hard against a high gear to turn the pedals, but rather spinning the cranks at a fast RPM, or "cadence," so that your leg muscles are not overstrained. All long-distance cyclists put a lot of effort into developing this ability to spin the cranks at a high cadence.

At first it will seem awkward, but with practice it will become second nature and you will find long rides more pleasant. The advantage that fit recreational cyclists and pros like Lance Armstrong have, of course, is that they can maintain that cadence in much higher gears, and may be able to maintain average speeds around 28 to 30 mph compared to speeds in the mid- to high teens that most ordinary riders might average. But even if you can only manage 10 mph with a heavy load, that's still 80 miles of travel in eight hours of the day, allowing plenty of extra time between daylight and dark for rest stops.

Toe Clips and Clipless Pedals A key difference equipment-wise between riding a bicycle casually around the block and setting out on a journey of a hundred miles or more is having some means of securing your feet to the pedals for a more efficient pedal stroke. This allows you to use some of your energy pulling up with one foot while pushing down with the other to spin the cranks. It also prevents your

feet from slipping off the pedals when sprinting or hill climbing and can help prevent a crash. Competitive cyclists and tourists alike have long understood the advantages of this, and today your options include the older toe clips and straps as well as high-tech clipless pedals that require special shoes. Toe clips use a metal or plastic partial enclosure that is bolted to the pedal, goes around the front part of your foot, and is tightened by adjustable straps that you can reach while riding. Toe clips can work with most any type of pedal that you could use without them, and allow you to ride in most types of shoes or even hiking boots. This is an advantage in a bug-out situation because you can still use the pedals with or without the toe clips and straps. Toe clips are a little awkward to adjust and take some getting used to, but the efficiency gains make it worth the effort to at least try them.

Toe clips have lost favor with serious cyclists since the introduction of clipless pedals and shoes. This system eliminates the clips and straps and instead involves a special pedal and matching insert in the sole of the shoe that lock together securely and cannot come lose except by a deliberate twist of the foot. The clipless system eliminates much of the hassle of toe clips and straps while creating a very secure connection to the pedals, but the downside is that the shoes are not designed for walking, and both the shoes and pedals are expensive. If you use this system you'll have to carry additional shoes or boots for walking, and if the locking mechanism fails or the shoes are lost, the small pedals are practically useless with ordinary shoes.

Quality Components and Proper Fit   No matter which type of bicycle you choose, it is important to find one of quality construction. You won't find this among the rows of cheap knockoffs from China at the big chain department stores, most of which will be styled to look like name-brand bikes, but will be heavy and fitted with inferior components that will likely fail with any serious use. The place to shop for new bicycles is in a real bicycle shop, where you will find the offerings of established manufacturers and a knowledgeable staff that knows how to assemble and adjust them properly. Bike shop bikes will have better-quality frames, all-aluminum wheels, and precision components like derailleurs and shifters. You don't have to buy the top-of-the-line models, but as with every other piece of equipment from firearms to tents and backpacks, you mostly get what you pay for and quality gear is worth the investment. Bike shops also stock a variety of accessories for their bikes and will have an inventory of spare parts so that any components you want swapped on your new bike can be installed before you take delivery of it.

Perhaps the biggest advantage of buying a bicycle from a bike shop is that the salespeople who work in these shops are usually riders and will know how to find the bike in the store that best fits your body dimensions and also how to fine-tune every adjustment to optimize this fit. Proper fit is essential to optimizing the potential of the rider and the bike, and includes parameters like frame size, handlebar stem length, crankset length, seat height, and so on. An improperly fitted bike will cause undue fatigue on long rides and possible injury to joints and muscles, while one that is perfectly adjusted will be a joy to ride all day.

Preparing a Bicycle as a Bug-Out Vehicle

To use a bicycle effectively as a bug-out vehicle, you will need a way to carry all your gear and supplies on the bike. Fortunately it is relatively simple to purchase a system of racks, panniers, and other bags like handlebar bags to distribute the load around the bicycle frame, or choose from a variety of trailers designed to be towed behind you with all your gear loaded on them. These luggage systems are highly refined and widely available to suit every type of bicycle and terrain, thanks to the popularity of bicycle touring both on and off pavement. Either carrying method is far superior to trying to ride a bicycle with your gear in a backpack, which puts too much strain on your body and compromises your safety when riding by raising your center of gravity too high.

Luggage Racks and Panniers   Racks and panniers are the most common arrangement used by bicycle tourists and have the advantage of keeping everything in a compact package without the extra wheels and length of a trailer. Touring panniers are designed to ride low and keep the weight of your gear centered near the axles on either side of the front and rear wheels. To carry the panniers properly, you will need both front and rear racks mounted on the bike. Many types of bicycles come with rear racks or at least the threaded eyelets on the frame to attach them to, but other than purpose-designed touring bikes, few have front rack eyelets on the forks. This is something to keep in mind when choosing a bicycle, but there are clamp systems and other ways to mount the racks you need if your bicycle does not have eyelets. To hold up under a heavy load, especially for long-distance travel in rough terrain, these racks need to be securely mounted and well made. The best ones are made of aluminum for light weight but with tubing made of a high-quality alloy and sufficiently thick that metal fatigue is not an issue. Expect to pay $50 to $100 or more for each rack, front and rear.

Bicycle panniers are purpose-made packs designed to fit precisely onto the racks and will have provisions for securely fastening them to the racks so that they do not shift or bounce off when you hit bumps or

potholes at high speed. The attachment method varies among manufacturers, but usually involves spring-loaded hooks or hooks and piv-
oting clamps that lock the bags in place. The shape of the panniers is
important, first for minimum wind resistance, and in the case of the rear
bags, to avoid interfering with the pedal stroke. Rear bags have a sloping cutaway section in the lower-forward quadrant to clear the rider's
heel on the pedal stroke. Quality panniers are made from a variety of
materials, including the Cordura fabric commonly used for backpacks
and the PVC-coated nylon fabric of the type used for kayaking and
whitewater drybags. Either type will work, but if your panniers are not
waterproof, everything inside them needs to be sealed in Ziplocs or
some other type of plastic bag. Keep in mind that no matter how big
your panniers are, if you are carrying a full complement of bug-out
gear and supplies, not everything is going to fit inside the bags. Bulky
but lightweight items like sleeping bags and rolled-up air mattresses
can be strapped down across the rear rack or atop of the front racks
without adversely affecting handling.

   Bicycle Trailers   Bicycle trailers offer an alternative means of
carrying your gear and can have many advantages over racks and
panniers when it comes to using bicycles as bug-out vehicles. For one,
a bicycle trailer is designed to carry all your stuff in one cargo area,
either a metal-framed rack or a frame with fabric bottom and sides.
This means that you can quickly throw in your bug-out backpack and
go without having to split your load up among four or more separate
bags. Most of these trailers also have a cargo area that can be adapted
to carry a wide variety of loads and oversized items you would not be
able to fit directly onto the bicycle using racks or panniers. An example
of the versatility they can offer is that you could use the bicycle and
trailer to haul firewood or jerry cans of water to your camp once you've
unloaded your gear and set up in your bug-out location.

   Bicycle trailers come in single-wheel and two-wheel variations
with different hitch systems for attaching them to the bicycle. An example of a heavy-duty cargo trailer that is popular with rough-terrain
bicycle tourists is the BOB Ibex single-wheeled trailer that has a 70 lb.
load capacity and 3 inches of suspension travel to handle the bumps.

This trailer attaches to the rear axle of the bicycle, and the single wheel decreases rolling resistance and handling problems on trails. It sells for around $439 with a custom-fitted dry bag for your cargo. Details can be found at www.bobgear.com.

Using a Bicycle as a Load-Carrying Vehicle   In discussing the idea of loading a bicycle with racks and panniers or pulling gear behind it with a trailer, I also want to point out the potential of a bicycle as a pure-load carrying vehicle. Though it is rarely seen in places like the United States, in undeveloped countries where bicycles are true workhorses and are used as taxis and all sorts of conveyances, bicycles are also seen carrying what most of us would view as impossible loads, with the owner walking alongside it and pushing, rather than riding. I mention this because in a bug-out situation where you may start out in a vehicle carrying bicycles and lots of other gear and supplies, there could be some scenario where you need to abandon the vehicle and move all the stuff inside some distance overland to a secure bug-out location. In this case, it might be possible to do so in one trip if you are walking and pushing the bicycle rather than trying to ride it. Once everything has been moved, you will then have use of the bicycle for transportation around the area.

Bicycle Maintenance and Roadside Repair   Compared to any motor vehicle, a bicycle is a relatively simple machine, but, even so, there are many components that can wear out, break, or otherwise fail. The most common issues are flat tires, bent rims, broken spokes, broken or stretched brake and derailleur cables, and worn hub or crankset bearings. Flat tires are an unavoidable part of any serious bicycle travel and you must carry what you need to fix them on the side of the road, including a pump, tire removal tools, spare tubes and patches, and, for longer trips, spare folding tires to replace the set you start out with. You can reduce the frequency of flats by using Kevlar-belted tires and heavy-duty tubes of the type favored by long-distance touring cyclists. Other spare parts to carry include extra spokes, brake and derailleur cables, and brake pads. In addition to the parts you will also need a compact kit with all the tools necessary to replace and adjust these components.

Maintenance and inspection is the key to staying ahead of any problems that might render your bicycle inoperable. Keep an eye on the condition of your tires and check for embedded bits of glass or thorns. Make sure the rims are true and inspect for dents and check the tension of the spokes. Brake pads should be inspected for wear and replaced when necessary. Keep the brake and derailleur cables lubricated and properly adjusted. The chain should be kept clean and lubricated for maximum life. Any knocking or grinding noises while riding could be a sign that it's time to overhaul your hubs or crankset. A list of the tools and spare parts you should have with you if you bug out by bicycle is included in the Bug-Out Bicycle Checklist.

Choosing a Bicycle

The popularity of many forms of both recreational and competitive bicycling has led to the development of a wide range of specialized bicycle types optimized for different activities, ranging from racing and commuting to touring and trail riding. Some of these types, like ultralight road racing machines, will hardly be suitable for bug-out purposes, but the technology that has been developed for the serious sport of bicycle racing has trickled down to every type of bicycle and benefits all riders. For potential bug-out vehicles, I will look at four different types of bicycles: touring bikes, mountain bikes, commuter or hybrid bikes, and recumbent bikes.

Touring Bicycles

Touring bicycles are simply derivatives of the road bicycles that are used for races and recreational and fitness riding. From a distance, they look much the same, usually featuring drop handlebars, skinny tires, narrow seats, and a lightweight frame. The touring bike, however, will have a more relaxed or stretched-out frame geometry to better absorb road shock and allow all-day riding comfort. It will be heavier than a high-tech racing bike, as the frame will likely be chrome-molybdenum steel or aluminum rather than carbon fiber or some combination of aluminum and carbon fiber. Chrome-moly is considered by many to be the best material for serious touring, as it will allow the frame to flex better to absorb bumps and won't break or weaken due to metal fatigue. Chrome-moly is heavier than aluminum, but a good touring bike with high-quality components will still weigh less than 30 lb.

The tires typically used for touring will be a bit wider than road-racing tires and the rims much stronger, with more spokes per wheel to handle the extra strain of a touring load. Touring frames come with threaded eyelets for front and rear racks, as well as mounting points for extra water bottles. Instead of the high, closely spaced gears of road racing bikes, they almost always have triple cranksets with a wide range of gearing to handle the steepest mountain roads with a load. The brakes are also stronger so they can stop all the extra weight of a loaded bike.

TOURING BIKE EXAMPLES
Surly Long Haul Trucker   In recent years, the Surly Long Haul Trucker has become one of the most popular touring bicycles on the market and its reputation as a reliable long-haul machine is well deserved. The heart of this bike is the chrome-moly steel frame that comes with brazed-on fittings for all the racks, bottle holders, and other

A classic touring bicycle with racks, panniers, and low gearing for carrying heavy loads

accessories you need and is offered in a range of sizes to fit every rider. The frame can be ordered to fit either 700c (622mm) road bike wheels or the more commonly available 26-inch wheels used on mountain bikes, which makes it easier to find tires and tubes. You can order a complete bicycle or just the frame through the company's dealers and build it up with the components you want. A complete bike runs around $1200. More information can be found on the Surly website at www.surlybikes.com.

REI Novarra Safari The Novarra Safari, which is available only through REI stores, is a rugged touring bicycle designed for "adventure touring" on paved or gravel roads and the kind of rough roads found in developing countries. Recently redesigned, it now has a stronger steel frame and comes in either 26-inch or 700c wheel size depending on the frame size. This bike is fitted with trekking-style handlebars, which offer multiple riding positions and the control of mountain bike flat bars. It weighs approximately 30 lb. depending on frame size and lists for $849. Full specs are available at www.rei.com.

Mountain Bikes

Mountain bikes are purpose-designed for off-road riding and are the bicycle equivalent of off-road motorcycles or ATVs. A mountain bike can take you down challenging single-track trails that no other vehicle except the smallest dirt bikes could negotiate, or handle fire roads or gravel with ease. They can also be ridden on pavement, of course, but will be much slower than a touring or hybrid bike because of the extra rolling resistance of the fat, knobby tires that allow them to do so well off-road.

There are many different variations of mountain bikes available today, most of which are designed for specific types of riding. Unfortunately, the most versatile, basic configuration that was popular when mountain bikes first became popular is hard to find now. These early bikes had strong rigid frames and rigid forks with no suspension. They got their off-road capability just from the strong rims and wide, aggressive tires combined with low gearing and were simpler and lighter weight than most of today's mountain bikes, which utilize suspension systems that can include both front and rear shocks. The earlier mountain bikes were easy to convert to touring machines because, like real touring bikes, they came with frame and fork eyelets to mount racks. The lack of suspension is an advantage when riding long distances, not only because of weight savings, but also because all the energy of your pedal stroke goes into forward motion without the flexing of shocks. Although these rigid-framed mountain bikes have gone out of fashion, you can still find good examples used or you can build one from a bare frame. You could also convert a front-suspension hard-tail mountain bike to rigid front forks.

Of all the mountain bikes available today with suspension systems, the "hardtail" type, which features a rigid frame with front fork shocks but no rear suspension, is more suited to long-distance riding than heavier, more complex models that feature rear suspension as well. People do tour on hardtail mountain bikes, and it is possible to set up a rack and pannier system on them using a special front rack designed to work with shocks. Or you could use one of the more rugged trailer designs that are built for mountain bike touring and camping. This type of mountain bike could serve well if most of your route will traverse rough terrain.

MOUNTAIN BIKE EXAMPLE

Specialized Rockhopper   The Specialized Rockhopper mountain bike has been in production for over 20 years in one form or another, and today represents a good buy in a hardtail, front-suspension bike built for general-purpose off-road use. In stock form it features an alloy frame, 24-speed drive train, and 26-inch wheels with 2-inch-wide tires. The base model with linear pull brakes starts at $640, with the disc brake models ranging from $940 to $1,350, depending on component groups. You can find a good example of a used Rockhopper for anywhere from about $150 to $300. Older Rockhoppers with their quality frames also make a good platform for conversion into long-distance road touring bikes. More info about the Rockhopper line can be found at www.specialized.com.

Hybrid or Commuter Bicycles

This class of bicycles evolved to address some of the limitations presented by road bikes and mountain bikes—machines that excel in the environments they were designed for, but do not cross over well to other uses. Hybrid or commuter bikes are mostly used for roads and streets, but have some of the ruggedness of mountain bikes to deal with potholes, curbs, and other obstacles of urban riding. Instead of knobby tires, they are usually fitted with wide tires that have a street tread for low rolling resistance. The riding position is upright, as on a mountain bike, which gives you good visibility and control in dense city traffic and the ability to perform quick evasive maneuvers similar to the riding techniques required on twisty off-road trails.

These bicycles could be called the "dual-sport" equivalent of bicycles, and, just like dual-sport motorcycles, individual models can be biased more toward road or off-road riding depending on your needs. Like touring bikes, bicycles designed specifically for commuting usually come with attachment points for luggage racks, and most also come with fenders for riding in inclement weather. If you like the upright riding position, such a bicycle can be a good platform for long-distance riding with minimal modifications compared to most mountain bikes.

COMMUTING BIKE EXAMPLE

Cannondale Bad Boy   The Cannondale Bad Boy line of commuting bikes consists of several models designed to take the hard knocks of urban commuting. With its matte-black finish that includes all-black wheels and components, it's not flashy but utilitarian, and could be a good choice for a no-nonsense bug-out bicycle. The disc brake version is designed to allow you to switch out wheels between 700c road wheels and 26-inch mountain bike wheels depending on the kind of riding you'll be doing. With the 26-inch wheels and knobby tires, this aluminum-framed commuter with no front or rear suspension has all the advantages of the old-style rigid-framed mountain bikes discussed above. The Bad Boy is also available with 29-inch wheels, which are becoming popular on this type of bike and on mountain bikes because they roll over obstacles better than smaller wheels. Cannondale is a top-notch bicycle manufacturer and the price for the Bad Boy is within reason for the quality you get at approximately $1,100, depending on the model and specifications. You can find out more at www.cannon dalebadboy.com.

Recumbent Bicycles

Recumbent bicycles are a completely different concept from conventional bikes. The name comes from the reclined riding position, which is attained by a lower seat and pedals that are forward of the rider's body instead of straight down under the seat as on a regular bicycle. Though still far from mainstream in the bicycle world, recumbents are becoming more common as more manufacturers offer a greater variety of models to choose from. Those who prefer them to conventional bicycles are usually of the belief that they are superior in every way, but like anything else, there are pros and cons to this type of bicycle and it is unlikely they will ever replace standard bikes.

Recumbents can be a good alternative for people who for some reason (such as an injury) physically cannot ride on an upright bicycle straddling a narrow seat. The seats on most recumbents are wide and comfortable, many of them made of mesh fabric, and put you in a laid-back position like lounging in a hammock or deck chair. In certain conditions, recumbents can be faster than upright bicycles because of the much lower windage. This is particularly true on downhills and long flat stretches. They can allow those who are less physically fit to manage long days with less fatigue, and for this reason some people do tour on them and some impressive trips have been completed on recumbent bikes. Areas where recumbents fall short are in steep uphill climbing, where you cannot get your body weight over the pedals, and in busy vehicle traffic, where the low position makes you hard to see and makes it hard for you to see around other vehicles. Another disadvantage of recumbents is that most of them are much more expensive than upright bicycles, starting at over a thousand dollars and averaging two to four thousand for those of high quality with good components.

Still, if you've never ridden a recumbent, it's worth trying one to see if you like it. You could make a good one work as a bug-out bicycle if you are so inclined, as some of the models used for touring pull a touring trailer or can be fitted with racks and panniers. The available designs vary widely and even include three-wheeled and four-wheeled versions. Find a shop that specializes in this type of bicycle and they will usually let you ride the models they have on hand so you can judge for yourself if this type of machine is for you.

RECUMBENT BICYCLE EXAMPLE

Bachetta Giro 26 ATT   Many people who use recumbents for touring favor the short-wheelbase designs such as this 47-inch wheelbase offering by Bachetta. Bachetta is a leader in the recumbent industry and this aluminum-framed example designed for touring and commuting is comparable in weight to many upright touring bikes at 28 lb. A point in favor of this particular recumbent is that it uses two equal-sized wheels in the common mountain bike size of 26 inches, making it easy to find replacement tires and tubes. Another advantage of these larger wheels is that they offer less rolling resistance and can negotiate rough terrain better than the smaller wheels used on many recumbents. The Giro 26 ATT has a wide range of gearing spread over 27 speeds to help you get up and down hills. It has a weight limit of just 230 lb. including your body weight, however, so you will have to take that into consideration if you want to carry all your bug-out gear. MSRP is $1,899 and more information can be found at www.bacchettabikes.com.

BUG-OUT BICYCLE CHECKLIST

BASIC RIDING GEAR:
- ❐ Helmet
- ❐ Eye protection (sunglasses)
- ❐ Bicycle shorts or pants that are comfortable in the saddle all day
- ❐ Footwear suited to the type of pedal system you are using
- ❐ Padded cycling gloves (to absorb handlebar shock)
- ❐ Wind/rain-protective outer layers
- ❐ Wicking inner layers for cold weather

BIKE ACCESSORIES AND LOAD-CARRYING OPTIONS:
- ❐ Mirror for left handlebar or helmet
- ❐ Fenders
- ❐ Water bottle cages and bottles
- ❐ Cycling computer or handlebar-mounted GPS
- ❐ Rear cargo/pannier rack
- ❐ Front pannier rack
- ❐ Front and rear panniers
- ❐ Handlebar bag
- ❐ Underseat bag
- ❐ Optional trailer if not using racks and panniers

TOOLS AND SPARE PARTS:
- ❐ Inner tubes and patch kit
- ❐ Spare folding tire(s)
- ❐ Hand pump
- ❐ Tire levers
- ❐ Pressure gauge
- ❐ Allen wrench set
- ❐ Spoke wrench
- ❐ Spare spokes (6 or more)
- ❐ 6" adjustable wrench
- ❐ Multitool
- ❐ Chain-breaker tool
- ❐ Replacement chain links
- ❐ Chain and general-purpose lubricant
- ❐ Spare brake and derailleur cables
- ❐ Spare brake pads
- ❐ Assorted nuts and bolts
- ❐ Nylon wire ties
- ❐ Duct tape

9

HUMAN-POWERED WATERCRAFT

Canoes, Sea Kayaks, and Rowing Vessels

If you're in a location where taking to the waterways may be a better option than overland travel, you should not overlook the many advantages of human-powered watercraft, especially canoes and sea kayaks. These advantages include simplicity, reliability, low initial cost, easy maintenance, and small size and weight that, in combination with shallow draft, allows them to go where other vessels cannot. Just as a bicycle could be kept going indefinitely as an overland vehicle in the aftermath of some SHTF or TEOTWAWKI event that renders fuel unobtainable, boats that can be paddled or rowed can function independently of technology and in the most remote environments. The simplest of these designs, especially canoes and some kayak designs that do not need a foot-controlled rudder, have no moving parts at all to wear out or break. Some of them, especially canoes, can still be built from scratch from materials found in nature, just as the natives who invented them did for thousands of years.

The stealth aspect of canoes and kayaks is a huge advantage in a bug-out scenario and in many environments could make them better than any other means of transportation available. As I pointed out in *Bug Out: The Complete Plan for Escaping a Catastrophic Disaster Before It's Too Late,* small streams, rivers, bayous, and other waterways that are rarely used by commercial or recreational boat traffic thread their way through suburban and rural landscapes all over America, often winding through dense woodlands and swamps that are cut off from roads and almost never visited by people living nearby. A small, silent boat could be quietly paddled along such waterways, taking you and your gear unnoticed through areas where you could never travel unseen overland. This is especially true if you paddle at night and hole up in streamside undergrowth and woods during the day. I have traveled hundreds of miles by sea kayak in just this way, pulling my boat up into the woods out of sight of the river to make camp and slipping past homes, farms, and ranches—even whole towns—undetected by those living on the banks. Paddling at night, I have also slipped unseen in the shadows past unsuspecting campers, beachgoers, fishermen, and others, often close enough to hear their conversations without them ever knowing I was there. Because they are so hard to see at night and so small that they do not show up on radar systems, especially in the rough seas of the open coast, sea kayaks have been used by special operations military forces such as the U.S. Navy SEALS for stealthy insertions into enemy territory. Seaworthy enough to be dropped off far offshore by helicopters or larger vessels, the kayaks can then be paddled in under cover of darkness by the assault team and sunk out of sight in shallow water near the shore. Most kayaks used for this purpose are of the folding type, with the capacity to carry two men and plenty of weapons and gear.

You can get the same stealth advantage as these teams by painting your boat and paddle flat black or camouflage or choosing a factory model finished this way. Such boats are often used by wildlife photographers, hunters, and fishermen, and if you paddle slowly and silently, you will be amazed at how closely you can approach animals without alarming them. This has obvious advantages when it comes to hunting in a survival situation. Boats that blend in are also easy to hide when you are not using them. The small size and light weight of a canoe or kayak will allow you to drag it up steep banks or carry it as far from the water as you need to conceal it from anyone who might pass by. This is an advantage of these boats that cannot be overemphasized, as they can truly allow you to paddle into a remote area and disappear.

Disadvantages of Canoes, Kayaks, and Other Human-Powered Watercraft

This type of boat has few disadvantages compared to larger boats, but there are some. The small size that makes them so versatile can be a disadvantage if you need a vessel that can haul more passengers and cargo. The crew and gear could, of course, be split up between several boats, but this wouldn't work if a number of the people in your party are children, elderly adults, or disabled individuals who cannot paddle or row.

The slower speed of human-powered watercraft can also be a disadvantage if you have to get out of an area fast, especially if leaving that area involves crossing a lot of exposed, open water where the stealth advantages of these boats won't be of benefit. In such cases, especially if you are trying to elude pursuers, you won't be able to outpace any kind of motor-powered boat or most sailboats if there is a favorable wind.

Some human-powered boats discussed in this chapter will also have limitations in their ability to traverse open water or deal with rough conditions. This applies mainly to open canoes, pirogues, and the smallest rowing vessels. All human-powered boats, even the incredibly seaworthy touring kayaks, are limited by human endurance, which will vary from person to person according to fitness and paddling skill. This can be a major factor in route planning, especially if your route involves long crossings of bays or sounds or passages between islands. Adverse wind and current can push human endurance to the limit and beyond, making some routes impossible. And while strong paddlers can travel upstream on rivers, it will always be more work and take longer than going downstream.

Key Considerations for Using Human-Powered Watercraft

Training and Techniques for Long-Distance Endurance   Most people reading about the long-distance canoe and kayak expeditions that today's adventurers undertake think of such exploits as epic stunts or foolhardy risks. I have heard comments to this effect time after time both during and after my own solo journeys of several thousand miles and constantly had to remind people that such travel is what these boats were designed for. Here in North America, the natives who lived along big rivers or coastlines thought nothing of paddling great distances for the purposes of trading, hunting, or raiding other tribes.

The key to long-distance paddling, just like long-distance bicycling or walking, is to develop efficiency and economy of motion—in this case the paddle stroke—and to learn to pace yourself at a rate you can maintain for hour after hour, day after day. I find that paddling generally requires about the same effort as walking at a normal pace, unless there is a contrary wind or current to fight against. At this level of effort, if you pause a few minutes and eat a high-energy snack every hour or hour and a half or so, you can keep the boat moving all day long. And if you think of a long journey as simply a string of daylong paddles done consecutively, you can see how you might be able to keep going indefinitely. This said, if you've never done a multi-day paddling trip, you should incorporate a few into your preparations so you know what you're getting into. If you are planning to bug out by human-powered watercraft, you should also paddle or row your chosen boat as often as possible to build up your endurance, even if it is only for short afternoon trips here and there.

Learn the Necessary Boat-Handling Skills   In addition to the physical fitness required to paddle long distances, you will also need to know how to keep the boat going in a straight line so that you are not wasting your energy with the paddle or oars fighting the natural tendency of the boat to turn off course. This turning can be caused by wind or current or simply by too much force on one side or the other in your stroke. In the case of canoes, to travel long distances without tiring you must learn how to do a correction stroke such as the guide stroke or J-stroke so that you can keep paddling on the same side of the boat without having to constantly switch sides. These skills take a concentrated effort and a bit of practice to learn to the point where they are second nature.

You will also need other boat-handling skills to control your canoe, kayak, or rowing vessel in the various conditions you can expect to encounter in your particular environment. For example, if you plan to canoe down rivers where you might encounter rapids, you must learn to read the water so you can pick the safest line through a long series of drops and whitewater, and you must know the basic sweeps and other strokes needed to quickly turn your boat to avoid danger. If you are planning to sea kayak the open coast, you will need a wide range of skills from weather forecasting to reading wind, tide, and surf patterns, and you will need to know brace strokes to keep from being knocked over in big waves, as well as Eskimo rolling techniques to right your boat after a capsize. You will also need to know how to do a "wet exit" if you cannot roll upright and how to do a self-rescue re-entry into the boat and get it going again. All these skills can be learned in advance by participating in recreational paddling, taking classes from instructors, or simply learning from more experienced paddling partners.

Poling a Canoe Upstream   Poles are actually the oldest form of boat propulsion and were undoubtedly first used by primitive people who discovered they could make a floating log or raft of logs go where they wanted it by pushing off from the bottom with a long pole. The simple boat pole still has its place on modern human-powered watercraft. Poling can be more efficient than paddling in some situations, particularly when traveling upstream in a canoe in swift currents. As long as the pole can reach the bottom and the canoe is stable enough to stand in, it is possible to travel upstream for great distances this way with much less effort than paddling. A good canoe pole may have to be 10–12 feet long, depending on the water depth, and can be improved if it is fitted with a splayed foot to keep it from digging into a soft bottom. Such poles are widely used with pirogues in the shallow swamps of south Louisiana, and it is still common to see the local natives poling dugout canoes upstream along rivers in the more remote jungle regions of the tropics.

Paddles and Oars   Many non-boaters routinely interchange the words "paddle" and "oar" as if they were both the same thing. The paddle is the next logical development of the pole, and can be as simple as a pole with one end flattened, allowing it to grab the water enough to propel the boat in places where you can't reach the bottom with a pole. Oars are an even later development; they are attached to the boat by lashings or oarlocks and work as levers to generate more propulsion force than paddles.

A canoe paddle can be anything from a simple flat board carved to the right shape to a high-tech composite creation made of exotic materials like carbon fiber and Kevlar. The main advantage of more sophisticated and expensive paddles is their much lighter weight and stiffness for a given weight. If you are traveling long distances by canoe, you will be wielding the paddle hour after hour, day after day, and every ounce of weight savings in the paddle will help decrease the fatigue you will feel from the effort. But when you choose a paddle, make sure it is designed to withstand the rigors of real-world touring, as some of the lightest paddles built for racing may not hold up over the long haul. Many experienced expedition paddlers still prefer wooden paddles, particularly those carved from a solid piece of hardwood, such as ash, with no glued laminations to fail. A well-made wooden paddle can also be lightweight and well balanced. The bottom of the barrel in canoe paddles is the cheap variety with aluminum shafts and molded plastic blades and handles, such as the type provided by most canoe rental outfitters. However, while such paddles are club-like and inelegant, they are quite durable, so having one or two for a spare in an emergency is not a bad idea.

Sea kayak paddles are more complex than canoe paddles, as they are double-ended and usually have the blades "feathered" or offset anywhere from 45 to 90 degrees to minimize wind resistance against the end that's pushing through the air while the other end is pulling through the water. More traditional "Greenland"-style kayak paddles do not need this offset, as the blades are long and narrow, rather than short and wide. Most modern touring kayak paddles are a compromise between the narrow Greenland style and the wide whitewater style needed to maximize grip in the water in rough conditions. You can think of different blade widths as gearing in a kayak paddle, much the same as the gearing on a bicycle. If you are out to paddle all day, possibly against the wind and sea, you need a lower gearing so you don't wear yourself out, and therefore a longer, narrower paddle blade. Big blades are for power sprints and rough-water maneuvering, but will cause fatigue and possibly joint injury over the long haul.

All kayak paddles are long by design and should be sized so that the paddler can stroke rhythmically with either end without having to lean or reach to avoid striking the sides of the kayak. The beam of the kayak, as well as the height of the paddler, will determine the optimum paddle length. Because they are so long, all higher-quality kayak paddles feature a quick-disconnect sleeve in the middle of the shaft that enables you to break them down into two pieces for storage or transport. You will definitely want to carry a spare two-piece paddle on the deck of the kayak, secured by bungee cords where it is accessible from the cockpit if the primary paddle is lost or broken.

Rowing oars are more useful than any type of paddle for boats that are wider or much heavier than canoes and kayaks. Such boats are also called "pulling boats" because the oarsman sits amidships, facing the stern, and propels the boat with a pulling stroke of two equal-sized oars attached to the gunwales. Oars can make human-powered propulsion feasible for much larger boats than canoes and kayaks, some of which have additional rowing stations for two or more oarsmen.

Canoes

Canoes in different variations were developed by indigenous people all over the world according to the types of materials available in their environment. Canoes have always been an ideal type of watercraft for people living a hunter-gatherer lifestyle, because they can be made with simple methods and tools from readily available materials. Dugout canoes carved out of a suitable log are the oldest types of canoe, and can be excellent boats if shaped by skilled hands. I have spent several days at a time on rivers in Central America paddling native dugouts and they are as efficient as any modern canoe while underway. Most are much larger than the canoes used for recreational paddling today and can carry entire families or several paddlers with a large load of cargo. The biggest disadvantage of even a small a dugout is its weight, which would make it unsuitable for carrying far overland or car-topping to the water.

Even modern canoes are the epitome of simplicity in boat design— just an open, double-ended hull with no moving parts and no interior structure other than thwarts to maintain rigidity and racks or brackets to support simple bench seats. Because they are open with no decks or hatches, canoes are easy to load and unload and to get in and out of. This makes them better than any other watercraft for negotiating narrow, winding, log-choked creeks, as well as traveling the Great North Woods lake country where the boat must be portaged overland from one lake to another. Open canoes are also easy to fish and hunt out of. Without the decks or the confined seating position of kayaks, you can stand in a canoe to get a better view or clearer shot at your quarry and most designs are stable enough to allow paddling from a standing position as well when it is necessary to scout the waters ahead for obstructions. Because they are paddled with a single-blade paddle from one side of the boat, canoes are the most silent of watercraft. A skilled paddler can move over the water without a sound, easily approaching unsuspecting game that would be difficult to stalk on foot.

DIFFERENCES IN CANOE DESIGN

Modern canoes have developed from their more utilitarian origins to become highly specialized craft optimized for a variety of recreational and competitive pursuits. When reading through a typical manufacturer's catalog, one could easily conclude that a different canoe is needed for every type of waterway. But if you stick to proven parameters in canoe design and ignore the latest trends, you can find a hull that might be a compromise in some areas, but will function well enough in all. The hull forms most likely to meet all your needs are usually those closest to the traditional shapes perfected over millennia by those who depended on them as a means of survival.

In boat design, as mentioned in previous chapters about larger craft, waterline length is directly proportional to speed, so the longer the hull, the easier it will move through the water. In the case of narrow canoe hulls, greater waterline length also increases stability and load-carrying ability, as well as improves straight-line tracking on open water. Conversely, too much waterline length decreases maneuverability, making it more difficult to negotiate the sharp bends of creeks and smaller rivers and thread through the obstacles of rapids. The best all-around canoes seem to fall in the range of 15 to 18 feet in length, with a maximum beam of around 33 to 37 inches. Although a wider canoe may appear more stable to the uninitiated, it will be slower to paddle and will actually have less secondary stability in really rough water. Other design considerations include the amount of rocker (the change in the hull's curvature) along the keel and the shape and height of the bow and stern ends. A straighter keel with slight or no rocker will track better and be faster on flat water than a banana-shaped hull designed to do tricks and spin on a dime in whitewater rapids. The bow and stern ends should be symmetrical and shaped with enough flare in them to provide lift over waves, both those taken head-on and the large following seas that can occur when paddling off the wind. The ends should be high enough to avoid shipping water and to deflect spray, but if too high they will catch too much wind and make the canoe difficult to paddle straight in open, exposed waters.

EXAMPLE OF A LONG-DISTANCE TRIPPING CANOE
Old Town Tripper 172   This is a classic example of a high-volume tandem canoe that is designed for traveling and can handle flat water or moderate rapids with ease. At 17 feet, 2 inches long and 37 inches wide, with a deep-V entry and 25-inch bow height, it falls within proven design parameters for a canoe that can carry two people and a heavy load of gear with minimal effort. Weighing 80 lb. empty, it can carry a total load of up to 1,550 lb.—more than enough for an extended stay in the wilderness. The hull is made of high-impact and abrasion-resistant Royalex for durability and low maintenance. MSRP is $1589.00 and more info is available at www.oldtowncanoe.com.

Sea Kayaks

Due to my extensive personal experience with them, I have a strong bias in favor of sea kayaks when it comes to human-powered watercraft. I've traveled alone for literally thousands of miles in a 17-foot Necky Tesla

An Arctic Tern, a DIY wooden sea kayak built from a kit by Pygmy Boats

along exposed coastlines, up- and downstream on major rivers, and island hopping in the open ocean. With this boat I've traveled from the Canadian North Woods to the Gulf Coast and through the West Indies from Florida to the Virgin Islands. I've seen first-hand how a seaworthy ocean kayak can venture out on days when the weather keeps larger craft in port, and how it can reach surf-bound rocky beaches and other coastal hideaways that are inaccessible by any other practical means.

My own adventures pale in comparison to some modern sea kayaking exploits, however, such as Ed Gillet's ocean crossing from California to Hawaii and Paul Caffyn's solo circumnavigation of the continent of Australia. Like the canoe, the modern sea kayak is a simple, lightweight vessel derived from aboriginal origins—in this case the natives of the arctic and sub-arctic regions of North America and Greenland. Modern adventurers have rediscovered the oceangoing kayak and its amazing capacity to do things no other vessel can. Lightweight and small enough to be carried to the beach on a lone paddler's shoulder, it is seaworthy enough to negotiate breaking surf and make long journeys on the open ocean.

The key to the kayak's extraordinary seaworthiness is the watertight deck and sealed cockpit. A decked boat with no place for water to enter can survive almost any wave, bobbing back to the surface like a cork even after being completely submerged. Unlike larger boats that depend solely on the shape of their hull or the weight of ballast to keep

The author's Necky Tesla, a long-distance touring sea kayak, at a remote island campsite

them upright in rough seas, in a kayak, the paddler literally becomes part of the boat and can use bracing techniques with the paddle to create outrigger stability or even right the boat after it is capsized to an inverted position. With a watertight spray skirt that seals the paddler to the boat at the waist, there is a seamless transition between paddler and boat with no place for water to enter.

Another feature you will notice on most touring-style sea kayaks is the small retractable rudder mounted on the stern. This rudder is not designed to steer the boat so much as to help it track straight. As mentioned in the key considerations, it's difficult to keep a paddle-powered boat tracking in a straight line due to wind, current, or a tendency to paddle too hard on one side or the other. If you have to fight with every other stroke to keep your kayak going straight, you will wear out much faster. A rudder with foot controls can make subtle corrections in your course and using it this way becomes subconscious over time and allows you to focus all your paddling effort into forward motion. Some kayaks utilize a retractable skeg (extension of the keel) instead of a rudder for the same purpose. Other kayak designs have hull forms that track so well that a rudder or skeg is not needed. One of these is the Arctic Tern 17 model described below. Rudders add moving parts to the boat that take away some of the simplicity, but modern manufacturers have learned how to build these parts strong enough withstand expedition use, so they are unlikely to give you trouble.

CHOOSING A SEA KAYAK

Just as with canoes, there are many different types of sea kayaks, but for serious travel or bug-out purposes the best choices are high-volume touring models that can carry the required gear and supplies and are long enough to be fast and efficient. This generally means a length of 17 or 18 feet and a beam of 23 to 25 inches. Avoid the more performance-oriented narrower boats, as they will not have sufficient volume for your gear. Larger tandem sea kayaks are also available if you are bugging out as a couple. These could be useful if one person is a significantly weaker or less experienced paddler, but if not, two people would be better served by the versatility of two separate kayaks that would have a greater combined payload than a large double.

One type of double kayak that is extremely useful and capable is the folding kayak, which is comprised of a take-apart wooden, aluminum, or plastic framework onto which a skin of waterproof canvas or other similar material is stretched. Modern folding kayaks feature tough Hypalon hull bottoms that can withstand hitting rocks and other objects as well as any kayak. These are the types of kayaks often chosen for military use, as already mentioned. They are typically beamier than hard-shell kayaks and consequently can carry a much heavier load. A disassembled kayak of this type could be easily carried in most other vehicles and larger boats as a backup means of bug-out transportation. They are expensive compared to hard-shell kayaks, but could be worth it if you need the folding feature.

SEA KAYAK DISADVANTAGES

Sea kayaks are a bit inconvenient compared to canoes because the watertight deck that makes them so seaworthy means that the cockpit opening has to be small and any access to the spaces beneath the fore and aft decks is through relatively small, watertight hatches. This means that you can't shove a loaded backpack or large duffel bag into a kayak the way you can casually toss it into a canoe. Instead, your gear will take more time to load through the hatches and will have to be divided into many small dry bags or other containers to take advantage of all the interior space below deck.

Sea kayaks are also more expensive than canoes and require more essential equipment simply to function, such as the more complex, double-ended paddle, the watertight spray skirt already mentioned, and safety gear such as bilge pumps and a paddle float that serves as a stability device for re-entry after a capsize. New expedition-type sea kayaks can cost anywhere from around $2,500 to $5,000 or more. The gear mentioned above—along with the other stuff you need to travel by kayak like dry bags, deck compass, GPS, PFD, flares, etc.—can add hundreds or thousands more. But there are good deals to be found in the used market, as most owners never subject their boats to the rigors of expedition use. A quality kayak made of good materials will last many years or even decades if not abused.

SOME TOURING SEA KAYAK EXAMPLES

Current Designs Solstice GT   Current Designs is a top-notch manufacturer of quality sea kayaks, and the Solstice GT is one of the best examples available today of a high-volume expedition kayak that can carry you and all your gear on practically all waters. At 17 feet, 7 inches long, with a maximum beam amidships of just over 24 inches, it can carry 475 lb. and has all the right design parameters for good cruising speed, steady tracking, and handling rough conditions. It comes standard with a foot-controlled rudder and is available in fiberglass construction, weighing 54 lb. for $3,199, or a lighter Kevlar version that comes in at 49 lb. for $3,599. More information on this and other Current Designs models is available at www.cdkayak.com.

Pygmy Arctic Tern 17 High Volume   If you want save some money on an excellent new kayak instead of shopping the used market, one of the best options to do so is to build your own from one of

Touring sea kayaks pulled up on a beach

the top-notch kits offered by Pygmy Boats. These kits allow even some-one without specialized boatbuilding skills to complete a high-quality, super-lightweight, and durable wood and fiberglass composite kayak that is equal to or better than any production sea kayak on the market. I currently own the standard version of the hard-chined Arctic Tern 17 that I built about 12 years ago, and it has proven to be a great-handling and seaworthy boat that is fast and easy to paddle. If I were doing it again today, I would choose the newer High Volume model instead for additional load-carrying capability. Completed, the Arctic Tern 17 High Volume will be lighter than any plastic or fiberglass kayak you can buy, at just 43 lb. The price for the complete kit with all the wood parts, epoxy, and fiberglass is $965. More about Pygmy Boats can be found online at www.pygmyboats.com.

Feathercraft K2 Expedition If you need a folding double kayak with an enormous 700 lb. load-carrying ability, then the Feathercraft K2 Expedition, which has been proven in some of the world's toughest marine environments, could be worth taking a look at. This big kayak packs down to 44"x23"x14" when disassembled, and weighs 87 lb. It comes with a foot-controlled rudder, two spray skirts, a repair kit, deck rigging, and many accessories. This type of folding kayak is typically more expensive than hard-shelled kayaks, and Feathercraft is a top-of-the-line maker of such boats. The price for this model, which is their flagship double, is $7,414.00. More information can be found at www .feathercraft.com.

Sit-On-Tops, Hybrids, and Pirogues

For long-distance travel by paddle, there is no question that full-sized canoes and touring-style kayaks as described above are the best choices. Either type of boat offers long waterline length for speed and glide between strokes, as well as good load-carrying capability for the gear and supplies needed on a long journey. However, there are other situations, such as negotiating twisting or confined waterways like small creeks, where long hulls designed to track straight are not optimal. In other situations, where operating in extremely rough water such as surf or rapids is required, some of the self-draining sit-on-top type kayaks that have become popular for saltwater fishing are more convenient than decked kayaks. Sit-on-top kayaks are wider and have more initial stability than touring kayaks, making them ideal platforms for fishing, hunting, and other tasks you may need a boat for in a survival situation. While some have a long waterline length and watertight storage compartments fore and aft, enabling them to function as touring kayaks, most are shorter and more compact for convenience of transport and maneuverability on the water. For bugging-out purposes, their best use would be as auxiliary craft carried on the decks of larger escape watercraft or liveaboard boats as discussed in previous chapters. In this role, they could be an invaluable tool and means of transportation to places the main vessel cannot go.

A new class of paddle craft usually referred to as "hybrids" or "crossovers" has evolved from the popularity of sit-on-top kayaks to meet the needs of those who want a drier ride and more protection for gear than a standard open sit-on-top. These hybrids are something of a cross between a canoe and a kayak. Unlike sit-on-tops, which have open, form-fitting cockpits with molded seats for one or two paddlers and maybe a storage compartment or two accessed by small hatches, hybrids have flexible interior space with canoe-like seats and room for backpacks and other oddly sized and shaped cargo. Most are designed to be extremely stable, with molded plastic hulls using a tunnel-hull type design that is almost like a mini-pontoon boat. This makes it possible to stand and do other things that would be impossible in most hulls only 12 to 14 feet long.

Pirogues are a traditional type of watercraft in about the same size range as many sit-on-tops or hybrids, but completely different in terms of their capabilities and intended purpose. Although the word "pirogue" has been used for many types of boats around the world, the one I'm referring to here is the Cajun pirogue evolved in the swamps of south Louisiana, most likely as a derivative of the native dugouts used in the region previously. Pirogues typically have double ends like canoes, but much lower freeboard and a narrow, flat bottom. They are designed to operate in calm waters only, and excel at negotiating the narrow, winding bayous and flooded forests typical of the Deep South, either by paddling or poling. Cajun fishermen typically carried them across the gunwales of their larger boats to get into more remote areas no other boat could reach. Used this way as an auxiliary craft, a pirogue might be quite helpful if you are planning to bug out into swamp country. Pirogues are simple craft, easy to build yourself for very little money from either plywood or the traditional material: cypress lumber.

EXAMPLE OF A HYBRID BOAT

Native Watercraft Ultimate 14.5 Tandem The Ultimate 14.5 Tandem is one of several designs in the Native Watercraft Ultimate line. This model has the advantage over the smaller ones of being convertible from a solo craft to a two-person seating and paddling configuration. This boat could be good choice as an auxiliary boat to carry on the deck of a larger boat or for those who need to operate on small waterways where larger canoes and kayaks would be awkward. The tunnel-hulled Ultimate 14.5 offers an incredibly stable platform in a boat that is only 30" wide and weighs 71 lb. It's easy to stand in without fear of capsizing and has a load-carrying capacity of 450 lb. The Ultimate 14.5 Tandem sells for $1,349 and the manufacturer's website is www.nativewatercraft.com.

Rowing Vessels

Most rowing vessels are quite different in their capabilities and design purpose than canoes and sea kayaks, but I'm including them here as they are the only other class of practical human-powered watercraft that might serve as bug-out boats. Most of them have few advantages over paddle craft, except in cases where you need a bigger boat to carry a lot of extra gear and supplies, or you have more small children than you can fit into a canoe and do not want to split up your family into two or more boats to accommodate everyone. Some rowing vessels, especially those descended from working craft used as ship's tenders, lifeboats, or fishing boats in the days before internal combustion engines, are quite seaworthy and are capable of undertaking serious voyages in most any conditions. Such boats include double-ended dories that can negotiate breaking surf or big river rapids as well as recreational canoes and kayaks.

Another use of rowing vessels is in the role of tenders, or dinghies, carried aboard larger craft. If your bug-out plans include any type of floating mobile retreat, such as a motor yacht, sailboat, or houseboat as discussed in Chapter Six, you will need to have some type of small boat aboard to get to shore from an anchorage, haul supplies to the mother ship, and perform any number of other tasks. While recreational boaters often prefer rubber inflatable dinghies, such as the typical Zodiac powered by an outboard, in a SHTF situation, fuel will be in short supply and inflatable boats will be too susceptible to damage and deterioration that can limit their useful life. A sturdy rowboat of wood or fiberglass is a better workhorse, and in this case a rowboat is a better vessel than a canoe or kayak because it can be boarded easily from alongside the big boat. Unlike canoes and kayaks, rowboats can be designed in very short lengths and still be efficient under the power of oars. Some dinghies less than ten feet long are easy to row and have

EQUIPMENT CHECKLIST
FOR HUMAN-POWERED BOATS

SAFETY AND
NAVIGATION EQUIPMENT:
- ❒ PFD (personal flotation device) for each person
- ❒ Handheld flares or 12-gauge flare gun
- ❒ Signal mirror
- ❒ Waterproof binoculars
- ❒ Hand-bearing compass
- ❒ Handheld GPS receiver/chart plotter
- ❒ Paper nautical charts of the region
- ❒ Sun protection (wide-brimmed hat and sunglasses)

TOOLS AND SPARE PARTS:
- ❒ Multitool with basic hand tools
- ❒ Hull repair kit and materials (specific to hull material type)
- ❒ Duct tape
- ❒ Marine silicone sealant
- ❒ Epoxy or other waterproof glue
- ❒ Spare hardware, cables, etc. (for seats, rudders and other moving parts)
- ❒ Folding saw, rasp, sandpaper, and other tools to make paddles and oars from wood
- ❒ Sewing kit for canvas and other fabric repairs
- ❒ Plenty of spare line (Dacron or nylon rope) in assorted sizes
- ❒ Spare bungee cords or lengths of shock cord

the advantage of taking up very little room when stowed on the decks of larger craft.

EXAMPLE OF A CAMP-CRUISING-TYPE ROWBOAT

Phil Bolger–Designed Gypsy　The 15-foot Gypsy, designed to be built in plywood with a fiberglass and epoxy sheathing over the hull, is an excellent lightweight rowboat that can be car-topped like a canoe, yet can carry a good load of gear for its size. With a beam of 4 feet and a sleek, low-windage profile, this is an easily driven boat you can row for long distances. If you add decks and watertight storage as my brother did when he built one, it can handle choppy coastal conditions as well. The Bolger Gypsy requires only five sheets of ¼-inch marine plywood for construction of the hull and is fast and easy to put together for a total cost of just a few hundred dollars. If you want to try your hand at building one, plans are $40 from www.instantboats.com.

CANOE-SPECIFIC EQUIPMENT:
- ❐ Paddle and spare paddle for each person
- ❐ Bailing scoop and sponge to remove water
- ❐ Dry bags and tie-down straps to secure gear
- ❐ Bow and stern painters for securing boat
- ❐ Accessible rescue knife
- ❐ Throwable rescue line and float

SEA KAYAK-SPECIFIC EQUIPMENT:
- ❐ Primary paddle
- ❐ Two-piece spare paddle secured on deck
- ❐ Watertight spray skirt
- ❐ PFD designed to work with kayak seating position
- ❐ Manual bilge pump secured within reach

- ❐ Bailing sponge
- ❐ Accessible rescue knife
- ❐ Deck rigging consisting of bungee cords and grab lines for self-rescue
- ❐ Bow and stern painters
- ❐ Paddle-float self-rescue device
- ❐ Deck-mounted navigation compass

ROWING VESSEL EQUIPMENT:
- ❐ Primary oars
- ❐ Spare pair of oars
- ❐ Spare set of oarlocks
- ❐ Anchor and rode for larger craft
- ❐ Boat hook
- ❐ Bow and stern painters
- ❐ Throwable PFD and line
- ❐ Pump, bailer, or bucket

Part IV

Fixed Retreats

10

SITE-BUILT NATURAL SHELTERS & LONGER-TERM PORTABLE SHELTERS

Most people think of bugging out in its most basic form, which involves packing everything you need to survive for at least a few days and possibly much longer into a bug-out bag (BOB), as I described in *Bug Out: The Complete Plan for Escaping a Catastrophic Disaster Before It's Too Late*. Since shelter is one of the primary needs in any kind of survival situation, and any bug-out plan should include preparations to meet this need, most well-stocked bug-out bags will include at least a versatile tarp, if not a lightweight back-packing-style tent to serve as temporary shelter while on the go.

It is always a good idea to have some form of shelter like this with you, even if your original plans involve bugging out with one of the various types of mobile retreats already discussed. Having a means of bivouacking on the go gives you great flexibility if you are unable to stick to your preplanned route or reach your preplanned bug-out location. You can survive this way if there is no other option, but it will not be as comfortable or as secure as bugging out to a location complete with a larger shelter that you have built or moved into the area in advance.

This chapter will cover two different types of shelters that can provide much greater long-term comfort than bugging out with a tent or tarp, but still offer flexibility in that they can be set up virtually anywhere, without requiring you to transport building materials or a prefab rigid structure to the site. The first type includes naturally occurring shelters such as caverns and rock overhangs that can be improved on with a little effort, and site-built shelters made from natural materials, the design and construction of which will vary greatly according to the climate and the natural resources available. In most cases these will be copies of, or variations of, proven designs used by indigenous people in the same kind of environment. This type of structure can also be built later, after you bug out into a remote location and find that you need more protection from the elements or need to stay in one location longer than you originally planned.

The second type of shelter covered here is the longer-term portable shelter—a take-down shelter that is bought or made in advance and moved into the bug-out location for assembly. These are generally much larger than backpacking or recreational camping-style tents and can be heated with a wood stove or a fire pit, extending the range of comfort and livability and making them suitable for four-season use in most areas. Such shelters include canvas wall tents, teepees, and yurts. This kind of portable shelter will be much too big and heavy to pack in on foot, but could be carried with you or taken into the area in advance if you are using pack animals or suitable bug-out vehicles such as ATVs or boats of some type to reach the area.

Essential Elements of
Shelter Construction and Location

Protection from the Elements   Keep in mind that the primary purpose of any shelter is to provide protection from the elements, and if it doesn't do that, it is of little use for anything else. This includes protection from the sun, from the cold, and from wind, rain, and snow.

Position Relative to Natural Features and Hazards   The shelter should be located so that it takes advantage of natural windbreaks if possible, as well as exposure to early morning sun to quickly warm it up after a chilly night. It should be out of the path of falling branches, dead trees, loose rocks, and avalanches, and above any flood plain or low area subject to flash flooding.

Free of Plant and Wildlife Hazards Ideally, your shelter will not be located near poisonous plants, areas of dense mosquito populations, or colonies or nests of other insect pests such as fire ants, wasps, or bees. If your bug-out location is in warm or swampy areas, it should be located off the ground or in open areas where snakes, alligators and other crawling animals can easily be seen. In areas with large predators such as bears and mountain lions, locate the shelter away from game trails and dens used by these animals.

Availability of Building Materials A site-built, primitive shelter will be much easier to construct if all the required materials are in the immediate vicinity and you don't have to spend a lot of time searching for them and moving them to the site. Try to use a construction method that works with the natural materials you have available close at hand.

Fire-Building and Firewood Supply The shelter should provide level space for sleeping and have room for a designated fire pit with ventilation for smoke. Large quantities of firewood should be available in the immediate vicinity, especially in winter or in colder regions, where your survival will depend on a reliable heat source.

Water Supply A reliable source of drinking water should be close by. Avoid setting up the shelter directly on the banks of rivers or streams, however, as these are natural travel corridors and may lead unwanted guests to your doorstep. Fast-moving water can also drown out the sounds of approaching danger, such as footsteps or voices. It's best to hide your camp out of site of the water source, but within reasonable distance for carrying water.

Strategic Location and Concealment Keep in mind that humans traveling in wild areas tend to take the path of least resistance, as do most animals, and will follow trails and waterways if possible, avoiding thickets, steep slopes, deep ravines, and other difficult areas. Make it unlikely that someone will stumble upon your shelter by locating it in difficult terrain or nearly impenetrable brush and forest. Use natural camouflage to conceal it by making it blend into the landscape as much as possible and avoid clearing out underbrush and making other alterations that will be obvious to anyone passing nearby.

Advance Work: Building, Moving Materials, and Hauling in Portable Shelters   Remember that the kinds of shelters discussed here will require more work to build or set up than the lightweight backpacking tents you might carry in a bug-out bag. Plan on several trips to your bug-out location in advance, first to find the ideal spot for the shelter, then to build it or at least haul in the tools and additional materials you might need later. If you're using a large portable shelter, you might also want to move it to the location and keep it packed and hidden, or if the area is sufficiently remote that it won't be found, even set it up in advance.

Natural Caves and Rock Shelters

The simplest type of long-term primitive shelter is one of the naturally occurring rock shelters that can often be found in mountainous areas or rocky, hilly terrain. Such shelters are typically rocky overhangs often found at the base of bluffs or cliffs or in the walls of river canyons or ravines. Some of these are shallow depressions just deep enough for an individual or a few people to get under, while others are large enough to shelter a large encampment. In North America, most of these large overhangs were well-known and used by the Native American tribes who once lived in the areas where they are found. Around many of them you can still find evidence of their ancient use as temporary or semi-permanent shelters in the form of artifacts, pottery shards, or flakes from Stone Age toolmaking. Such rocky overhangs are ideal shelters in many ways, as their rock walls provide natural windbreaks and reflect heat from fire pits. They are also often strategically located, overlooking rivers or canyons, and/or difficult to get to, sometimes bordering on inaccessible. Today, most of the larger rock shelters of this type that were known to be ancient dwelling places are well-known to area residents, and even many of them that are deep in wilderness areas have trails leading to them. These would obviously not make good bug-out locations. But despite this, in any area where such rock overhangs occur, there will usually be many more smaller ones in addition to the large, spectacular examples, and many of these will be far off the beaten path and seldom if ever visited.

One of the most interesting things I've ever come across while backpacking was just such a rock shelter in a remote part of the Gila Wilderness in New Mexico. Following an established trail along a creek with steep slopes covered in ponderosa pine forest on either side, I just happened to stop at a random spot for a drink of water and a brief rest. As I stood looking around and catching my breath, I noticed something that didn't seem quite right on the mountainside several hundred feet above the trail. It looked like it could be a cave, but I couldn't be sure. It would have been impossible to reach it with the heavy backpack, so I left my gear behind and scrambled up the slope to the dark area in the rock wall. Much to my surprise, when I finally reached it, I found a large rock overhang with a barricade of sharpened logs forming a palisade across its open front. It had clearly been someone's frontier home or camp, and when I went through a narrow opening in the wall I found blackened cooking utensils around a fire pit, along with many Prince Edward tobacco cans dating from the 1920s. It appeared that no one had been in the shelter since the original inhabitant left it, and I never would have spotted it if I had not paused at that exact spot midway on a 30-mile loop hike. Whoever built the barricade across the entrance was probably trying to keep out bears or mountain lions. From the history of the area, I concluded that it was most likely the semi-permanent camp of a silver prospector, as the area was not far from the tiny town of Mogollon, where there was once a lot of mining activity.

This modified natural rock shelter struck me as a perfect setup for living in that particular area. Requiring much less work than building a cabin, it had an interior that was well-protected from wind, rain, and snow and easy to heat with a central fire pit that would vent naturally at the peak of the opening. The log palisade added a measure of security and defensibility, and the stream below was within a reasonable distance to haul water.

If you are lucky enough to be in an area where your bug-out location may include natural features such as rock shelters and caverns, it will be easier to scout out and locate one of these than to build or haul in any other kind of structure, and probably will offer more shelter or security as well. However, you should be very careful when entering such an opening for the first time, especially a dark cavern or a rock shelter with a cave entrance opening into it. Wild animals know the value of such places as well, and you could inadvertently stumble upon a bear or mountain lion den and find yourself in a very dangerous position. Before approaching any opening you can't see into, look around the surrounding area carefully for tracks, droppings, or other signs of animals. Rattlesnakes are another danger you may encounter in these kinds of places, as are wasps or bees. Use caution, approach slowly, and don't enter a dark hole without a flashlight or torch. Also, make sure the overhanging rock is stable—avoid crumbling, fragmented rock that may cave in. In areas where there are no rock cliffs or bluffs, such as the river bottom swamplands in the Southeast, you may find similar overhangs at the base of clay bluffs. Most of these would not be safe to use as a long-term shelter, but sometimes you can find good short-term shelter in clay banks, especially in places where the roots of large trees are holding the bank together but floodwaters have carved out "caverns" beneath them.

You can effectively increase the protection of a natural rock overhang without doing all the hard work of felling large trees to build an elaborate palisade like the frontier dwelling I found in New Mexico. Other materials, such as stacked rocks or deadfall and brush from the surrounding area, can serve as a windbreak while effectively concealing the shelter if arranged in a haphazard fashion that appears natural. Stacking logs or rocks adjacent to the fire pit you build can help concentrate the heat in a smaller area so you won't need to burn as much fuel.

Primitive Structures: Temporary Shelters and Semi-Permanent Dwellings

In most potential backcountry bug-out locations, there simply aren't any natural shelters to be found; or if there are, they are often unsuitable for the purpose for one reason or another. They may be insufficiently remote to be secure, not easily accessible without dangerous climbing, or not close enough to food or water sources. This lack of an adequate amount of natural shelter led primitive cultures all over the world to develop ingenious structures suited to their particular environments and designed to make use of whatever natural materials could be found there. Examples include the bark houses of the Woodland Indians of eastern North America, the igloos made of ice by the Eskimos and Inuit of the Arctic, and huts of bamboo and thatch built by tribes in the tropical zones. Every environment you might conceivably bug out to offers some kind of natural building material that could be used to make a temporary or permanent shelter. Studying the designs and construction methods can be a fascinating exercise, and actually going out and building such a structure will go a long way toward increasing your confidence in your survival skills should you ever have to bug out without the convenience of your mobile retreat or high-tech fabric and frame tent.

DEBRIS HUTS: QUICK-TO-BUILD EMERGENCY SHELTERS

The debris hut is the simplest primitive shelter you can build, and knowing how to make one could save your life if you are caught out in the wild in cold weather without modern gear or a means to make fire. This is essentially a cocoon of natural insulating material that keeps out the cold and holds in your body heat much as a sleeping bag does. It's not a comfortable place to spend a lot of time but it can suffice as a place to sleep while you work on a larger shelter. I've tested these on more than one occasion in temperatures below freezing and discovered that they work well. Building one starts with setting up a low, sloping ridgepole, with one end on the ground and the other supported by a tree, stump, or A-frame of two shorter poles. You then make a framework by leaning large sticks against the ridgepole, angled out to the ground on either side to provide enough space for sleeping, but not so big that there is too much airspace for your body heat to warm. The next step is to pile on the insulation, which can consist of leaves, brush, tree bark, leafy boughs, grasses, and sticks of assorted sizes (hence the name "debris" hut). The insulation layers should add up to two or three feet thick, steeply angled down from the ridgepole to shed rain and snow.

LEAN-TO SHELTERS

The lean-to is another basic shelter that is easy to build and can serve as a quick overnight campsite or a more long-term shelter, depending on its size and the care you take in its construction. It is essentially a sloping roof, the high side supported by a horizontal pole held up by two trees or poles and the low side terminating on the ground, forming not only a roof overhead, but a wall or windbreak on one side. It can be left in this configuration or partially enclosed with sidewalls for better wind protection. A fire built near the front opening can be kept protected from the rain, yet will still vent well. A small reflector wall of stacked logs or stones built on the opposite side of the fire can help retain heat within the lean-to. After you secure the top horizontal pole, building the rest of the lean-to is simple, and involves placing several long poles of equal length from the ridge to the ground, keeping the spacing close enough that you can then lash on cross members to support the roofing material. The roof itself can be made of large slabs of bark, evergreen boughs interwoven and stacked deeply, or thatching of grasses, reeds, or suitable long leaves such as palmettos.

THATCHED-ROOF HUTS

Thatch roofing in many variations can be used on most any primitive shelter from the simplest lean-to shelter to the largest raised-platform hut or tree house. Most people immediately think of palm trees when they think of thatched huts, and it's true that large palm fronds make ideal thatching material. But you don't have to bug out to a tropical island to make use of this roofing method. Thatching can be done with many types of plant materials, including most reeds and grasses, as well as the more obvious choices you might find if you are in the southeastern portion of the U.S., such as cattails or palmetto leaves. Once you have a framework of lashed support poles for a roof, you can adapt the structure to suit the materials you have available by lashing on smaller saplings as crosspieces to fix the thatching material to. The distance between these crosspieces will be determined by the length of the bundles of grass or other material. The longer the thatching material, the faster the roofing process will go. Applying the thatching is similar to laying shingles: you start at the bottom, lashing the bundles on while packing them as close together as possible. The next row overlaps the first crosspiece and the top edge of the first row of thatching. If the bundles are closely packed and thick enough, and the slope of the roof is steep enough, a thatched roof will be dry even in the heaviest rain.

RAISED PLATFORM HUTS AND TREE HOUSES

In some environments, particularly in hot and humid areas such as the swamp country of the Deep South or jungle regions, indigenous people often built their shelters off the ground. This serves two purposes: better air circulation and ventilation for enduring sweltering hot nights, and getting sleeping areas above mud or standing water on the forest floor, not to mention all the undesirable insects, snakes, and other creatures common in such places. While traveling in the Mosquitia region of Honduras and Nicaragua, I spent many nights in such raised-platform huts and found them to be comfortable and dry even in torrential tropical downpours. In this area, entire villages consisted of such houses, elevated on a framework of wooden poles, the floors and walls made of split bamboo and the roofs of palm thatch. Most of the platforms that form the floors were less than ten feet off the ground. Unless you have dangerous animals to worry about, even a platform two or three feet off the ground will have the desired benefits.

An easier way to build such a raised platform shelter is to use standing trees as the support poles rather than cutting and setting posts. If you are in a forest area, this is easy to do, and structures can be built between any number of trees, from two to four or more, depending on the size of the platform you need. Horizontal beams can be made from large saplings or small trees of a size that you can cut with a machete, as long as the span between support trees is not too great. The easiest way to attach them in a wilderness situation where you probably won't have nails or lag screws is to lash them, either with rope you brought for the purpose or with vines or rope made from natural fibers found in the area. Using natural materials will be much more time-consuming and require more skill, so if you are planning to build this kind of shelter, it is a good idea to bring enough rope with you. Lashing rope can be as small as $^3/_{16}$ or ¼-inch as long as it is of a strong synthetic material such as nylon or Dacron. Several turns around each connection will hold a considerable weight. The floor platform can be finished with a structural framework of additional poles lashed across these main beams, followed by a matting of smaller branches or saplings placed close enough together to allow standing, sitting, and sleeping on the floor.

You can use the same support trees to lash on a horizontal ridgepole for a roof, either of an A-frame or lean-to style. An interlaced framework of saplings or branches here forms the base for a roof that can be thatched with palmetto leaves, bundles of grass or reeds, or layers of bark or evergreen boughs, depending on what's available in the area.

This same kind of structure lashed between tree trunks could technically be called a tree house, especially if it is elevated high off the ground. The main reasons some primitive groups built tree houses were to get far enough off the ground to be safe from predators or to make defense against other groups easier. In a bug-out situation, you might consider a tree house shelter for concealment purposes, especially in places like hardwood bottomland forests where there are lots of big, leafy trees. With the help of a friend, I once built such a tree house about 40 feet off the ground in a huge beech tree. We hauled the support poles up one at a time by rope and lashed them between the spreading branches of the tree to form the floor platform. The closest limb to the forest floor was 20 feet high, and we accessed the tree house by climbing a large wild grapevine that grew alongside the trunk. From the ground, the platform was well concealed by the canopy and would not be noticed by anyone passing through unless they were specifically looking for it.

STACKED LOG OR ROCK HOGANS

If you need something more substantial than a lean-to or raised platform hut, particularly in mountainous or cold regions, you could build a simple but sturdy type of shelter called a "hogan" with stacked logs or rocks. The hogan most people think of is the round adobe or log structure favored by the Native Americans of the southwestern U.S., but it doesn't have to be round and it can be any size you need. A hogan is quicker and easier to build than a traditional log cabin because it does not require large logs of uniform size or the notching and assembly techniques needed for log cabin building. The stacked-log hogan is constructed by setting stakes in the ground to define the perimeter of the structure and to hold the logs in position, as they are stacked between the stakes. The logs are mortared into place and sealed by a mixture of mud and grasses or clay. The roof can be thatch, bark, or a heavy layer of logs and stacked debris with the same mixture of make-shift mortar locking it all in place and sealing it. Large stacked rocks can be used for the walls if they are more readily available than logs. Either type of hogan can be made sturdy enough to serve as a long-term wilderness home in the same way that a log cabin might.

Mixing Modern Materials and Methods with the Primitive

Although there are many people who enjoy studying primitive technology and methods, learning ancient skills, and putting them into practice as a survival drill or for research, the kind of survival situations that would require you to bug out to a wild location are not conducive to purist practices. While it would be great if you were skilled enough to walk naked into the wilderness and procure everything you need for survival without the aid of modern tools or materials, most people do not have a lifetime to devote to learning these skills. When it comes to building a dry, leak-proof roof, for instance, it's amazing what a plastic tarp or two can do for your chances of success. Keep this in mind when you consider building a primitive shelter. Even if you don't want to pack in one of the complete portable shelters discussed in the next section, you can merge the modern with the primitive by carrying a few materials to "cheat" with. Modern synthetic rope, as has already been mentioned, is invaluable in lashing structural members together.

You could also carry in nails, screws, and other hardware and the tools to use them. Plastic or canvas tarps, rolls of Visquine plastic sheeting, roofing felt, and other modern building materials can all be incorporated into your primitive bug-out shelter. I've seen every combination of this imaginable in my travels in Latin America and the Caribbean. None of the Miskito Indians or others I've met living in remote locations would turn down the opportunity to get their hands on a piece of plastic in any form, and even in remote villages where all travel is by dugout canoe, sheets of tin roofing hauled upriver from the coast could be seen on a few of the bamboo houses.

Wall or "Cabin" Tents

The comfort level that a good heavy-duty canvas tent can offer for both short- and long-term living should not be underestimated. This kind of tent bears little resemblance to the ultra-light nylon fabric tents most people use for recreational camping or backpacking. Traditional heavy-canvas wall tents have been around a lot longer, but fell out of favor when lighter materials were introduced because they are much heavier and bulkier when packed and quite a bit harder to set up, often requiring poles cut on site as part of their structure. For long-term use, however, this is not an issue and once it's set up it has many advantages in terms of comfort, including ability to heat the interior and cook inside with a wood stove.

Modern wall tents are still widely used by hunting outfitters and others who need an all-season base camp in a remote location, and are available in a wide variety of sizes and configurations. The best material to look for is heavy 12-oz. natural canvas, which breathes well and provides insulation. Some of these tents are available with or without frames and poles. If you are planning to move the tent into a really remote backcountry location, it may be best to choose one without poles and then cut your own poles on-site. Most of these wall tents do not come with floors, but do have a 10–12" wide "sod" cloth made of vinyl that is sewn to the bottom edge of the walls and used to seal them to the ground, both to keep out the cold and to keep small animals from getting in. Another essential feature is the stovepipe to connect to your wood stove, along with a rain cap and spark arrestor for the open end of the pipe.

EXAMPLE OF A MODERN CANVAS WALL TENT

Western Wall Tents 12x14x5 ft. Magnum   This is a heavy-duty tent made of treated 12-oz. canvas with reinforced corners and ridge and a stovepipe jack, sod cloth, and zippered screen doors. It comes with tent stakes, tensioning ropes, and a bag, but no frame. Shipping weight is listed at 85 lb., which gives you some idea how it compares to ultralight backpacking tents. The price starts at $797.00, depending on options. More information is available at www.westernwalltents.com.

Canvas Teepees (or Tipis)

The original teepees used by many Native American tribes in the western U.S. were made of sewn buffalo hides stretched around a conical framework of long, slender poles. Teepees were ideal shelters for the open plains, as they could easily be taken down and moved to follow the game herds, they were sturdy enough to withstand high winds, and their steep sides worked well to shed snow. The peak of a teepee creates a natural chimney to funnel smoke from a central fire pit out the top of the shelter, and the round floor plan allows maximum use of space for sleeping and storage. Today you can buy a modern teepee faithful to the original design but made of heavy treated canvas just like the wall tents described above. These teepees are popular with those who attend mountain man rendezvous, Native American powwows, and other such festivals, but they are also sometimes used as full-time alternative housing. The demand for functional teepees that really work as serious shelters has led to many manufactured or custom options if you decide that a teepee is more to your liking than a traditional wall tent.

One disadvantage of teepees compared to wall tents is the number and length of the poles required, especially for the larger-diameter versions. For example, a 24-foot diameter teepee that could house a family will require some 17 to 20 poles of up to 30 feet in length. Needless to say, these will be inconvenient to pack far into the backcountry, and finding suitable timber that is straight, strong, and lightweight enough will take some work as well. Packing the poles in by dragging them behind a horse, as the Indians did, may be feasible if the terrain is not too difficult, but a teepee would probably work best in a location you could access with some sort of motor vehicle that had roof racks for the poles.

MODERN TEEPEE EXAMPLE

Nomadics Tipi Makers 20-foot Tipi Package   This is a complete package for a 20-foot-diameter teepee with everything you need except the poles. It comes in different grades of canvas from 13 oz. to 20 oz. army duck, with the price varying from around $1,000 to $1,300. A bundle of 17 27-foot poles can be added for an additional $343. The packing weight of the canvas cover varies from 62 to 85 lb., depending on the grade. The 20-foot model will accommodate four people comfortably for long-term use. Larger and smaller sizes are available and more information can be found at www.tipi.com.

Modern Yurts

A yurt is classified as a type of tent, but is much stronger and much more weathertight, making it suitable for a long-term or permanent shelter. Like the teepee, the modern yurt is descended from the ancient version used by nomadic tribes, in this case those of Central Asia. The modern yurt is a high-tech structure built with architectural fabrics and a highly engineered framework that gives it nearly the strength of a permanent building. The design uses the principles of tension and compression to make a lightweight structure that can stand up to heavy wind, rain, and snow, and the circular walls and domed roof are highly efficient with regard to airflow and heating. They are often set up on permanent wood decks, but are still portable shelters and could be packed into and set up in remote locations—though with more difficulty than something like a wall tent, probably taking days rather than hours. A modern yurt can be a comfortable long-term bug-out retreat or even a full-time home, but is not the best choice if you plan to move to different locations often.

MODERN YURT EXAMPLE

Rainier Raven 24-foot Yurt   This is a 24-foot diameter modern yurt that has 7' 4" high walls and is designed to withstand winds up to 95 mph and snow loads of up to 280 lb. per square foot. It comes with a fiberglass door that locks with a standard residential-style lock. The shipping weight is listed at 2,500 lb., which gives you some idea of what's involved in moving and setting up a modern yurt of this size. The 24-foot Raven is listed at $8,000, but there are a large number of options available that can change this price significantly. You can learn more at www.rainieryurts.com.

11

SECURE BUG-OUT SHELTERS

The secure type of fixed shelter is usually thought of as part of a "bug-in" plan, rather than part of preparations for bugging out. For most people planning to bug in, their secure shelter will be their home, or perhaps a vacation home or cabin. In the context of bugging out, the kinds of secure shelters covered here are generally smaller than full-time homes and are located somewhere other than your full-time residence, preferably in a remote, off-grid location where few people would have reason to go and your presence can go unnoticed. This would be the type of structure that you could build on some undeveloped land you might own or have access to, perhaps as an agreement with a family member or friend, or a lease arrangement such as the sort that hunting clubs work out with large individual or corporate land owners. Setting up such a shelter on public lands, such as national forest or BLM lands, is generally not a good plan, though you might get away with a low-profile version in some of the really big and remote backcountry areas of the West or in Alaska.

By "secure" shelters, I'm referring to rigid permanent or semi-permanent structures that have a door or doors that you can lock to protect your gear and supplies when you are away, or while you are occupying it, to add a level of protection against intruders that you would not have in a shelter like a tent or primitive structure. The degree of security such shelters can offer varies greatly by the type, design, and construction materials, as will be discussed in this chapter. They can range from a simple shack or converted portable storage building to a reinforced underground bunker. Naturally, such rigid structures can in most cases also offer better protection from the elements than most primitive or moveable shelters such as tents, teepees, or yurts. They can also be better sealed to keep out insects and other pests, as well as larger animals that might smell the stored food inside and attempt to raid your supplies.

Disadvantages of Secure Bug-Out Shelters

While secure bug-out shelters can make bugging out much less stressful than heading out into the wilderness with nothing but what you can carry, the fact that such a shelter must be fixed in one location automatically negates one of the primary purposes of bugging out, which is having the flexibility to adapt to changing circumstances. No matter how well you plan and how perfect your chosen location seems to be, you still have no way of knowing what events may occur. Who is to say whether that particular location will be safe in a major SHTF event or if it will actually end up being ground zero for a natural or manmade disaster? Nature is impossible to predict, as is the course of action that will be taken by governments, military forces, or ordinary citizens forced out of their homes by events beyond their control. In a mobile retreat or in a more primitive camping mode, you have the option to keep moving as events unfold. Of course, you have this option with a secure retreat as well, as long as you are willing to abandon it when the time comes and you have some sort of backup plan.

Secure Bug-Out Shelter Considerations

Although there are no guarantees you will be able to stay in your secure bug-out shelter, thorough planning and research can increase your odds. The guidelines that follow can help you choose a shelter site that will give you a better chance of getting through a crisis without needing to move.

Make Sure You Can Get to the Shelter When You Need It As part of your overall bug-out plan, a secure bug-out shelter will work best if you are lucky enough to have an ideal place to build one and a reliable means to reach it from your everyday living or working location. Unless you already live in a rural area, you will undoubtedly have to travel to reach it, but the farther you have to travel in a SHTF scenario, the greater the risks involved. Know in advance the route you will take and be familiar with as many alternative routes as possible. Make sure your escape bug-out vehicle is ready to go and have a backup transportation option as well.

Choose the Most Remote Location Possible   The shelter location should be far from large cities and population centers and not directly accessible from interstate highways, freeways, or other main highway arteries connecting cities together. It should ideally be surrounded by large tracts of undeveloped and uninhabited land, or at least sparsely populated rural countryside. People fleeing cities in the wake of a major breakdown will know to head for the countryside to look for food and other resources, and any farms or rural lands close by and accessible to large populations of refugees will likely be overrun early on.

Undeveloped Areas Are Less Regulated   Another advantage of remote, sparsely populated and underdeveloped rural areas is that you can get away with building unconventional structures that may not meet code requirements and other regulations that are becoming more restrictive all the time, even in most rural areas. But though they are getting harder to find, there are still counties in the U.S. where you can build what you want to on your land without permits. As long as you don't require insurance on the structure or a connection to the power grid or other public utilities, you may be able to keep the location and even the existence of your shelter secret.

Know Your Neighbors   If the site for your secure bug-out shelter meets the recommendations above, chances are you won't have many, if any, immediate neighbors. The fewer people who know about your shelter the better, but before choosing a site it is wise to know who those closest neighbors are and attempt to determine if they could possibly be of help or if they might become a threat in a SHTF situation. If you are new to the area and have just acquired the land, this may be more difficult than a situation where you are inheriting family land or buying a parcel from a friend, but a little time spent talking with people can tell you a lot. In most remote rural areas, people who choose to live there have an independent spirit and mostly want to be left alone to live the way they want to. But they may come to your aid in a crisis after you get to know them, just as you should be willing to help them if required.

Water Supply   Be sure that the site you choose for your secure shelter has a reliable, year-round water supply. Keep in mind that part of the reason there are vast tracts of uninhabited land and cheap parcels of land for sale in arid regions of the country is that there is no natural water supply, easy access to ground water, or reasonable way to bring a waterline in. Before buying property that does not have access to a permanent stream or spring, find out how deep you will have to drill to have a reliable well and how much it will cost. If there is any appreciable rainfall in the region, consider a cistern as well, with a system of gutters on the roof of your bug-out shelter or some other means of collecting as much rainfall as possible.

Firewood and Natural Material Resources   Unless you plan on hauling in a prefab shelter or manufactured building materials for every part of your shelter, you should take into consideration the natural building material resources of the land, including timber, rock, and clay. Having such materials on site can reduce the cost of building and the difficulty of moving materials into remote areas, but you will need the tools and skills to utilize them. Regardless of whether you build with local timber on the property, you will need a large supply of available wood, especially in cold regions or mountains. If there is not enough on hand, you can start bringing in firewood well in advance of any anticipated need. As long as it is properly stacked and protected from the weather you can stockpile enough that you won't have to worry about it for several seasons.

Game, Fish, and Wild Plant Foods   Availability of wild game is an important consideration for any good bug-out location, especially if you are preparing for a long-term stay. While you can stock enough supplies to survive for a considerable length of time in most secure shelters, it's always a good idea to supplement your larder with hunting, fishing, and foraging. Generally, if the area is remote enough to meet the other qualifications for a bug-out location, there will be game around, and in every region of the country there are at least some edible plant foods that should be easy to locate and harvest. If you have access to waters that contain fish and other aquatic life such as crawfish, frogs, or waterfowl, that's even better. Before settling on a site to build your secure shelter on, scout the potential area to see what food resources you can find.

Stockpile Supplies, Tools, and Extra Gear   One of the primary advantages of a secure bug-out shelter is that it gives you a place to store and protect a lot of additional goods that will make survival much easier, especially in the early stages of a SHTF ordeal. Having enough food for several weeks or months will take a lot of the pressure off after you bug out to your shelter by eliminating the need to forage, hunt, and fish right away. In addition, you can give yourself more options in the way of hunting weapons, traps, fishing gear, tools, extra clothing, medical supplies, and anything else you may need in a long-term survival situation. Just be sure you have the basics with you at all times when you are traveling to your well-stocked bug-out shelter, in case you cannot reach it for some reason or you arrive to find it destroyed or raided by others.

Types of Secure Bug-Out Shelters

The possibilities for building or converting existing structures into secure bug-out shelters are nearly unlimited, and as the popularity of survival preparation grows, new and unique ideas are constantly showing up on blogs, websites, and YouTube videos. In addition to those who are interested in survivalism, there are other enthusiasts promoting the idea of "micro" houses and cabins or other minimalist structures for economic and environmentalist reasons, leading to all sorts of innovative designs and ideas that could be applied to the secure bug-out shelter concept. Some of these shelters are the kind you build from scratch using either conventional or unconventional building materials. Others are converted from prefab structures that were never intended to be shelters or living quarters, including everything from storage buildings to steel shipping containers.

Low-Cost DIY Cabins and Micro Houses

Designing and building your secure bug-out shelter from scratch gives you the most flexibility in making the accommodations fit your and your family's needs. Building from scratch also allows you to invest labor and materials into the structure over a period of time, working on weekends or vacation trips to your building site. Many such structures can be built small to provide basic shelter right away, but later expanded as time and money permits or your needs change to require more space. They can be built using conventional materials and methods, or you can save money and time by taking a more unconventional route. The following sections give a few examples.

Pole Building Pole building is a construction method that dates back to the Stone Age and, as already discussed in the previous chapter, is still a viable way to build primitive shelters in the wilderness using cut poles set in the ground or standing trees. As a modern construction method, pole building is still popular because of its low cost relative to conventional buildings on slab or masonry foundations. The poles are the foundation, and using this method you can build with no excavation on steep slopes, over ground subject to flooding, and on many other types of terrain unsuited to a foundation. Pole building is a method that will work for everything from the smallest storage shed to the most elaborate permanent home. Like the primitive versions, elevated pole buildings work great in hot, humid climates and in environments where it is desirable to build several feet above the ground. As a bonus, the space beneath can be used for a shaded outdoor living area, or for work or storage space. If you want to go even higher, you can also apply the principles of pole building to constructing a tree house, using all live trees or a mix of standing trees and poles to form the base for the platform you require.

Post and Beam Construction Post and beam construction is similar to pole building construction except that it entails using square posts as the load-bearing structural members to support the roof and walls. This method can be used on a conventional foundation, on a platform set on poles, or as a stand-alone foundation, with the posts set into holes in the ground the way poles are in pole buildings. It is a faster method of building than conventional stud-wall framing, and is more economical in terms of materials, because the posts can be set several feet apart and tied together with minimal horizontal framing members to which vertical board and batten siding planks are fastened directly. Modern pressure-treated lumber eliminates the need to worry about wood decay in the buried posts, and with proper design, post and beam construction can be used to make any size permanent building.

Cordwood Masonry Cordwood masonry is an unconventional yet time-tested building method that can be used to construct low-cost shelters and dwellings that have fortress-like strength and efficient insulation properties. Short logs (12 to 24 inches long) are laid widthwise in a wall like a stack of firewood (hence the name) and are held together by mortar. Because the logs can vary in diameter and type of wood, and do not even have to be particularly straight, they are much easier to gather than the long, straight logs needed to build a traditional log cabin. For long-lasting durability, however, the logs should be debarked and seasoned before use. In the finished walls, the ends of the logs are visible, sometimes protruding a bit beyond the mortar. This building method is well suited to both rectangular and round structures.

Straw Bale Construction Straw bale construction is another unconventional building method that dates back many centuries but has recently found favor among those seeking to build energy-efficient homes and other structures that have minimal environmental impact in their material use. Bales of straw are stacked to form the walls, held in place with wire and metal rebar, and encapsulated by mortar and stucco to form a rigid structure. Straw bale construction can have the advantage of superior insulation properties because of the thickness of the walls, and it can be a cheap material to build with if you have a readily available source of wheat, rye, or oat straw. It would be ideal on the plains or prairies and works best in drier climates because of rot concerns, though I have seen some well-built examples that seemed to be holding up just fine in my humid and rainy home state of Mississippi.

Rammed Earth Construction Rammed earth construction is another way of building with materials found on the site. This process traditionally involves using wooden forms to build walls with a mixture of earth, sand, gravel, and clay that is compressed between the forms to make a solid structure that can then stand on its own when the forms are removed. Modern rammed earth construction uses cement in the mix for additional binding and stabilization properties. The compression of the walls is done by hand with a ramming pole or with a pneumatic ram that makes the job much easier. Although the walls can be reinforced with rebar, bamboo, or wood, they are typically strong enough on their own, ranging from 12 to 24 inches thick in a house-sized structure. Rammed earth construction is a low-cost building method that works in most environments and has great thermal and soundproofing properties. It is also unaffected by rain once it is cured and is impervious to attack by insects or fire. Full curing of the walls can take months or years, but eventually they will resemble and have most of the properties of solid rock.

Converted Structures

Many existing vehicles and objects designed to transport goods or people can be transformed into unique fixed shelters or homes that can be functional as well as inexpensive and quick to convert. Some of these vehicles or parts of vehicles can even be obtained for free if they were abandoned or destined for the scrapyard.

MARINE SHIPPING CONTAINERS

By some estimates, as much as 90 percent of the world's trade goods are moved about the globe in steel shipping containers. These containers are widely available as surplus or sometimes damaged goods no longer used by the shipping companies, and in recent years people have been using them to create innovative, low-cost housing and other structures. Steel containers obviously have the advantage of solid construction, making them relatively easy to convert into secure bug-out shelters. Shipping containers can be buried, partially buried, or stacked vertically to form multistory buildings, or several can be cut apart and welded into larger structures—the possibilities are as limitless as your imagination. Such containers come in many configurations and sizes, but the most common are the 40-foot and 20-foot dry freight containers. A standard 40-foot container will be 8' wide by 8 ½' tall, with the inside about a foot smaller in all dimensions (totaling 2375 cubic feet). Considering the size and heavy-duty construction, as well as the weather-tight heavy steel doors that come on them, shipping containers are a bargain compared to what it would cost to build such a structure from scratch. You'll probably get a better deal on a used one, including delivery, if you live reasonably near a port city, but because of the standardization of sizes, shipping containers can be moved by truck or rail to any location.

Before they became so popular, you could buy used shipping containers for very little money, sometimes just a few hundred dollars, but lately I've seen prices ranging from under $1,500 to over $3,000. Some companies offer new containers in this price range but the price of delivery can vary greatly. Most can give you a quote including delivery so you can plan your total costs. To convert a shipping container into a livable shelter, you will need a means of cutting openings for windows and other ventilation and maybe an extra door or two. Welding skills and equipment will give you many more customization options when working with these steel containers. Some survivalists using these for secure bug-out shelters have created fortified bunkers out of them by encasing them in concrete blocks and cement, keeping in mind that the steel wall alone will not stop bullets from high-powered rifles. Overall, steel shipping containers are well worth considering if your land is accessible by truck or perhaps a tractor that can pull a trailer to move the container to the site.

BUSES, RAIL CARS, BOATS, AIRCRAFT, AND OTHER ABANDONED VEHICLES

As discussed in Chapter Five, many types of vehicles can be converted into DIY mobile retreats. Many types of large vehicles that are abandoned or beyond repair can also serve as a basic structure that can be converted into a fixed retreat or home. Such conversions have become almost as popular as building homes out of shipping containers and have the advantage that they might already have functioning windows, doors, and other necessities that shipping containers lack. Abandoned vehicles like this can in many cases be had for free or for very little money, especially if you have the means to move them out of the owner's way to your retreat site. Look for old buses and other fleet vehicles at junkyards or storage yards and make an offer. In coastal areas, hurricane-damaged vessels from luxury motor yachts to oceangoing sailboats are often written off by insurance companies and moved to boatyards before being cut up and scrapped. You may be able to get one for free just for moving it and saving them the trouble. A little creativity can go a long way in adapting such a vehicle into a secure bug-out shelter and blending it into the landscape. For example, you could bury a deep-keeled sailboat up to the waterline and have a sturdy home that would be impervious to almost anything nature could throw at it. The modifications that you could make to such vehicles and boats are endless. Some people even add on parts of conventional buildings to create more living space inside.

Prefab Structures and Kit Houses

If you don't have the time or the inclination to build from scratch, assembling a kit house or storage building or simply purchasing a complete building that can be moved intact or set up by the company selling it could be an attractive option. This will certainly be faster than building from plans or even converting containers or vehicles as described above.

STORAGE SHEDS, BARNS, AND METAL BUILDINGS

Today there are more options than ever before in prefab buildings or kits that you can purchase and assemble yourself or have assembled upon delivery. Some of the smaller storage sheds and outbuildings are nailed or screwed together using traditional house-framing materials and built on skids so they can be loaded onto a trailer or flatbed truck and moved intact. You can find such buildings at any big-box home improvement store or on the lots of dealers or manufacturers. This is cheap and fast way to get a finished building that can be converted into a livable camp house or secure bug-out shelter. While most of these buildings are not designed to be cabins, the addition of insulation and interior walls, as well as ceilings and better floors, could convert one into functional living quarters. Larger wooden sheds and barns are also available from most of the same companies, but since they are too big to readily transport, they will have to be put together on-site. A typical example of the type of small, transportable shed you might find for sale at a big box store is an 8x16-foot cedar-sided shed with a door and windows for around $3,500. Many of these stores will delivery such prefab sheds at no extra cost if your property is within reasonable distance.

Perhaps the cheapest way to get a large structure on your property if you need more space is to buy a metal building, either in kit form or from a company that will set it up for you on your site. Such buildings are designed to be used for everything from workshop and storage space to commercial office or retail space. Compared to wood-frame structures, these offer much more enclosed, secure, and dry space for the same amount of money, and maintenance is minimal to none. Converting one of the basic structures that is designed for storage into a livable shelter is mainly a matter of insulating the walls and ceiling and finishing the inside. To give you an idea of how reasonably some of these large metal buildings are priced, you can visit the websites of a number of companies that offer them and get a quote that includes delivery and setup on your site by entering the zip code of your property.

KATRINA COTTAGES

After Hurricane Katrina decimated the Mississippi Gulf Coast in 2005, tens of thousands of FEMA trailers (actually commercial RV trailers) were brought in by the government to serve as temporary housing for displaced homeowners. These trailers were not satisfactory long-term accommodations for most people, and a new industry sprang up to produce "Katrina Cottages" to meet the demand for housing until the area could be rebuilt. Originally designed for emergency relief, these Katrina Cottages have caught on and become popular for everything from hunting camps to guest houses. Much more substantial than any RV trailer or mobile home, they are designed to be easily transported by truck, yet are built to specifications that are engineered to withstand hurricane-force winds. The original design was for a one bedroom, one bath, 308 square foot unit, 14 feet wide by 30 feet long (including an 8-foot front porch), but today you can buy complete Katrina Cottages or plans to build your own in a range of larger sizes as well. If you need a home-like, secure bug-out shelter on your property in a hurry, purchasing one of these units complete could be the way to go. You can find more information about Katrina Cottages by doing a web search for "Katrina Cottage" or visiting www.katrinacottagehousing.org.

LOG CABIN KITS

Another type of kit-built structure to consider is the log cabin. Complete kits for building your own log cabin are available in all sizes all the way up to luxury homes. A small cabin kit could make a solid bug-out shelter and will come with preprocessed logs that have been peeled, treated, and prepared for assembly. Erecting such a log cabin will be faster than trying to put together a traditional log cabin by felling your own trees and laboriously preparing all the logs, but it will also cost a lot more than building from your own timber. In general, log cabins are much sturdier and easier to secure against intruders than some of the lightweight storage buildings and other prefab options mentioned, but exactly how much depends on the size of the logs used in the construction. Larger logs also have good insulation properties, which is why cabins built this way have always worked so well in cold climates and mountainous regions. There are many manufacturers of such cabin kits, all with varying reputations as to the quality of their products. Before investing in one, it would be wise to try to find an example of the design you're interested in that is actually in use so you can get some owner feedback and check out the details yourself.

Underground Structures and Bunkers

Many people consider building partially or fully underground to be the best way to ensure safety in a survival retreat. Digging in has been an essential military strategy since the invention of projectile weapons, and especially explosive projectiles. A defensive position can be as simple as a one-man foxhole or as elaborate as a reinforced concrete bunker buried deep in the ground or in a mountainside. Underground structures can have advantages other than defense, however. An underground home or shelter can be warmer in the winter and cooler in the summer than an above-ground building as well as safer in storms, particularly violent wind events such as tornadoes. Going underground also makes it easier to blend in with the landscape and to completely hide a large structure, if desired.

DUGOUT SHELTERS

The simplest type of underground shelter is the dugout. Dugout shelters can be partially or completely underground, and in the most basic form consist of a large hole four feet or so deep with timber or masonry-reinforced walls that protrude above the ground just enough to provide headroom and support for a roof. Dugouts were common frontier homes in places like the Great Plains where building materials were scarce and building below ground level provided better protection from cold wind and storms. As bug-out shelters, even though they are not completely underground, dugouts can be much easier to conceal than taller structures, and with creativity, you can build one that blends in perfectly with the landscape, especially if it is incorporated into the side of a hill. They can also offer obvious advantages for defense against attackers due to their lower profile and the fact that several feet of earth in the lower sections will stop bullets and most other weapons that might be brought to use against your retreat. But unlike structures buried completely underground, dugouts enable you to incorporate defensive positions where you can see your attackers and return fire.

UNDERGROUND BUNKERS/FALLOUT SHELTERS

The ultimate in defensive secure bug-out shelters is the underground bunker, bomb shelter, or fallout shelter. Such shelters were especially popular during the Cold War when the threat of a nuclear attack seemed imminent, and plans for building your own can be found dating back to the 1950s. Most of these shelters will at minimum be under several feet of dirt and built of reinforced concrete several inches thick. Though it would be labor-intensive, you could dig out and build your own underground bunker or you can purchase a prefab or site-built one from one of the many companies that are in business to address the concerns of those who think they might need this level of protection. Fully underground shelters like this require a lot of planning with regards to plumbing, drainage, ventilation, and air filtration, as well as access and escape. In some types of events, such a shelter could be the only thing that will save your life and those of your family, but in other cases it could well become a deathtrap with no escape if someone finds out it's there and that it may be full of supplies and other necessities they covet in a post-SHTF situation. Be aware that any such shelter has some weakness to attack, which could be as simple as someone pouring gasoline down one of the ventilation pipes and setting it afire. The best bet when relying on this type of shelter is to build it in secret and in such a way that it is well-concealed, perhaps hidden beneath some conventional structure expected to be seen on a rural property, such as a cabin or barn.

BIBLIOGRAPHY & RECOMMENDED READING

ESCAPE VEHICLES

Adams, Carl. *The Essential Guide to Dual Sport Motorcycling: Everything You Need to Buy, Ride, and Enjoy the World's Most Versatile Motorcycles.* Center Conway, NH: Whitehorse, 2008.

Allen, Jim. *Four-Wheeler's Bible.* 2nd ed. Minneapolis, MN: Motorbooks, 2009.

Alvord, Douglas. *Beachcruising: An Illustrated Guide to the Boats, Gear, Navigation Techniques, Cuisine, and Comforts of Small Boat Cruising.* Camden, ME: International Marine, 1992.

Brand, Paul. *How to Repair Your Pickup or SUV.* Minneapolis, MN: Motorbooks, 2008.

Cardwell, J. D. *Sailing Big on a Small Sailboat.* 2nd ed. Dobbs Ferry, NY: Sheridan House, 1997.

Coyner, Dale. *The Essential Guide to Motorcycle Travel: Tips, Technology, Advanced Techniques.* Center Conway, NH: Whitehorse, 2007.

DeLong, Brad. *4-Wheel Freedom: The Art of Off-Road Driving.* Boulder, CO: Paladin, 1997.

Gray, Michael E. and Linda E. Gray. *Auto Upkeep: Basic Car Care, Maintenance, and Repair.* 2nd ed. Ozark, MO: Rolling Hills, 2007.

Hough, David L. *Proficient Motorcycling: The Ultimate Guide to Riding Well.* 2nd ed. Irvine, CA: BowTie, 2008.

Little, Ida, and Michael Walsh. *Beachcruising and Coastal Camping.* Rockledge, FL: Wescott Cove, 1992.

McKnew, Ed. *The Boat Buyer's Guide to Trailerable Fishing Boats: Pictures, Floorplans, Specifications, Reviews, and Prices for More Than 600 Boats, 18 to 27 Feet Long.* Camden, ME: International Marine/Ragged Mountain, 2006.

Sweet, Robert. *Powerboat Handling Illustrated: How to Make Your Boat Do Exactly What You Want It to Do*. Camden, ME: International Marine/Ragged Mountain, 2006.

Vance, Randy. *Power Boating for Dummies*. Hoboken, NJ: Wiley, 2009.

Wicks, Robert and Greg Baker. *Adventure Riding Techniques: The Essential Guide to All the Skills You Need for Off-Road Adventure Riding*. Newbury Park, CA: Haynes, 2009.

MOBILE RETREATS

Baker, Kim and Sunny Baker. *The RVer's Bible: Everything You Need to Know About Choosing, Using, and Enjoying Your RV*. New York: Fireside, 1997.

Beck, Roger D. *Some Turtles Have Nice Shells: A Picture Book of Handbuilt Housetrucks and Housebuses*. Eugene, OR: Pine Hill Graphics, 2002.

Buehler, George. *Bueler's Backyard Boatbuilding*. Camden, ME: International Marine/Ragged Mountain, 1991.

Casey, Don and Lew Hackler. *Sensible Cruising: The Thoreau Approach; A Philosophical and Practical Approach to Cruising*. Camden, ME: International Marine/Ragged Mountain, 1990.

Kretschmer, John. *Used Boat Notebook: From the Pages of Sailing Magazine, Reviews of 40 Used Boats Plus a Detailed Look at Ten Great Used Boats to Sail Around the World*. Dobbs Ferry, NY: Sheriden House, 2002.

Livingston, Bob. *RV Repair and Maintenance Manual*. Rev ed. Ventura, CA: Trailer Life Books, 2002.

Mate, Ferenc and Candace Mate. *The Finely Fitted Yacht: The Boat Improvement Manual, Volumes 1 and 2*. Pflugerville, TX: Albatross, 1944.

Moeller, Bill and Jan Moeller. *The Complete Book of Boondock RVing: Camping Off the Beaten Path*. Camden, ME: Ragged Mountain, 2008.

Moitessier, Bernard. *A Sea Vagabond's World*. Dobb's Ferry, NJ: Sheridan House, 1998.

Pallidini, Jodi. *Roll Your Own: The Complete Guide to Living in a Truck, Bus, Van, or Camper*. New York: MacMillan, 1974.

Parker, Reuel B. *The New Cold-Molded Boatbuilding: From Lofting to Launching*. Brooklin, ME: Wooden Boat Publications, 2005.

———. *The Sharpie Book*. Camden, ME: International Marine/Ragged Mountain, 1993.

Vigor, John. *The Seaworthy Offshore Sailboat: A Guide to Essential Features, Gear, and Handling*. Camden, ME: Ragged Mountain, 2001.

———. *Twenty Small Sailboats to Take You Anywhere*. Arcata, CA: Paradise Cay, 1999.

ALTERNATIVE AND BACKUP VEHICLES

Burch, David. *Fundamentals of Kayak Navigation*. Seattle, WA: Pacific Search, 1987.

Burke, Edmund R. and Ed Pavelka. *The Complete Book of Long-Distance Cycling: Build the Strength, Skills and Confidence to Ride as Far as You Want*. Emmaus, PA: Rodale Books, 2000.

Casper, Steve. *ATVs: Everything You Need to Know*. Minneapolis, MN: Motorbooks, 2005.

Davidson, James West and John Rugge. *The Complete Wilderness Paddler*. New York: Vintage, 1982.

Donaldson, Doug. *Bicycling Magazine's Guide to Bike Touring: Everything You Need to Know to Travel Anywhere on a Bike*. Emmaus, PA: Rodale Books, 2005.

Dowd, John. *Sea Kayaking: A Manuel for Long-Distance Touring*. Victoria, BC, Canada: Greystone Books, 1986.

Downs, Todd. *The Bicycling Guide to Complete Bicycle Maintenance and Repair For Road and Mountain Bikes*. 5th ed. Emmaus, PA: Rodale Books, 2005.

Hallam, James. *Snowmobiling: The Sledder's Complete Handbook*. Abbotsford, BC, Canada: Fun on Snow Publications, 1999.

Hutchinson, Derek C. *Expedition Kayaking*. 4th ed. Old Saybrook, CT: Globe Pequot Press, 1999.

Jacobson, Cliff. *Expedition Canoeing: A Guide to Canoeing Wild Rivers in North America*. 4th ed. Falcon, 2005.

Lovett, Richard. *The Essential Touring Cyclist: A Complete Guide for the Bicycle Traveler*. 2nd ed. Camden, ME: International Marine/Ragged Mountain, 2000.

Mason, Bill. *Path of the Paddle: An Illustrated Guide to the Art of Canoeing*. Revised ed. Buffalo, NY: Firefly Books, 2001.

———. *Song of the Paddle: An Illustrated Guide to Wilderness Camping*. Revised ed. Buffalo, NY: Firefly Books, 2004.

Null, Scott and Joel McBride. *Kayak Fishing: The Ultimate Guide*. 2nd ed. East Petersburg, PA: Fox Chapel, 2011.

FIXED RETREATS

Brown, Tom. *Tom Brown's Field Guide to Living with the Earth*. New York: Berkley Books, 1986.

———. *Tom Brown's Field Guide to Wilderness Survival*. New York: Berkley Books, 1987.

Creekmore, M. D. *Dirt-Cheap Survival Retreat: One Man's Solution*. Boulder, CO: Paladin Press, 2011.

Kahn, Lloyd. *Home Work: Handbuilt Shelter*. Bolinas, CA: Shelter, 2004.

———. *Shelter*. Shelter Publications, 2nd ed. Bolinas, CA: Shelter, 2000.

Lacinski, Paul and Michel Bergeron. *Serious Straw Bale: A Home Construction Guide for All Climates*. White River Junction, VT: Chelsea Green, 2000.

Nelson, Peter. *Tree houses: The Art and Craft of Living Out on a Limb*. New York: Mariner Books, 1994.

Oehler, Mike. *The Fifty Dollar and Up Underground House Book*. 4th ed. Bonners Ferry, ID: Mole Publishing, 1981.

Olsen, Larry Dean. *Outdoor Survival Skills*. Provo, UT: Brigham Young University, 1976.

Roy, Rob. *Cordwood Building: The State of the Art*. Gabriola Island, BC, Canada: New Society, 2003.

———. *Earth-Sheltered Houses: How to Build an Affordable Underground Home*. Gabriola Island, BC, Canada: New Society Publishers, 2006.

Shafer, Jay. *The Small House Book*. 2nd ed. Boyes Hot Springs, CA: Tumbleweed Tiny House, 2009.

Stiles, David and Jeanie Stiles. *Rustic Retreats: A Build-It-Yourself Guide*. North Adams, MA: Storey Publishing, 1998.

Wolfe, Ralph. *Low Cost Pole Building Construction: The Complete How-To Book*. Pownal, TV: Storey Books, 1980.

OTHER ESSENTIAL SURVIVAL REFERENCES

Burns, Bob and Mike Burns. *Wilderness Navigation: Finding Your Way Using Map, Compass, Altimeter and GPS*. 2nd ed. Seattle, WA: Mountaineers Books, 2004.

Carr, Bernie. *The Prepper's Pocket Guide: 101 Easy Things You Can Do to Ready Your Home for a Disaster.* Berkeley, CA: Ulysses, 2011.

Chesbro, Michael. *Wilderness Evasion: A Guide to Hiding Out and Eluding Pursuit in Remote Areas.* Boulder, CO: Paladin, 2002.

Craighead, Frank C. *How to Survive on Land and Sea.* United States Naval Institute, 1984.

Forgey, William. *Wilderness Medicine, Beyond First Aid.* 5th ed. Guilford, CT: Globe Pequot, 1999.

Gibbons, Euell. *Euell Gibbons' Beachcomber's Handbook.* David McKay, 1967.

Gonzales, Laurence. *Deep Survival: Who Lives, Who Dies, and Why.* New York: W.W. Norton, 2004.

Hinch, Stephen *W. Outdoor Navigation With GPS.* 2nd ed. Birmingham, AL: Wilderness Press, 2007.

Kesselheim, Alan. *Trail Food: Drying and Cooking Food for Backpacking and Paddling.* Camden, ME: Ragged Mountain, 1998.

Layton, Peggy. *Emergency Food Storage and Survival Handbook: Everything You Need to Know to Keep Your Family Safe in a Crisis.* Roseville, CA: Prima Publishing, 2002.

Lundin, Cody. *When All Hell Breaks Loose: Stuff You Need to Survive When Disaster Strikes.* Layton, UT: Gibbs Smith, 2007.

Maxwell, Jane, Carol Thuman, and David Werner. *Where There Is No Doctor: A Village Health Care Handbook.* Revised ed. Berkeley, CA: Hesperian Foundation, 1992.

McCann, John D. *Build the Perfect Survival Kit.* Iola, WI: Krause, 2005.

McNab, Chris. *Special Forces Survival Guide: Wilderness Survival Skills from the World's Most Elite Military Units.* Berkeley, CA: Ulysses, 2008.

Nestor, Tony. *Desert Survival Tips, Tricks, and Skills.* Flagstaff, AZ: Diamond Creek, 2003.

———. *The Modern Hunter-Gatherer: A Practical Guide to Living Off The Land.* Flagstaff, AZ: Diamond Creek, 2009.

Rawles, James Wesley. *How to Survive the End of the World as We Know It: Tactics, Techniques, and Technologies for Uncertain Times.* New York: Plume, 2009.

Sherwood, Ben. *The Survivor's Club: The Secrets and Science that Could Save Your Life*. New York: Grand Central, 2010.

Stein, Matthew. *When Technology Fails: A Manual for Self-Reliance, Sustainability, and Surviving the Long Emergency*. Revised ed. White River Junction, VT: Chelsea Green, 2008.

Wiseman, John. *SAS Survival Handbook: For Any Climate, in Any Situation*. Revised ed. New York: Harper Paperbacks, 2009.

PHOTO CREDITS

INDEX